Finding Oasis
Within the
Wilderness
of Our
Socio-Political
Ideologies

JOHN ARIS ELELEME

Copyright © 2024 John Aris Eleleme
All rights reserved
First Edition

Fulton Books
Meadville, PA

Published by Fulton Books 2024

ISBN 979-8-89427-329-7 (paperback)
ISBN 979-8-89427-330-3 (digital)

Printed in the United States of America

AUTHOR'S NOTE

This book is a project privately funded by the author. The research work, interviews conducted, writing processes followed, and logical arrangement done were accomplished through the personal perseverance of the author.

ABSTRACT

This book was written to impress on the minds of citizens of the United States of America, the rise of America as an economic and military power on a virgin land, an empire of states such as the world had never seen. How democracy has helped to build a nation that is the most powerful nation in history can best be explained by the difference between "perfect union" and "inclusive union." It lays out the journey of America toward becoming the greatest military and economic power in world history. It explains the pitfalls hindering the journey to a more perfect union and honestly looks at them from the general view of "We the People!" Although democracy and the constitution are viewed in the lens of political institutions, these terms could define our ways of life, culture, traditions, and status as a nation within the league of nations. Consequently, this is not a religious book, per se, but references made to religion, cultures, traditions, and sociopolitical ideologies are meant to buttress the points stated and present pictural explanations for readers to appreciate the lessons portrayed. Deeply imbedded in its pages are the factors that have created divisiveness among Americans, as well as impeded in many ways our journey toward "a more perfect union." Portraying a visual image of looking at those impediments as a wilderness and the possible solutions as an oasis within the wilderness. It is by imbibing and applying the deep-rooted spiritual lessons of an oasis that we can overcome the obstacles in our journey toward a more perfect union.

The lessons portrayed within the pages of this book are meant to inspire within us the tendency that all men were created equal and demand equal treatment for all. It is written for the understanding of a layman in the street, to impress on the mind that the government of the United States of America is owned by the people and the country or republic belongs to all the citizens. The power of our democracy is that of the people and not that of politicians or special groups. The ideas expressed are not for political debate by academicians, politicians, or constitutional law experts but for the citizens' civic understanding of who they are within this sociopolitical system known as the United States of America.

CONTENTS

Introduction xi

Chapter 1: A Journey of a Thousand Miles 1
    Every Journey Begins with a Step 1
    Our Journey through the Wilderness of Life 4
    Oasis in the Wilderness! 8
    An Oasis with a Republic or Democracy or Both 17
    Are You a Democrat or a Republican or Both? 20
    Civic Responsibilities of a Democratic-Republican 21

Chapter 2: Toward a More Perfect Union 23
    The Preamble of the Constitution Begins as an Agreement 23
    Can Perfection Be Achieved within the Wilderness of
    Imperfection? 25
    Declaring Our Independence from the Wilderness of
    Controls 30

Chapter 3: Order in the Oasis: Pillars of Power and Functions ... 42
    We the People! 42
    American Democratic Institutions 44
    The People's House, the Congress 47
    The People's House, the White House 54
    The People's Court, the Supreme Court 65

Chapter 4: Expanding the Oasis against Encroaching
                 Wilderness: The Bill of Rights 72
    The Bill of Rights 73

All for One and One for All! 76
An Oasis of Life, Not the Wilderness of Death 78
The Fight to Keep Our Democracy Depends on Us 83
Neighbors and Neighborhoods within Our Oasis of Life........89

Chapter 5: Wilderness of Misinformation and Disinformation ..94
Communication: Give Some! Take Some! 95
Wilderness of Misinformation and Lies 98
The Jungle of Disinformation, Conspiracy Theories,
and Manipulation 106
Countering Bad Rhetoric with the Truth..............................111
The Oasis of Truth and Freedom...116

Chapter 6: The Peoples' Oasis: Freedom, Liberty, and
Equal Justice...125
"I Wish You Are Either Hot or Cold…" 126
Lukewarmness Is Unacceptable!...135
For Anyone to Be Free, All Must Be Free! 138
Leave No Citizen Behind, Liberate All!..................................142

Chapter 7: True Justice Must Be Equal or No Justice! 158
Retributive Justice: Vindictive or Justification? 162
Distributive Justice: Fairness or Pretense? 166
Procedural Justice: Truthful or Subjective? 169
Restorative Justice: Punitive or Reclamation?........................172

Chapter 8: Restoring the Oasis within Our Wilderness............180
The United States of America—a Country, a Nation,
or Both? 180
Restoring the Soul of the United States of America 184

Chapter 9: Making Our Oasis Better than Before 194
The American Dream: Reality or Just a Dream? 195
Transferring Our American Dream to the Next Generation..201
Let Us Meet in the Town Hall to Make Our Oasis Better.....206
Passing the Baton to the New Generation 209

Chapter 10: Power in the Oasis Is the People's Power 218
    Overcoming the Wilderness of Ideological Differences 221
    Finding the Oasis within Our Sociopolitical Wilderness! 231
    In God We Trust! In the Constitution We Unite! 234
    Be Awake to the Whims of Evil in Our Society! Resist
    It! Condemn It! Destroy It! 240

Chapter 11: Applying the Principles of "Oasis" in Our
              Sociopolitical System 246
    Separating the True Guardians of the Constitution
    from Corrupt Deceivers 249
    Repairing the Breaches of Our Congressional Dysfunction ..260
    Finding Oasis in the Wilderness: The Conclusion of
    the Whole Matter 268
    Let the Oasis Blossom, Let Freedom Reign, and Let
    Peace Be Still 274

INTRODUCTION

In our daily interactions, associations, and transactions, we have come across the words "republic" and "democracy," but their meanings to us differ in terms of how much information, education, and experience acquired by each and everyone. Although in America we hear these words, refer to them, and even participate in their activities, an average citizen finds it difficult to define or understand how they are related to our daily lives. In my interaction with various people of diverse cultures and education over the years, the general understanding of how these words relate to the understanding of our system of government unfortunately exhibits more deficiency than expected. However, the difference between naturalized citizens' and born citizens' understanding of the terms stems from their pathways to citizenship rather than how much knowledge of the system they acquired through any civic education. Since civic education is ignored by the people who are supposed to initiate, develop, and expand its impact in preparing our young people for their new role of the custodians of democracy, born citizens are more confused and frustrated about democracy.

As a matter of fact, the various requirements as stated by the Immigration and Citizenship Bureau includes a good knowledge of American history, constitution, and civic responsibilities. An applicant is required to pass various tests and assessments to prepare them to fully participate or carry out their civic duties. Some attend workshops and conferences to gain more knowledge about their new country to-be. These and many other requirements expand an applicant's knowledge of the adopted country far beyond most people born in the United States of America. On the other hand, citizens born in America tend to lack the basic knowledge of our system of government, its structure, and civic requirements. Unfortunately, politicians across the board take undue advantage of these limitations to exert their will on the people instead of the other way around. For instance, so many Americans believe that the president can do everything through executive order without understanding the limitations of such actions, and thereby place heavy blames on the President of the United States (or POTUS), if their problems are not solved when demanded. Hence, the low poll ratings of some American presidents, if not all, after their first year in office is directly related to this pitfall, as well as other factors. The predicament of uninformed citizenry always led to failure of any political system. And lack of coordination of any systemic function will lead to systemic failures as experts in all fields can easily attest.

We as a nation are struggling to understand the structure of our government as set out in our constitution by the Founding Fathers due to the events that led to the establishment of the system in the first place. The near annihilation of Native Americans by the European Powers as they embarked on forcefully taking over the land through the colonial wars that led to the thirteen colonies proved that this country was established in bloodshed. Bloodshed that resulted from the greed and self-centeredness of the first Europeans who arrived the continental America. Besides, slavery and distortion also contributed immensely to the disparities that exist today. It was a miracle that the continental America made the decision to design our government as a democracy instead of a monarchy or autocracy, however imperfect.

Americans should understand that it was a prototype and not a finished design. It required continuous improvement, amendment, development, and generational modernization. In simple terms, the constitution is a dynamic document and not a dead piece of paper that only describes the beginning of a nation and not its progress. The resistance to change is fully ascertained to the fact that it was originally designed by White men to benefit White men and their immediate families. Any other ethnic group was regarded as second class, if not third class. In retrospect, since American constitution is subject to change and amendment as the generations roll by, the

Finding Oasis Within the Wilderness of our Sociopolitical Ideologies

process of updating the constitution should not have been made so rigid as to require two-third of the senate and two-third of the state legislatures to amend or ratify. On the other hand, having a simple majority to amend the constitution would alienate minority groups or disenfranchise ethnic interests. The forefathers of our country could not find the balance in this situation, hence, left the issue to subsequent generations to resolve but with their hands rigidly tied up by the founders' self-centered and fraudulent resolutions.

If Americans are to find the solution, there must be a process of troubleshooting, scrutinizing the structure, and honestly reforming the parts to achieve a more functional democratic system for our government. From modern understanding of systems, we can ascertain that every system has pitfalls, overload issues, and abnormal use that may lead to error signals or possible shutdowns. Modern problems require modern solutions and not archaic strategies, and only the modern generation can provide the platform for it. It is imperative that our country must learn to symbiotically understand, appreciate, and initiate our most important resource, the young people, into the culture of governance and nation building.

We can move toward a more perfect union if we can understand diversity within our democratic system, the spread of our human resources, and how to become inclusive and not exclusive. Unity comes as a subset of understanding and appreciating the subjects involved in bonding. It may take a longer time or a split of time to achieve this principle depending on our openness to each other's cultural, religious, and statutory differences. As the saying goes, "United we stand, divided we fall!" We the citizens and the people of the United States of America must understand that the bond that leads to a more perfect union requires hard work from all to build a strong and egalitarian society.

As you take more steps to reading this book, you will be provided with the opportunity to look deeper into yourself, find that inner understanding of how our existence is tied to that of our country, the United States of America, and the part you are expected to play in making it the best nation on earth. The children of Israel were punished by God to wander in the wilderness for forty years due to their disobedience and unbelief. Probably, many could not fathom out the reasons why they had to go through the wilderness experience in the first place, but they had to dig deep enough to find the answers. The wilderness became a training ground for the Israelites to learn about the God of their fathers and their forefathers; it served as the consequence for their sins of disobedience, and most of all, for those who disobeyed to perish and give way for the new generation. Within those forty years, he took care of them in a way a father should: providing manna for food, oasis for fresh water, and protection in the day with the pillar of cloud and in the night with the pillar of fire and making their cloths new every morning such that they had no need for new ones. The Lord created oases at every spot they chose to rest, and with the strike of Moses's staff turned barren rocks into watersheds.

For nearly two hundred and fifty years, the United States of America has been cropping in a wilderness in search of the truth of who we are, why our republic was established, and where is the focus of our journey and how can we get there. Like the children of Israel, America's progress toward a more perfect union is being resisted or slowed by people's individual or group philosophies that are contrary to that of our democratic principles and general cultural values. They complain about the evidence of truth, accusing the victims of their crimes of being the reasons they committed the offense, they attack the government at any chance at their reach, and they show no mercy or compassion to their fellow citizens. In the case of Israel, it took a generation (forty years) to eliminate the problematic population, but it will take America several generations to eliminate the ideological sentiments that move people to perpetrating this evil. Therefore, our work to ramp up all our efforts begins now!

CHAPTER 1

A Journey of a Thousand Miles

Every Journey Begins with a Step

In every instance, people, things, and ideologies make progress to either achieve better standards of their functions or to cover a wider range of their influences. As wisely stated, "A journey of a thousand miles begins with a step!" This statement is true for almost everything we do or try to accomplish. Sexual relations between a man and a woman begins the process of life followed by pregnancy, then birth of a child. It is a natural phenomenon that we are so unconsciously familiar with but may find it difficult to explain to a child where babies come from. However, the child picks up bits and pieces of this knowledge as he grows and makes full sense of the process at his point of maturation.

Similarly, the process of acquiring knowledge or skills begins with the very basic stage of a beginner to an advanced beginner or intermediate stage through to the proficient stage then the advanced stage or expert level to the master's stage. All the steps profoundly indicate progressive movement from level to level which requires persistence in performance, increase in effectiveness, and effort by the individual. Our desires drive the effort needed to scale every step in the journey, without which progress cannot be achieved.

By the same token, building or constructing any object begins with a plan which may be a draft of the design, finance, duration of project, or location of the project. A building begins with the foundation to the elevation, then the roofing and fittings, finally furnishing. Each stage requires time and effort by the building manager to satisfy the requirements. Without planning, the whole project is bound to fail before it begins. Every journey that we make begins with the first step, and without the next step and the next, progress cannot be achieved, destination cannot be reached, and our purpose cannot be realized. Therefore, the process of our journey toward any destination involves focusing on the details of the plans, reflecting on the strategies within the process, evaluating portions of the progress made, and determining the next move toward our destination. We

should be aware that everyone's journey may be different and should not be compared to others but to one's inner desires and inspiration.

Relatively, we can reflect on several journeys that we had taken in the past for any reason best known to us as individuals or groups. In most instances, we had to begin somewhere or somehow, but we needed to take the first step to jump-start our journey. Unfortunately, many do not realize that life is a journey. Some journeys may be smooth and incidentless or challenging and filled with difficulties or better still an adventure. No matter how we undertake our journey, our final destinations are embodiment of hope, freedom, liberty, security, and better life.

Sometimes, our achievements may be the beginning of a new journey: education becomes a means to an end and not an end on its own, acquired skills requiring applications to succeed but not a guarantee of success. Also being an American citizen or a born American is not a certainty for privileges but an opportunity to access the rights and resources accorded you under the laws of the United States of America. Our journeys are not privileges but hard work, persistence, progressive effort, flexible adaptation to new situations, and total focus on achieving our goals as we go through the processes in our plans to reach the thousandth mile or our destination.

The United States of America is a nation of journeys made by diverse people from all over the world. A unique nation of immigrants from inception till now, our history is laden with real-life stories of exceptional movement of individuals and groups from Europe, Asia, Africa, and South America to this great nation. Many come to improve their lifestyles while others come to avoid persecution and war. Unfortunately, many were forced, against their own will, to come and serve others for no reason than greed and inhumanity of man against their fellow men. Similarly, some groups journey for the purpose of preserving their existence, right to life, and to domicile in their ancestral lands. Whether the focus is group movement or individual journey, we all experience the difficulties within the wilderness of our travels.

Our Journey through the Wilderness of Life

Some group journeys are embedded in the history of America such that deleting the accounts will adversely distort the whole history of the United States of America. From the moment England separated from the Roman Catholic Church to form the Church of England, other separatists emerged that led to numerous confrontations among religious groups. The 1500s proved to be a century of religious upheaval and spiritual awakening in England and other parts of Europe. Consequently, the Puritans and the Pilgrims decided to take the first step to religious freedom by leaving their homeland in 1609 for Leiden, Holland.

Finding Oasis Within the Wilderness of our Sociopolitical Ideologies

Without many favors in the Dutch land for freedom they sort, the next ten years of their sojourn in Holland was more of a wilderness of thorns and thistles. Through thick and thin, the Pilgrims and the Puritans made the leap of faith to the new world, embarking on a treacherous journey across the Atlantic Ocean, in a small ship that history had made famous for their courage than its enormity, the *Mayflower*. They landed in the Massachusetts region in September of 1620, contrary to their destination to the territory of Virginia as the storm blew their boat off course.

The significance of the Pilgrims' and the Puritans' journey to North America and the establishment of our great nation was their believe in freedom of worship, liberty of all men, ability of the people to choose their leaders, democracy without dominance, and peoples' rights to live freely without constraints. They journeyed through the wilderness for their beliefs and desire for freedom and a better lifestyle. However, within their ranks were the mixed population whose intentions were more ulterior than the rest and decided to forcefully attack the natives for reasons of domination and acquisition of lands that didn't belong to them. The continuous war with the natives lasted for centuries. The cruelty of the colonials toward the Native Americans, as well as the defenses mounted against the European Invaders factored into shaping the structure of the new nation. Both groups journeyed through the wilderness of life from different perspectives. They journeyed to reach better destinations, no matter what that destination may be.

In contrast to the story of the European Pilgrims and Puritans is the story of the enslaved Africans forcefully transported to North America against their will. They made the treacherous journeys across the Atlantic Ocean not for their beliefs but the beliefs of other people who choose to deprive them of their God-given freedom, take away their liberty and free will, and steal from their most natural resources—strength to work for a living as well as generate wealth. The black people's journey is one that continues to rigmarole through the desert because the archenemy of mankind continues to incite evil in the hearts of descendants of the original perpetrators to resist and torment the Black people. Although this book is not focusing on the slavery of the Africans and the racism against the African Americans, but all through the existence of the colonial America to the United States, injustice against these people from the continent of Africa seems to know no end. The Africans went through not just the wilderness of life but persecution and dehumanization within the oasis of hope.

Equally important for us to review is the treacherous journeys made by the Jewish people as they flee persecution in Europe and other parts of the world. The holocaust spearheaded by Adolf Hitler that took the lives of over six million Jews cannot be forgotten in a hurry. This crime against humanity is the worst example of evil where men took pleasure in exterminating their fellow men. The helpless Jews went through the wilderness of hardship and dehumanization as they flee from their enemies in search of freedom, liberty, justice, and security in the new world.

Although, we had mentioned this in the preceding paragraphs, we cannot forget the journey of the Native American tribes as they confronted the invading migrants from Europe. They welcome those like the early Pilgrims and Puritans who came in peace but engaged in unending conflicts with the mixed crowd of pirates, Vikings, mercenaries, and slavers. It is estimated that more than fifty-six million natives were killed by the European settlers between AD 1492 and early 1600s. These devastating crimes were perpetuated in the North, Central, and Southern regions of the Americas. The origin of the Thanksgiving ceremony in a way was a story told to cover up the devastating killings of the native tribes by the colonials. However, history of the events may not be as straightforward as should be depending on who is telling it; evidence have shown the horrible travels of the tribes through the wilderness of wars, sufferings, hunger, and death. The cruelty and inhumanity of those from Europe led to the genocide of the natives.

In addition, the movement of the first Asians, specifically the Filipinos to the continent of America in the late fifteen hundreds and early sixteen hundreds, uniquely marked a portion of American history that is too important to ignore. They boarded Spanish ships to America under dehumanized conditions and met racial discrimination and hate from mostly immigrants from Europe. In the 1850s, Chinese workers migrated to the United States, first to work in the gold mines but also to take agricultural jobs and factory work, especially in the garment industry. Although the first Chinese people that landed on the continental America were crewmen on mercantile ships, the later travelers came to better their life and to chart economic connections for their homeland. For whatever reason that brought them to America, their journeys through the wilderness of life were as tedious as any other groups.

Equally important to the group movements are the individual and family movements from all over the world. It can be inferred that immigrants contributed to building America because of the individual talents, developed or untapped skills, and business as well as technological know-hows that contributed to American ingenuity. Albert Einstein, one of the greatest physicists in the history of this country, was a German-born theoretical physicist who had Swiss and German citizenships before moving to the United States of America in 1933 and became a citizen in 1940. His achievements in science led to the development of the atomic bomb through the "Manhattan Project" initiative. We also owe the theory of relativity, $E=mc^2$, to his genius and research excellence in the areas of continuum mechanics, thermodynamics, electrodynamics, and gravitational pull on objects.

Albert Einstein journeyed through the wilderness of rejection by his native Germany and was hated by the Nazis government because of his Jewish heritage. Germany's loss became America's gain. His contributions to science and technology earned him the Nobel Prize and world recognition. In America, he joined the fight against racism and dehumanization of the minority by the majority, shining his influence on the continuous human journey to confirm that all men were created equal and with God-given rights that must not be tampered with by other individuals or groups or governments.

Like a flowing stream, many individuals had made their journeys through the wilderness of life as they migrated to the United States of America for reasons best known to them. Sergey Brin from Russia, cofounder of Google; Levi Strauss from Germany who founded the Levi Jeans Company; Dikembe Mutombo from the Democratic

Republic of Congo, one of the best shot blockers in NBA history; and Joseph Pulitzer from Hungary, founder of the famous Pulitzer Prize for journalism. Also, we can make mention of Isabel Allende from Peru, Jan Koum from Ukraine, Arianna Huffington from Greece, Mariano Rivera from Panama, Arnold Schwarzenegger from Austria, Steve Chen from Taiwan, Jawed Karim from East Germany, Guetty Felin from Haiti, Chimamanda Ngozi Adichie from Nigeria, Lupita Nyong'o from Kenya, Wyclef Jean from Haiti, and the list continues.

The abovementioned and many more, including you and I, have in no small ways contributed to the building of this empire of states. Some came from war-torn countries with hope for the future. Others suffered indignity and rejection from their tormentors while others came for the opportunity to hone their talents in a conducive environment. Most importantly, many come for religious freedom. In all these instances the first step was taken to begin our difficult but hopeful journeys through the wilderness to get to this destination—America.

Oasis in the Wilderness!

"Oh, that men could praise the Lord for his goodness, and for his wonderful works to the children of men! Let them exalt him also in the congregation of the people and praise him in the assembly of the elders. He turned rivers into a wilderness, and the water springs into dry ground; a fruitful land into barrenness, for the wickedness of them that dwell therein. He turned the wilderness into standing water, and dry ground into water springs. And there he makes the hungry to dwell, that they may prepare a city for habitation; and sow the fields, and plant vineyards, which may yield fruits of increase. He blessed them also, so that they are multiplied greatly; and suffered not their cattle to decrease" (Ps. 107:32–38).

These beautiful Psalms surely depict that in every journey we make, the Creator of all things provides rest and refreshing moments even in the wilderness. Those who have at any time journeyed through a wilderness or a desert land can testify that the desire for

Finding Oasis Within the Wilderness of our Sociopolitical Ideologies

water, food, and rest can be overwhelming. The sight of a mirage can incite hope and demoralize as well. In some cases, the traveler develops a sense of hopelessness that the journey may not come to an end, and the heightened bodily needs of water, food, and rest could become the deciding factor for courage to persevere or give up the adventure.

There is nothing more exciting to a desert traveler than the sight of a looming oasis. The possibility of recuperating from the strains of his journey and the desire to quench his taste, satisfy his hunger, and acquire provisions for the remaining journey ahead of him feels like salvation to the wayfarer. Although most of us may not understand the feeling, we can understand the feeling of knowing that help is on the way for any difficulty or hardship we may encounter in our individual journeys.

To explain the relationship between a wilderness and an oasis, it is important to picture an oasis as a fertile land in a desert. Available water comes from wells dug by people or a seemingly natural water source from rocks or waterfalls that flows through streams into lakes of water. It provides habitats for desert plants, such as palms, pomegranates, peaches, citrus trees, apricot trees, plum trees, nectarines trees, desert apple trees, and coconut trees.

Similarly, the fertility of an oasis provides the natural conditions for desert animals to thrive. Some animals, such as dromedary camels, desert goats, antelope jackrabbits, may serve useful purposes for man while others, such as scorpions, yucca moth, sidewinder snakes, sand cats, and bobcats, serve only trouble to man but useful in other ways.

Like "oasis in the wilderness," the United States of America has served as a nation of relieve to many people who had journeyed to reach her shores. A nation whose natural and human resources provide the environment for individuals or groups to dream and have their dreams realized by hard work and talent investment. A nation whose constitution promises freedom, liberty, equal justice, and fairness to all its people. A nation who supposedly "a shining city on a hill" that provides examples and leadership to all the world. When God promises, he fulfills. His promise of an oasis in the wilderness is fully embodied in the rise and growth of the United States of America into the most powerful economic and military empire the world has ever seen. He promised, "The Lord shall open unto thee his good treasure, the heaven to give the rain unto thy land in his season, and to bless all the work of thine hand: and thou shalt lend unto many nations, and thou shalt not borrow. And the Lord shall make thee the head, and not the tail, and thou shalt be above only, and thou shalt not be beneath: if that thou hearken unto the Commandments of the Lord thy God, which I command thee this day, to observe, and to do them" (Deut. 28:12–13).

Finding Oasis Within the Wilderness of our Sociopolitical Ideologies

The same promise made to the Israelites is equally directed to us today as spiritual beneficiaries. We can appreciate an oasis in our wilderness of difficulties, struggle for freedom and liberty, and fight for justice anywhere injustice is experienced or perceived. As an oasis incites hope in a weary traveler, the vision of our destinations inspires courage and perseverance as we take steps to reach them.

The best characteristic of an oasis is that it serves plants, animals, and humans without restrictions, providing natural food and water for all to survive and thrive. Since the water flows from natural sources, the probability of drying up is quite low if not tampered with human abuse.

As it is written, "But he also can turn a barren wilderness into an oasis with water! He can make springs flow into desert lands and turn them into fertile valleys so that cities spring up, and he gives it all to those who are hungry" (Ps. 107:35–36). God provides each one of us the opportunity to thrive in the oasis when we take the responsibility of tending and caring for the source. He gives it all to those who are hungry, hungry for freedom, liberty, justice, and dignity. He gives it to everyone who hungers for righteousness, peace, security, and hope for an egalitarian society.

Not only that cities may spring up around oases but do grow and expand into great settlements. Some of the greatest cities that sprang up around oases in a desert include Las Vegas, Nevada; Palm Springs, California; Karachi, Pakistan; Santa Fe, New Mexico;

Finding Oasis Within the Wilderness of our Sociopolitical Ideologies

Casablanca, Morocco; Dubai, United Arab Emirate; and Phoenix, Arizona, to mention but a few. These cities grew as people of various cultural, religious, ethnic, and racial identities flock to them for trade, homes, and conducive atmosphere for prosperity. Population explosion in these cities is because of favorable conditions envisioned not by the climatic or geographic features that surrounds them but other factors, such as trading routes, central access connecting many destinations, or a potpourri of cultures.

On the contrary, an oasis may dry up and become unattractive to any living thing due to human or natural factors. As Psalms 107:33–34 states, "Whenever he chooses, he can dry up a river and turn the land into a desert Or he can take a fruitful land and make it into a saltwater swamp, all because of the wickedness of those who dwell there."

If peoples' vision is marred by hate, lawlessness, corruption, selfishness, and disregard for environmental protection, the oasis becomes unattractive and repugnant to all living things. Just as great habitations could spring up and grow around oases, beautiful cities could as well be destroyed by the negative and abusive behavior of man.

History has in many ways recorded the fall of great empires due more to internal rumblings than enemies' attacks. The great Babylonian Empire fell because of infighting and sabotage from within. Medi-Persia crumbled due to cruelty. Greece, after Alexander the Great, came to an end because his generals divided the empire among themselves with continuous infighting. The Han Empire, Mongol Empire, Ottoman Empire, Spanish Empire, Russian Empire, British Empire, and the great Roman Empire collapsed due to economic, political, social, cultural, or environmental reasons that they could not find solutions to or prevention of due to human factors.

These empires have similar characteristics that led to their rise and fall: they were monarchies or autocracies that displayed authority of powerful individuals who were almost worshipped as gods.

They depended on conquest to expand or preserve their territories, fill their treasuries with wealth, expand their influences far and wide, and multiply their dominance over all other jurisdictions around them. Consequently, their cruel methods that led to their rise also served as their cataclysmic fall. John Foster Dulles stated, "The world will never have lasting peace so long as men reserve for war, the finest human qualities. Peace, no less than war, requires idealism and self-sacrifice and a righteous and dynamic faith." Some of most talented men and women were reserved for armies and trained to be commanders and generals that commanded great armies in history. Wars and rumors of wars reigned supreme, and stories of combatant victories and devastating defeats ruled the minds of the people. These periods in world history were periods of crises, devastating pandemics, political tumults, and uncertainties. The world needed a sense of direction, peace, economic growth, stability, population safety, and a new world order. In retrospect, all these may not be accomplished without political stability and new ways of ruling that are not authoritarian.

Unfortunately, many countries were rooted in monarchies, such as realms, kingdoms, empires, and regions, that were ruled by powerful men and women across ages: Julius Caesar of Rome, Suleiman I of the Ottoman Empire, James I of England, John III of Poland-Lithuania, Meiji of Japan, Gustav II Adolf of Sweden, Augustus Caesar, Cyrus II of Persia, Frederick II of Prussia, Victoria of the United Kingdom, Louis XIV of France, to mention but a few. Although some of these monarchs ruled with compassion toward their subjects, many led their countries with iron fists. In almost all instances, citizens had no say in their governance but obey orders to avoid death. The people were limited in ways of talent growth and generation of wealth for which any sign of acquisition of wealth attracted the interest of an envious king or emperor. Similarly, the growth of science and development of technology during the reign of monarchs were slower than the rate of expected growth until the period of Renaissance in Western Europe. Development of new technologies or making scientific statements that were contrary to popular beliefs were not viewed kindly, particularly if they debunked popular religious and traditional beliefs.

Consequently, many individuals and groups of people eloped to other lands or new environments for new opportunities and security. They wandered in the wilderness of persecution, intimidation, deprivation, dehumanization in search of liberty, freedom, and justice for themselves and their posterities. They moved for the sake of having a say in their governance through representation and equal access to resources, such as lands, clean water, and minerals. As a matter of fact, each of them took the leap of faith knowingly or unknowingly believing the promises from Psalms 107:36–38, "He turned the wilderness into standing water, and dry ground into water springs. And there he makes the hungry to dwell, that they may prepare a city for habitation; and sow the fields, and plant vineyards, which may yield fruits of increase. He blessed them also, so that they are multiplied greatly; and suffered not their cattle to decrease." Therefore, wherever favorable conditions abound movement of people from far and wide must be expected. The question was "How do we maintain order and rulership within these habitations?" They wanted something different from the autocracy of Europe, the old world. They desired a system of government where the people can control their destiny, choose their leaders, have a say in their governance, and make sure that the basic rights of the citizens are protected.

An Oasis with a Republic or Democracy or Both

The Founding Fathers of the United States of America came from all over the world, and the original owners of the land or Native Americans were also a part of the foundation of this great country. All the activities, whether human or natural, contributed to laying the foundation. Tribal wars and wars between the colonies raged furiously for two or more centuries before they realized that the wilderness of Europe, what they were running away from, had followed them to the new world. It became expedient to get rid of the British, dislodge the French from the stolen lands, keep the Germans at bay, and defeat the Spanish intruders to start a new nation. A nation where power belongs to the people, managed by the people's representatives, and for the service of all the people. This oasis needed a structure of power, a means of controlling the power, and the basis for peaceful transfer of power from one administration to another. Here was the nightmare for the Founding Fathers: inculcating diverse cultures, traditions, religions, and philosophies to form a government that is practical, efficient, and inclusive. We can only imagine the debates, disagreements, confrontations, or sparing opinions that characterized the processes in forming the new nation. The demanding issue before the establishment of the country was how the nation should be governed. How can power remain with the people without autocracy creeping in? How should the people be represented in their governance to avoid sectional dominance? Which system of government will provide solutions to these problems as well as take into consideration the variation in culture, tradition, or religion?

The idea of creating a monarchy in America was completely out of the way. Repeating the mistakes of Europe was not entertained at any limit, and handing over power to one individual or to a group of selected people will, unfortunately, recreate the failings of Europe in America. Consequently, they toiled through the wilderness of ideas, philosophies, considerations, debates, argumentations, and conflicts as they searched for the best form of government for the new nation. The question was, "Do we form a Republic or a Democracy or a Democratic-Republic?"

They were desperate to come up with a decision that was acceptable to all the representatives of the people. A series of meetings, regional or central, including constitutional conferences and individual contacts permeated the whole process of founding this great nation. As at the time, none of the participants could imagine what their efforts were going to produce. Yet they persevere in all ways possible to settle on "a Democratic-Republic." They were not highly educated or aristocratic people, yet they had a vision of a country where all men have the right to participate in their governance, own properties, dream dreams, and work hard to realize their dreams.

Throughout human history, God has always shown that he can use imperfect men and women to achieve great things. He used poor and uneducated fishermen to spread the gospel to all the world, inspired a lowly shepherd boy, David, to defend the honor of his people Israel, and he put a great army on flight using three hundred men with bullhorns, led by a humble and lowly Gideon. When he chooses to form the greatest nation that the world had ever seen, he inspired them to choose a republic and not a monarchy, apply a representative democracy, not an autocracy in governance. Since no country in history had ever united these ideas, American democracy became an experiment. An experiment that may be destined to fail or succeed. Consequently, it started as a system of trial and error, subject to amendments, and dependent on the basic acceptable values of the founding generation and for generations to come.

Agreeably, the people settled for a republic, a form of government in which "supreme power is held by the people and their elected representatives," according to the online encyclopedia resource, Wikipedia. In a general term a republic is considered "public matter," not the private concern or property of rulers. It belongs to all the people of the country or domain. To stress this again, a republic is a form of government in which "supreme power is held by the people and their elected representatives." In a republic, the country is considered a "public matter," not the private concern or property of the rulers."

Republic originates from two Latin words, *les publica*, meaning public property or owned by the people of the country. Also the people settled for democracy to be the driving structure for the new republic.

Although the definition of democracy and republic tends to be similar in meaning, there are differences that can separate the two. According to Wikipedia's definition, "Democracy is a form of government in which the people have the authority to deliberate and decide legislation, or to choose governing officials to do so." Simply put, "it is the government of the people, by the people, for the people!" The word democracy originates from two Greek words *demos*, which means people, and *kratos*, which means power. Combined, it means "power of the people." Here, the way of governing, the laws of governing, and representatives to govern remains the will and decision of the people. It is your government, it is my government, and all together, it is our government. Just as the Greek word *demos* designate all the citizens living within a city, state, or a country, democracy surely involves all the citizens. Also, as the word *kratos* represents strength, rule, power, or dominance, the supreme authority in a democracy is vested in all the citizens.

Despite the close similarity in the definition of both terms, democracy and republic, the difference is that one is a physical property of the people and the other is administrative structural property of the people. In a republic, domiciliate of the landmass, the political dominion of all the regions that defines the country, and the right to purchase and own property is solely that of the people and not the government or powerful individuals. Also, religion, economy, cultural beliefs, and traditions, major factors in determining any republic, are considered before a nation is established. In both cases, the power solely rests on the people. However, the people must understand the power, how to wield it, and what to wield it for.

Are You a Democrat or a Republican or Both?

The American experiment was meant to be improved from one generation to another and amendments to the structure and functions of its parts updated as knowledge increases. To make the amendments, the people must understand the structure, functions, and the role that each citizen plays in the process. In many instances, citizens get caught up in the disparity of identifying what or where to lean on. It has been a wilderness of misunderstanding, infighting, resistance, and even physical confrontations as America continues to grow toward a more perfect union.

Since America is a republic and it belongs to all Americans and American citizens, logically it implies that all the people are republicans. Similarly, as democracy is the property of the people, it means all the people are democrats. Therefore, all the American people can be identified as "Democratic-Republicans." There is no question that this technical description is scientific and logical. The United States of America is a Democratic-Republic based on the uniqueness of the chosen structure of its civilization. Understandably, this makes America a unique country among all the nations of the world. It is a nation of diverse races, multiple ethnicities, and a variety of cultures. Historically, the only country in the world where its extended diversity is a foundation to its greatness is the USA.

In contrast, being a democrat does not technically identify you as a member of the Democratic Party. Also being a republican does not infer that you are a member of the Republican Party. These are political platforms or what we may refer to as political clubs. They are created based on political philosophies and beliefs that may change depending on socioeconomic factors and generational differences. We can be rest assured that we the people are similar in our views of a functional republic more than we are ready to agree; we are all democratic republicans. It is the responsibility of all the citizens to uphold the constitution and laws of the land and to defend our Democratic-Republic against all enemies, foreign or domestic.

Civic Responsibilities of a Democratic-Republican

It is important for every American citizen, born or naturalized, to understand that the responsibility of upholding the constitution and laws of the country and protecting the integrity and domiciliate of the nation rests on all the people. "Citizenship is the state of being vested with the rights, privileges, and duties of a citizen, but it can also be defined as the character of an individual viewed as a member of society. While US citizenship provides many rights, it also involves many responsibilities." According to the Kansas State Secretary of State Office, although some responsibilities are required by law, many more are inert and are based on our patriotism. Obeying laws is both required and inert responsibility. This assertion is fully stated thus, "Civic duties ensure that democratic values written into the constitution and the Bill of Rights are upheld. Responsibilities include both those that are voluntary as well as those required by law."

Obeying the laws of the land implies understanding and keeping the statutory requirements of all the laws, federal, state, or city ordinances no matter our status in the community. We must always be ready to pay the fine for breaking the rules and laws of the land. According to Theodore Roosevelt (twenty-sixth president of the United States), "The first requisite of a good citizen in this republic of ours is that he shall be able and willing to pull his weight." To be ready to follow the rules, serve when required or needed and express his or her love for the country beyond self and family.

The United States is a land ruled by laws, not by persons. It is a democracy and not an autocracy, that is why it cannot be ruled by individual persons without the authority of the people. However, the responsibility of creating laws and implementing them rests on the representatives selected by the people. Without laws, we the people will be stocked in the wilderness of lawlessness, chaos, incivility, violence, injustice, and continuous erosion of civilization. President Franklin D. Roosevelt once stated, "Let us never forget that government is ourselves and not an alien power over us. The ultimate rulers of our democracy are not a president and senators and congressmen and government officials, but the voters of this country." It is you, it is me, and it is all the people that hold the power and authority to rule. Therefore, the responsibility of upholding our laws starts and ends with us the people.

CHAPTER 2

Toward a More Perfect Union

The Preamble of the Constitution Begins as an Agreement

"We the people of the United States, in order to form a more perfect union, establish justice, ensure domestic tranquility, provide for the common defense, promote the general welfare, and secure the blessings of liberty to ourselves and our posterity, do ordain and establish this Constitution for the United States of America." As a matter of reference, it is one of the most important documents the world has ever seen since it is the agreement that established the most powerful economic and military empire of states in history. The constitution is an agreement, as well as a document that enshrines the rights to live, work, rear our children, and achieve our individual dreams for all the people of this great country. "We the people!" is an introduction to the agreement that has no adjectival description of who the people are supposed to be. It did not say "We the White people" of the United States of America or "We the Black people" or "We the Asian people" or "We the Brown people" of the United States of America. Rather than make any specifics, it described all the people domiciled in the country at the time the country was established and the constitution written. Technically, that included the Native Americans, Latin Americans, African Americans, Asian Americans, and the European Americans. Also, this includes all people who will at one time, or the other, immigrate to this beautiful land of the free and the home of the brave.

Notably, the preamble displays the expression "and secure the blessings of liberty to ourselves and our posterity." This by implication means that the agreement includes our descendants for generations to come. Let's make this simpler by considering a land agreement of a very large region purchased by the first generation of people of different races and backgrounds which bestows all the rights and privileges of use on all involved and their descendants, and by specific instructions, it cannot be sold out or divided with prejudice but must be developed for the benefit of the family and generations to come. As a dynamic document, the Constitution of the United States of

Finding Oasis Within the Wilderness of our Sociopolitical Ideologies

America is subject to change, corrections, updates, and improvement as the generations roll in and out of the system. However, this promise had a conflict, maintaining slavery of the Black people broke the promise of liberty and freedom and needed to be abolished as a cruel practice before proceeding to a new beginning. Unfortunately, this conflict was settled on the battlefield where thousands of Americans were sacrificed on the altar of greed and human cruelty. The fiercest and most devastating war ever fought on the continent of North America, the American Civil War of 1861–1865, reminded and continues to remind all Americans that the fight for the blessings of liberty, freedom, equality, and equal justice under the law cannot be taken for granted. They are not guaranteed due to our imperfection as human beings we must determine to keep them if we must continue to enjoy these rights and privileges.

Can Perfection Be Achieved within the Wilderness of Imperfection?

The expression "Towards a more perfect union!" in the preamble of the constitution has been a topic of debate among experts in the legal community, historians, and social scientists in our history. Some have argued that no human activity can reach perfection with our imperfections as human beings. As a matter of fact, we are prone to errors in all forms of human activities no matter how much care is taken in working toward their goals. On the other hand, others believe that we can persistently work toward achieving higher standards with consistency. However, to fully appreciate the concept we need to provide the simplest definition of both terms and conditions required to combine them.

What is a union? We have in many instances encounter the word union and have as well associated ourselves with organizations that are based on this concept. As clearly stated in the *Merriam-Webster Dictionary*, union is "an act or instance of uniting or joining two or more things into one, such as the formation of a single political unit from two or more separate and independent units; a unity in marriage, the growing together of severed parts by a unified condition; combining or junction—into a gracious union of excellence and strength; something that is made into one, or something formed by a combination or coalition of parts or members, such as, a confederation of independent entities (such as nations or people) for some common purpose; a political unit constituting an organic whole formed usually from units which were previously governed separately (such as American colonies) and which have surrendered or delegated their principal powers to the government of the whole or to a newly created government (such as the US in 1789)." Consequently, we can infer that union is bringing parts or things with same purposes to form a whole. It is important to note that a bond cannot be formed without similar characteristics, interests, or goals.

There can never be a bond between armed robbers and bankers; neither can a bond be formed between good and bad or associated laziness and hard work. Bonding in human sense requires similarity in purpose, characteristics, and free will of the subjects involved. It involves more than being like each other but being more inclusive than exclusive, appreciating each other's weaknesses as well as strengths, and promoting all the values we have in common than our differences. Let's consider a Venn diagram which is a picture of sets and their combinations.

As illustration, let's consider three sets of cultural or traditional values:

Group A
Democracy, liberty, unity, diversity, individualism, equality, freedom, and self-government, innovation

Group B
Freedom, liberty, unity, diversity, individualism, equality, self-government, change, democracy, representative assembly, patriotism, equal justice, and progress

Group C
Courage, liberty, unity, diversity, individualism, equality, self-government, equal justice, patriotism, and fairness

Finding Oasis Within the Wilderness of our Sociopolitical Ideologies

Within each group are certain fundamental values that are paramount. They may not have every value in common but share certain values that make the sets similar in characteristics. For example, Group A has certain values common to Group B but not in Group C, and Group B shares certain values with Group C not with Group A. However, there are common values shared among the three groups that tie them together as intersection of values or a bond.

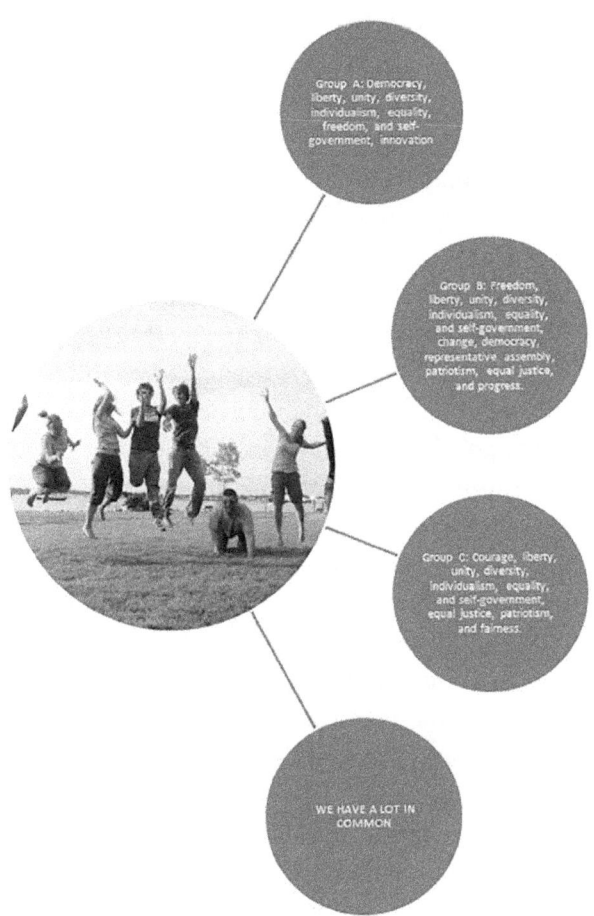

The idea of movement toward a more perfect union begins with values that bind us together as human beings, a people, groups, communities, and as individuals. Even with dissimilar life-forms, there are always things or values we hold dear that make us living things. The beautiful thing about bonds is that they can either be grown or diminished because of the dynamic nature of existence.

Whatever values bind us together, growing within the bond is extremely important to keep or strengthen the relationship. As I mentioned, there can never be a growth toward a more perfect union without an inclusive union. In a marriage, individuals involved must get together to court each other, identify values that can bind them together, as well as disparity in opposite values that may pull them apart. They may finally decide to get married or break up the relationship as they weigh each other's strengths and weaknesses.

However, marriage is not an end on its own but a means to an end. Many people may be troubled by this truth, but it is critical that we view marriage as the first step in reaching a more enduring bond in our relationships. Both partners have the obligation to continue to build on the values that bind them together and eliminate or improve on those that separate them. As beautifully stated in the scriptures, "Therefore a man shall leave his father and his mother and hold fast to his wife, and they shall become one flesh" (Gen. 2:24). It requires letting go of personal drives for common drives, as well as focusing on common goals without the interference of personal ones. It is a lifelong journey that involves lots of obstacles, thorns, thistles, bends and corners, ups and downs, and as many failures as successes. It involves making changes and amendments to our personal philosophies as we grow.

As in marriage, our union under the constitution is a contract or an agreement that requires the concern of all involved—individuals, communities, states, regions, and institutions to form the bond of values that are shared by all. The journey began with the first thirteen British colonies signing the contract: Virginia, Massachusetts, Rhode Island, Connecticut, New Hampshire, New York, New Jersey, Pennsylvania, Delaware, Maryland, North Carolina, South Carolina, and Georgia. Today, the union is made of fifty states, including island regions of the United States of America. As binding as this contract may be, it is subject to continuous changes, improvement, updates, and amendments because it is a dynamic document and not an immutable law. It hovers over everyone from the Founding Fathers to our generation of today and over generations to come. The crop of the matter is that it is subject to adaptation to each of the generations for which it serves.

For our bond to grow toward a more perfect union, we the people must make visible and progressive effort to grow and expand the factors that bind us together as a nation and reduce or decrease those that disunite us. It is the responsibility of all the people to make the sacrifice for the general good of all. If you as a citizen insist that your culture and tradition must be the dominant one, then you are not building toward a more perfect union. If any race among the multiple races in our country continues to advocate for supremacy over all others, the bond will be weakened by distrust and resentment among the citizenries. We cannot make progress toward a more perfect union if fear of our neighbors and fellow community members dominate our thoughts and activities. Unfortunately, we could continue to croup through the wilderness of hate, suspicion, division, and resentment or instead discover and expand the oasis of knowledge, love, peace, understanding, acceptability, and harmony that leads to a better and more inclusive union.

If the human desire to dominate any system of governance persists, representative democracy will remain a dream or an idea. A situation where a qualified Black person in a community with majority White citizens is not voted in to represent the people because of his race is a cultural and racial wilderness. Also, the unjustified practice of having a certain race continuously represents a community of minorities becoming a wilderness of deprivation can be intolerable. When people are deprived of their rights and privileges, they begin to fight back furiously to regain them. They may fight for years, decades, or centuries; it will not abort until justice is achieved or respites are given. The fight to abolish slavery led America to the civil war, which was a very devastating experience for all involved, the perpetrators and the victims alike. Its effect is still overwhelming on the people today as it was between 1860 and 1865 because so many people are still wallowing in the wilderness of hate and resentment. We the people of the United States of America must, for the sake of a better union, travel toward the oasis of repentance, humanity, forgiveness, restoration, reformation, and acceptance of diversity. Without which our progress toward a more perfect union may hit a snag or abruptly come to an end.

Factually, true forgiveness requires true repentance. Dr. Ron Allchin stated that, "Genuine repentance is crucial to the success of restoration of a relationship. Without it, the rebuilt relationship will almost certainly crumble with even more devastating results. It suggests wrongdoing, apologies, forgiveness, and change." Has America as a nation repented from the wrongdoing meted out to the enslaved Africans and their descendants? Or the massacre of the Native American tribes ever been recognized as evil against humanity? If there were any attempt at repentance, the continuous perpetration of the same wrongdoing in form of racism does not suggest any change in the descendants of the perpetrators. "Be not deceived; God is not mocked: for whatsoever a man soweth, that shall he also reap" (Gal. 6:7). Until we fix or resolve those issues, our growth to a stronger bond may remain unattainable.

We the people of the United States of America cannot deceive ourselves by pretending that those atrocities were not committed. The mere fact that certain people in the union are trying everything in their bags of tricks to suppress the history of slavery, racism, discrimination, or massacre of certain minority groups would not hide the truth but will remain an unrepented sin. It is insane for anyone to believe that wiping cleans a crime scene and will delete the crime from history or relieve the perpetrators from guilt. No, it will continue to pulsate the facts that something happened and needs to be accounted for.

Declaring Our Independence from the Wilderness of Controls

The Declaration of Independence document paints a better picture of what America symbolizes in human history. An idea! An idea that really digs into the Creator's will on how we should admin-

Finding Oasis Within the Wilderness of our Sociopolitical Ideologies

ister our existence. Without doubt, every human being possesses the inert desire for peaceful existence, freedom of expression, liberty in fulfilling one's dreams, sense of security and safety, and freedom to pursue individual happiness. To plant the tree that would bear the fruits of this idea, America needed to separate from the wilderness of autocracy (King George IV), corruption of European aristocrats, continuous violence of war, and suppressive tendencies of the colonial masters. We needed to remind ourselves that all men were created equal, and this equality must be preserved.

As important as the Declaration of Independence was to the establishment of this great country, most American citizens don't exactly know the text of this document and how it relates to the structure and functions of our republic. If you have never read this document before, this could be your opportunity to appreciate the statement in its entirety. If you had read it before, this provides another opportunity for you to review and gain more insight into its relevance to our system of governance.

In Congress, July 4, 1776, the unanimous Declaration of the thirteen United States of America

> *When in the Course of human events, it becomes necessary for one people to dissolve the political bands which have connected them with another, and to assume among the powers of the earth, the separate and equal station to which the Laws of Nature and of Nature's God entitle them, a decent respect to the opinions of mankind requires that they should declare the causes which impel them to the separation.*

Note: Although this declaration was made by a majority White population of the first thirteen states, the statement refers to mankind which include all the races. Maybe they did not realize that the declaration was on behalf of all mankind. In truth, as the demography continues to change from one generation to another, all the people no matter their differences, are under this umbrella of rights.

We hold these truths to be self-evident, that all men are created equal, that they are endowed by their Creator with certain unalienable Rights, that among these are Life, Liberty and the pursuit of Happiness—That to secure these rights, Governments are instituted among Men, deriving their just powers from the consent of the governed, that whenever any Form of Government becomes destructive of these ends, it is the Right of the People to alter or to abolish it, and to institute a new government, laying its foundation on such principles and organizing its powers in such form, as to them shall seem most likely to affect their Safety and Happiness. Prudence, indeed, will dictate that Governments long established should not be changed for light and transient causes; and accordingly, all experience hath shewn, that mankind is more disposed to suffer, while evils are sufferable, than to right themselves by abolishing the forms to which they are accustomed. But when a long train of abuses and usurpations, pursuing invariably the same Object evinces a design to reduce them under absolute Despotism, it is their right, it is their duty, to throw off such Government, and to provide new Guards for their future security. Such has been the patient sufferance of these Colonies; and such is now the necessity which constrains them to alter their former Systems of Government. The history of the present King of Great Britain is a history of repeated injuries and usurpations, all having in direct object the establishment of an absolute Tyranny over these States. To prove this, let Facts be submitted to a candid world.

Finding Oasis Within the Wilderness of our Sociopolitical Ideologies

Note: "We hold these truths to be self-evident, that all men are created equal, that they are endowed by their Creator with certain unalienable Rights, that among these are Life, Liberty and the pursuit of Happiness." Thus, the self-evidence inferred is based on the natural inclinations of mankind as originally intended by God. To be human, we all have equal number of eyes, ears, hands, legs, and all the external or internal organs. The blood that flows in every human being is "red" no matter the color of your skin, your physical appearance, the language that you speak, or your sociocultural inclinations. According to Genesis 1:27, "So God created man in his own image, in the image of God created he him; male and female created he them"; the equality of all mankind lies in the fact that we reflect God or his image.

It is not the will of the Almighty that man should dominate another man or enslave anyone. The evidence of human rights is embedded in the scriptures and in nature as indicated, "And God blessed them, and God said unto them, 'Be fruitful, and multiply, and replenish the earth, and subdue it: and have dominion over the fish of the sea, and over the fowl of the air, and over every living thing that moved upon the earth.' And God said, 'Behold, I have given you every herb bearing seed, which is upon the face of all the earth, and every tree, in the which is the fruit of a tree yielding seed; to you it shall be for meat. And to every beast of the earth, and to every fowl of the air, and to everything that crept upon the earth, wherein there is life, I have given every green herb for meat: and it was so'" (Gen. 1:28–30). These rights are for all mankind, and any attempt to deprive anyone of these rights amounts to disobedience to God's commandment.

The grievance continues:

> *He has refused his Assent to Laws, the most wholesome and necessary for the public good.*
>
> *He has forbidden his Governors to pass Laws of immediate and pressing importance, unless suspended in their operation till his Assent should be obtained; and when so suspended, he has utterly neglected to attend to them.*
>
> *He has refused to pass other Laws for the accommodation of large districts of people, unless those people would relinquish the right of Representation in the Legislature, a right inestimable to them and formidable to tyrants only.*
>
> *He has called together legislative bodies at places unusual, uncomfortable, and distant from the depository of their public Records, for the sole purpose of fatiguing them into compliance with his measures.*

He has dissolved Representative Houses repeatedly, for opposing with manly firmness his invasions on the rights of the people.

He has refused for a long time, after such dissolutions, to cause others to be elected; whereby the Legislative powers, incapable of Annihilation, have returned to the People at large for their exercise; the State remaining in the meantime exposed to all the dangers of invasion from without, and convulsions within.

He has endeavored to prevent the population of these States; for that purpose, obstructing the Laws for Naturalization of Foreigners; refusing to pass others to encourage their migrations hither, and raising the conditions of new Appropriations of Lands.

He has obstructed the Administration of Justice, by refusing his Assent to Laws for establishing Judiciary powers.

He has made Judges dependent on his Will alone, for the tenure of their offices, and the amount and payment of their salaries.

He has erected a multitude of New Offices and sent hither swarms of Officers to harass our people and eat out their substance.

He has kept among us, in times of peace, Standing Armies without the Consent of our legislatures.

He has affected to render the Military independent of and superior to the Civil power.

He has combined with others to subject us to a jurisdiction foreign to our constitution, and unacknowledged by our laws, giving his Assent to their Acts of pretended Legislation:

For Quartering large bodies of armed troops among us:

For protecting them, by a mock Trial, from punishment for any Murders which they should commit on the Inhabitants of these States:

For cutting off our Trade with all parts of the world:

For imposing Taxes on us without our Consent:

For depriving us in many cases, of the benefits of Trial by Jury:

For transporting us beyond Seas to be tried for pretended offences

For abolishing the free System of English Laws in a neighboring Province, establishing therein an Arbitrary government, and enlarging its Boundaries to render it at once an example and fit instrument for introducing the same absolute rule into these Colonies:

For taking away our Charters, abolishing our most valuable Laws, and altering fundamentally the Forms of our Governments:

For suspending our own Legislatures and declaring themselves invested with power to legislate for us in all cases whatsoever.

He has abdicated Government here, by declaring us out of his Protection and waging War against us.

He has plundered our seas, ravaged our Coasts, burnt our towns, and destroyed the lives of our people.

He is at this time transporting large Armies of foreign Mercenaries to complete the works of death, desolation and tyranny, already begun with circumstances of Cruelty & perfidy scarcely paralleled in the most barbarous ages, and totally unworthy the Head of a civilized nation.

He has constrained our fellow Citizens taken Captive on the high Seas to bear Arms against their Country, to become the executioners of their friends and Brethren, or to fall themselves by their Hands.

He has excited domestic insurrections amongst us and has endeavored to bring on the inhabitants of our frontiers, the merciless Indian Savages, whose known rule of warfare, is an undistinguished destruction of all ages, sexes and conditions.

In every stage of these Oppressions We have Petitioned for Redress in the most humbled terms: Our repeated Petitions have been answered only by repeated injury. A Prince whose character is thus marked by every act which may define a Tyrant, is unfit to be the ruler of a free people.

Nor have We been wanting in attentions to our British brethren. We have warned them from time to time of attempts by their legislature to extend an unwarrantable jurisdiction over us. We reminded them of the circumstances of our emigration and settlement here. We have appealed to their native justice and magnanimity, and we have conjured them by the ties of our common kindred to disavow these usurpations, which would inevitably interrupt our connections and correspondence. They too have been deaf to the voice of justice and of consanguinity. We must, therefore, acquiesce in the necessity, which denounces our Separation, and hold them, as we hold the rest of mankind, Enemies in War, in Peace Friends.

We, therefore, the Representatives of the united States of America, in General Congress, Assembled, appealing to the Supreme Judge of the world for the rectitude of our intentions, do, in the Name, and by Authority of the good People of these Colonies, solemnly publish and declare, That these United Colonies are, and of Right ought to be Free and Independent States; that they are Absolved from all Allegiance to the British Crown, and that all political connection between them and the State of

Great Britain, is and ought to be totally dissolved; and that as Free and Independent States, they have full Power to levy War, conclude Peace, contract Alliances, establish Commerce, and to do all other Acts and Things which Independent States may of right to do. And for the support of this Declaration, with a firm reliance on the protection of divine Providence, we mutually pledge to each other our Lives, our Fortunes, and our sacred Honor.

(Source: National Archives. https://www.archives.gov/founding-docs/declaration-transcript)

Note: All the allegations, accusations, and complaints labeled against the British monarchy before the final separation were fully justified. King George IV acted as a monarch which he was, with the characteristics of autocracy which placed all the power to rule on one person. His rule was contrary to the desire of the people to be free and to pursue their happiness: stringent taxing, excessive use of force to compel the people to give up their possessions and resources in feeding and quartering an army of foreign mercenaries, subject only to the king and his appointed officials, proclaiming unjust laws to control the people and refusing to make laws that would have brought order and prosperity to the hardworking people of the colonies.

Declaring independence from the cruelty of their colonial masters and forcefully executing their will through the revolution war of 19 April 1775 to 3 September 1783 could be viewed as a divine intervention for the sake of the unalienable human and civil rights that the people duly deserved. The concluding statement of the declaration as written, "We, therefore, the Representatives of the united States of America, in General Congress, Assembled, appealing to the Supreme Judge of the world for the rectitude of our intentions, do, in the Name, and by Authority of the good People of these Colonies, solemnly publish and declare, That these United Colonies are, and of Right ought to be Free and Independent States..." drew the line that King George IV and the British could not cross. However, American people are still fighting, even within a democracy, to uphold our God-given rights and benefits.

Writing a declaration statement for the purpose of justifying the reasons for separating from the British Empire and becoming an independent nation did not provide sufficient evidence that the new country was going to be the solution to all the problems mentioned. American democracy was an idea that started as an experiment influenced by both human imperfection and human triumphs. From one generation to another, progress was made to upgrade the institutions of democracy, expand the inclusiveness of the people's representation in the government, and provide conducive atmospheres for all to pursue their happiness. But the people are still left with the situation of fighting to uphold their rights in every generation bedeviled by some people who tend to lean toward autocracy and cruelty instead of freedom, liberty, and equal justice under the law.

Throughout history, autocracy has been in controversy with democracy. Resistance of the few against the will and desire of most of the people persist in all human endeavors, with every intent to dominate the majority at all costs. They may arise as individuals that take over dominion to rule the rest with iron fists or as a group of people who make claims to birthrights as their basis to controlling and subduing everyone else. Today we can still observe these human conditions in laws created by some to control others, resources being looted by few to the alienation of some communities, and structural injustice perpetrated by society's elites to marginalize certain ethnicities.

For America to be truly independent and free, all the people must be freed from whatever chain of restrictions that are put in their ankles. The founders demanded complete independence from

Great Britain but enslaved the Africans, restricted economic progress to only male-gendered White people, reduced the women to homemaking, to be seen and not to be heard, and fraudulently restricted voting rights to only land and property owners (owning people as property included). Their stands were against true freedom, liberty, equality, and justice. The irony of it was that they wanted independence for themselves and not necessarily for all other groups outside the assumed inner circle of beneficiaries. A government of such pedigree would have been worse than the autocracy of a monarchy.

They needed a constitution to spell out the intricacies of a new, unique, and contrastable government, structured to achieve all that they accused King George of not doing, and to right all the wrongs that they were agitated by, in their dealings with the British Empire. However, their human greed and self-centeredness was in the way. They fought furiously among themselves, debated unendingly over issues that were more cultural than practical, and spent countless hours achieving less to nothing. Unable to proceed as a group, the constitutional conference resorted to the capabilities of three prominent members of the body: James Madison, John Adams, and Thomas Jefferson to write the constitution of the new country. As incomplete and imperfect as the document was, it was a step in the right direction. Therefore, it demanded continuous amendment to become a more befitting document for the preservation of the rights of the people and the establishment of a true democracy for the United States of America.

Although America has endured centuries of sociopolitical difficulties like any other civilization in history, the ability to overcome such difficulties always lies with the new generation. They toil, research, and apply new knowledge and skills to bring solutions to the problems encountered or even perpetrated by the past generation while at the same time generating their own problems for the future generations. Problems that cannot be resolved in the present always find solutions in the future. However, the most modern situation the country is experiencing is the dichotomy between the generations that are coexisting due to the increase in generational lifespan. The older generations want to hold on to power, and the new generations are either less interested in government or are systematically deprived of the civic education required to initiate them into the responsibilities of leadership. These struggle to hold power by the older generation has tended to create a lot of vacuums that would become serious issues that will create political wilderness for the United States of America.

If the younger generation does not understand the political power structure in our political system, how would they handle the baton when the self-serving older generation finally moves on? Today we have presidential candidates who are more than seventy years old vying for the presidency after two presidents over seventy years of age already occupied the White House.

CHAPTER 3

Order in the Oasis: Pillars of Power and Functions

We the People!

Based on the Declaration of Independence as well as the people's rights to exist and to pursue their own happiness without any subjugation by authorities of a monarch, American democracy was born. At the pinnacle of the power structure is the people, all the people, and not sections. The rights, welfare, and prosperity of the people is paramount in this structured government. In a way, we could say that "the people" is the boss or the owner of this business.

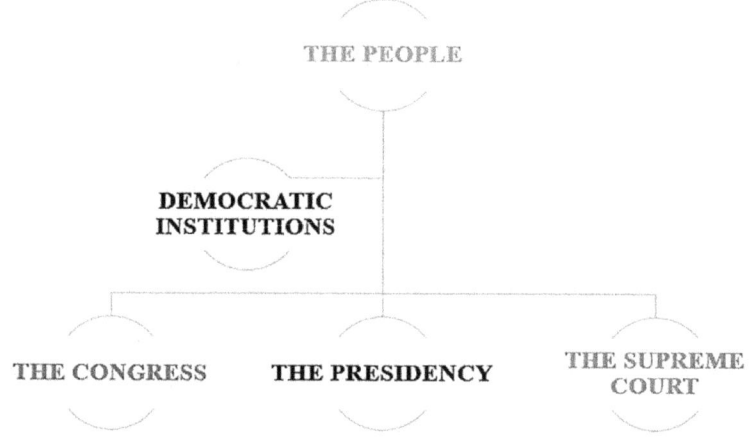

Finding Oasis Within the Wilderness of our Sociopolitical Ideologies

Government is the business of the people, and the republic is the sole property of the people of the United States of America. In this business, every American citizen owns a unit share in the commonwealth of the republic, and the shares are represented symbolically and practically as "one vote." Like a check, every vote determines the will of the people. Where the majority decides every outcome, the minority benefits from the decision as well. The beautiful thing about this oasis is that decisions are not determined based on dominant races, rather on the general views of all the people. However, the wilderness of autocracy, greed, biases, racism, discrimination, and corruption creeps in at the slightest opportunity. Therefore, the more people participate in the process of managing their business, the better they can fight against these encroaching deserts of destruction and expand the oasis.

The power of the people can only work when all the people bond together as one force to attack the wilderness of destruction. Plato stated that "One of the penalties for refusing to participate in politics is that you end up being governed by your inferiors." When you refuse to vote for the right candidates, be ready to accept the wrong ones. Having a say in your business, protecting its integrity, and pushing for a better performance consistently is important in growing toward a more perfect union. "Politics is not a game. It is an earnest business" (Winston Churchill). It requires dedication and honesty from both the owners and the managers. It requires serious and dedicated political administrators to manage effectively and not corrupt, self-serving, undedicated individuals whose main aim is to destabilize and steal from the people the benefits of their government. The government is supposed to serve the people and not otherwise. It requires the people who are the real owners of the government to be alert to the business of governance and be ready to demand accountability from whosoever they elected to manage their business. They must not allow political differences or ideologies create divisiveness among them such that their ability to control the power of government is diminished by corruption or corrupted officials who are always ready to take undue advantage of any loophole in the system.

American Democratic Institutions

Since democracy is the business of the people, democratic institutions are subjects to the will of the people as well. They are institutions established to develop and protect democracy and the people's rights. You may have some ideas what they are, or you may not realize that they are important for democracy to thrive: legislative bodies, electoral boards, executive bodies and institutions, police commissions, ombudsman institutions, human right councils, check and balance systems, press institutions, investigative bodies, departments of justice, courts, and judiciary bodies, to mention but a few.

Generally, the definition of "institution" is that it is "a society or organization founded for a religious, educational, social, or similar purposes." They are meant to serve the people privately or publicly. But what are democratic institutions? Why are they important? Who do they serve? Simply stated, "A democratic institution would be the procedures or routines of democratic system that defines how it functions." However, its definition means more than portrayed. They are institutions that drive our democracy to function to the levels or standards that allow growth and progress toward a more perfect union of the people.

In addition, they define the processes by which democracy can function efficiently and accessible to all the people. From the enactment of laws to their executions, investigation of civil offenses to the application of consequences, democratic institutions play major roles in applying fairness and equality status of all Americans.

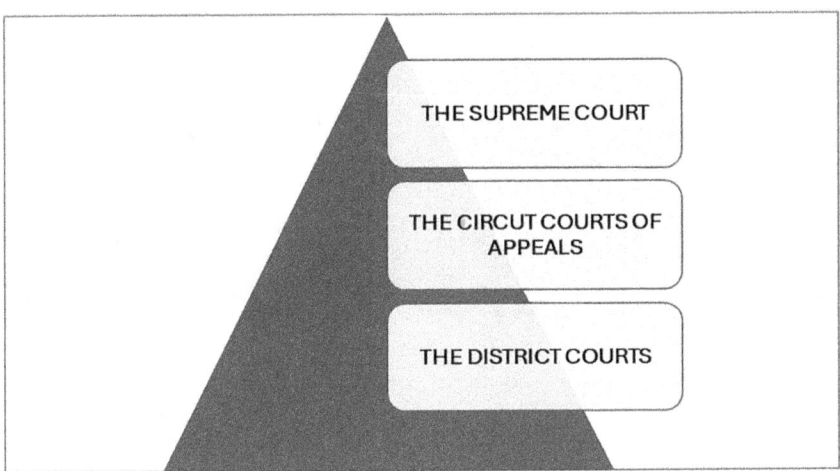

The court system, for example, follows levels of case resolutions that implement or protect the rights of the people even under trials. The hierarchy of the court system displays an arrangement that allows cases to be determined from the lowest court to the highest court in the land. If the conflicts are not resolved in the lower court, they are moved to the next higher courts, appeals courts, or the Supreme Court.

Investigative and policing bodies like the Federal Bureau of Investigation, police departments, sheriff departments, and other law enforcement units are authorized to investigate crimes, protect lives and property, and maintain order in society. While others like Secret Service are meant to check financial crimes and provide protection to high-ranking civil officials like the president and the vice president of the United States of America. All these institutions and more operate based on our major democratic values: freedom, liberty, equal justice, and fairness under the law. Unfortunately, we must not leave out the encroaching wilderness of corruption, racism, discrimination, biases, misjudgment, manipulation of data, as well as cover-ups. These institutions are not perfect, but they still possess competency in carrying out their functions despite the human imperfection that riddles the system.

It is important for every American and American citizen to understand the importance and functions of democratic institutions in relation to us as Democratic-Republicans, owners of the republic and owners of the government. If we are very familiar with the departments in our jobs and businesses, we must be fully acquainted with the functions of our democratic institutions and how they serve us. We the people must push for the institutions to work more effectively and fairly for all the citizens. If we don't take notice of the injustice committed in our law enforcement institutions, policymaking agencies, people's welfare departments, public health institutions, educational institutions, to mention but a few, we may not be able to fight for their eradication. Having insight, no matter how limited, is necessary for us to hold these institutions accountable when they underperform or go against the principles of our democracy and cultural values.

Really, the republic must function according to the will of the people, not that of the politicians. It must operate based on the core values of our society. According to Charles W. Pickering, "A healthy democracy requires a decent society; it requires that we are honorable, generous, tolerant and respectful." Therefore, our democratic institutions must reflect our values and democratic principles. Unfortunately, no matter how positive the values may be, their integration and implementation tend to be elusive due to either structural defects or human errors.

The People's House, the Congress

The importance of the congress to all the people of the United States of America cannot be overemphasized. It is the people's house where laws are created to govern and resolve constituency problems. So let's remind us of the preamble of the constitution: "We the People of the United States, in Order to form a more perfect Union, establish Justice, ensure domestic Tranquility, provide for the common defense, promote the general Welfare, and secure the Blessings of Liberty to ourselves and our Posterity, do ordain and establish this Constitution for the United States of America." It is where the representatives of all the people congregate to carry out the will of the people as stated.

The establishment of the congress is duly imbedded in the constitutional Article I, Sections 1–10. If you desire to understand the importance and functions of the constitutional establishment of the congress, you may refer to https://constitutionus.com/. Whether it's about the makeup of the chambers, the representatives from each constituency, district, or state, your understanding of the importance of electing qualified officials to hold office on your behalf cannot be overstressed. They are expected to be your eyes, ears, and voice in this congregation of representatives. As stated in Article I, Section 1, "All legislative Powers herein granted shall be vested in a Congress of the United States, which shall consist of a Senate and House of Representatives." This is not the power of the politicians but your power as the owners of the government. The execution of this power must be to the benefit of the republic, that is all the states and all the people that are domiciled in the United States of America as a country. Therefore, our citizenship includes holding the government accountable for their actions.

The Senate is the upper chamber of the congress. According to Article II, Section 3,

> *The Senate of the United States shall be composed of two Senators from each State, chosen by the Legislature thereof, for six Years; and each Senator shall have one Vote.*
>
> *Immediately after they shall be assembled in Consequence of the first Election, they shall be divided as equally as may be into three Classes. The Seats of the Senators of the first Class shall be vacated at the Expiration of the second Year, of the second Class at the Expiration of the fourth Year, and of the third Class at the Expiration of the sixth Year, so that one third may be chosen every second Year; and if Vacancies happen by Resignation, or otherwise, during the Recess of the Legislature of any State, the Executive thereof may make temporary Appointments until the next Meeting of the Legislature, which shall then fill such Vacancies.*
>
> *No Person shall be a Senator who shall not have attained to the Age of thirty Years and been nine Years a Citizen of the United States, and who shall not, when elected, be an Inhabitant of that State for which he shall be chosen.*
>
> *The Vice President of the United States shall be President of the Senate, but shall have no Vote, unless they be equally divided.*
>
> *The Senate shall choose their other Officers, and also a President pro tempore, in the Absence of the Vice President, or when he shall exercise the Office of President of the United States.*
>
> *The Senate shall have the sole Power to try all Impeachments. When sitting for that Purpose, they shall be on Oath or Affirmation. When the President of the United States is tried, the Chief*

> *Justice shall preside: And no Person shall be convicted without the Concurrence of two thirds of the Members present.*
>
> *Judgment in Cases of impeachment shall not extend further than to removal from Office, and disqualification to hold and enjoy any Office of honor, Trust or Profit under the United States: but the Party convicted shall nevertheless be liable and subject to Indictment, Trial, Judgment and Punishment, according to Law.*

The Senate is set as an equity power of all the states since every state is entitled to two Senate representatives; the power of making decisions is equal no matter what the population or economic status are. However, when these authorities are expressed in certain situations, smaller states seem to exhume the power to obstruct the will of the majority. Throughout the history of the Senate, a lot more impasses have been achieved than actual bipartisan victories. Although designed to balance the power of the states, the cultural and economic factors tend to make their application more of a "pullback" force than a "push-forward" and progressive trajectory momentum.

Finding Oasis Within the Wilderness of our Sociopolitical Ideologies

The House of Representatives is the lower chamber of the congress. According to Article I, Section 2 of the constitution, it is the chamber with more grassroot representation of the people than the Senate. Presently, a total of four hundred and thirty-five districts are represented in the House of Representatives. As the power base of the people, the function of this chamber is very extensive, as well as more accessible to the citizens than the Senate.

> *The House of Representatives shall be composed of Members chosen every second Year by the People of the several States, and the Electors in each State shall have the Qualifications requisite for Electors of the most numerous Branch of the State Legislature.*
>
> *No Person shall be a Representative who shall not have attained to the Age of twenty-five Years and been seven Years a Citizen of the United States, and who shall not, when elected, be an Inhabitant of that State in which he shall be chosen.*
>
> *Representatives and direct Taxes shall be apportioned among the several States which may be included within this Union, according to their respective Numbers, which shall be determined by adding to the whole Number of free Persons, including those bound to Service for a Term of Years, and excluding Indians not taxed, three fifths of all other Persons (Remedied through the 14th Amendment). The actual Enumeration shall be made within three Years after the first Meeting of the Congress of the United States, and within every subsequent Term of ten Years, in such Manner as they shall by Law direct. The Number of Representatives shall not exceed one for every thirty Thousand, but each State shall have at Least one Representative; and until such enumeration shall be made, the State of New Hampshire shall be entitled to choose three, Massachusetts eight, Rhode-Island and Providence*

Plantations one, Connecticut five, New-York six, New Jersey four, Pennsylvania eight, Delaware one, Maryland six, Virginia ten, North Carolina five, South Carolina five, and Georgia three.

When vacancies happen in the Representation from any State, the Executive Authority thereof shall issue Writs of Election to fill such Vacancies.

The House of Representatives shall choose their Speaker and other Officers; and shall have the sole Power of Impeachment.

In retrospect, Congress functions for the following reasons: lawmaking, representing the people, performing oversight, helping constituents, and educating the public. The primary function of Congress, which is lawmaking, is one which this body struggles to perform due to contentious debates over what should be considered as law for all to obey. "It is better, as far as getting the vote is concerned, I believe, to have a small, united group than an immense debating society" (Alice Paul). The wilderness that exists in the Congress is unimaginable, and it really needs an oasis of collaboration and cooperation to function as was intended. In a wilderness, nothing is easy, and habitation is nearly impossible.

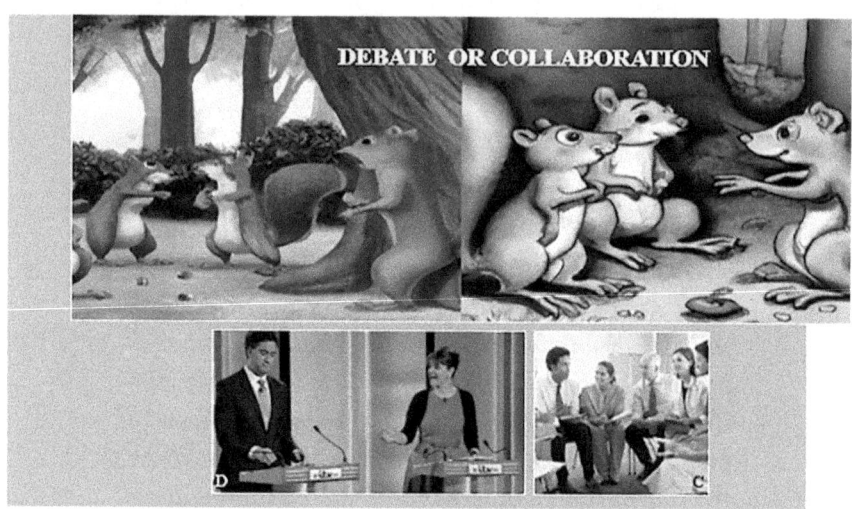

Finding Oasis Within the Wilderness of our Sociopolitical Ideologies

According to George P. Shultz, "Nothing ever gets settled in this town. A seething debating society in which the debate never stops, in which people never give up, including me. And so that's the atmosphere in which you administer." We the people can change all that by electing the right minds and skills to represent our community in Congress, as well as set up discussion protocols and collaborative structures that induce positive problem-solving principles for the Congress to function efficiently.

What the founders never anticipated was the problem of gerrymandering. The two major political platforms have unfortunately engaged in excessive political gerrymandering tactics meant to put the opposition at a representative disadvantage. As expressively stated in the constitution, every community of a population of up to thirty thousand residents or more is entitled to a district representation in the Congress. The issue may not be on the actual population but on how the redistricting maps are drawn. Some party impositions have over the years engaged in the unjust habits of splitting communities that tended to vote more for the opposition into districts that puts such communities in a representation disadvantages. Those communities lose political power of not being able to elect representatives of their choice but forced to cast votes that will never produce candidates the people desire to send to Congress. In many instances, such communities become dissatisfied with politics and become redundant, frustrated, and possibly become very aggressive with any political move by the opposition. Community progress is stalled, the will of the people trample upon, and systematically the power of the people to rule is taken away by corrupt politicians. If the will of the American people at the grassroots are unjustly tampered upon and their political power stolen, then the will of all American people has been subverted by corruption; for injustice anywhere is injustice everywhere.

Although many political minds have suggested that redistricting must be done by an independent redistricting commission, the fact remains that human errors, cultural and sociopolitical influences may continue to drastically influence any decision made by such a commission. However, attaching any such commission to the National

Population Commission will take away the influence of the political parties from the redistricting process and allow the commission to carry out a fair and equitable redistricting job that will be satisfactory to all the political shareholders. It will be the actual population data that will determine the maps and not the political will of the parties. Also, having a range of population spread needed for decision-making is important to avoid little discrepancies. For example, a community whose population went down from thirty thousand to twenty-eight thousand cannot be redistributed into other districts but can still maintain its district status without many changes. However, it is justifiable if the population went down to fifteen thousand or less.

On the other hand, if there is an increase in population from thirty thousand to about thirty-five thousand, the increase is insignificant and must not trigger any redistribution. But a population increase from thirty thousand to fifty thousand is significant and should trigger redistribution and redistricting, creating one more district from the increase. Therefore, it is a statistically proficient institution like the National Population Commission or Bureau that will provide the data analysis needed to make these important decisions and not the political parties. The Congress, the political parties, the people, and other political shareholders must mutter the political will to make these changes that will bring equity and trust into the whole process of population distribution and redistricting.

The People's House, the White House

Most people believe that the presidency is the most important pillar of American democracy. I beg to differ with many reasons based more on power structure and authority. The presidency may be the most politically appealing, but its authority is limited in comparison with the Congress and the Supreme Court. Its function depends on the lawmaking of the Congress and what is allowed in the constitution, defended by the Supreme Court and the court system. However, without the presidency, the functions of the other pillars may derail or not function at all because it requires a central office to execute policies and laws, administer the total welfare, security, and prosperity of the republic. The president may be the most powerful office holder in the country but does not have an absolute power or absolute authority to make decisions without consulting the Congress and upholding the constitution.

The origin of the word "president" tends to reflect a position or a person who leads out in a meeting or a gathering of people for specific purposes. "A president of a company is typically the primary leader of the day-to-day operations of a business, agency, institution, school, etc. Like a political president, he or she is often one of the most visible people in the organization" (Kate Lopaze, The Job Network). Historically, the word president, "found in Latin in the present participle *praesidentum*, in relation to the verb *praesidēre*, understood as presiding in the action from a high hierarchical position, formed by the elements *prae*, which refers to something previous or earlier and that in this context indicates being in front, and *sedere*, interpreted as "to sit," with roots in the Indo-European word *sed* for "to sit" and completed by the suffix -nt, to make it function as a noun."

"It is a position that represents the highest authority of the state, as well as at the corporate level, placing the individual in absolute display and prominence, demanding a high degree of responsibility and commitment in the making of their decisions and actions" (Benjamin Veschi, Founder and Author of Etymology.net). In the early Continental Congress of America (1774–1789), it was more of a ceremonial position to preside over meetings and day-to-day administration of the Congress and national correspondence of the continental government. Consequently, the establishment and implementation of the United States Constitution upon the ratification of the states, the position of the president became and is still the most powerful office in the land.

The establishment of the presidency in Article II (Sections 1–3) with Section 1, Clause 3 being replaced by the Twelfth Amendment and Section 1, Clause 6 redressed with the Twentieth Amendment and the Twenty-Fifth Amendment.

Article II, Section 1

1. The executive Power shall be vested in a President of the United States of America. He shall hold his Office during the Term of four Years, and, together with the Vice President, chosen for the same Term, be elected, as follows:
2. Each State shall appoint, in such Manner as the Legislature thereof may direct, several Electors, equal to the whole Number of Senators and Representatives to which the State may be entitled in the Congress: but no Senator or Representative, or Person holding an Office of Trust or Profit under the United States, shall be appointed an Elector.
3. The Electors shall meet in their respective States, and vote by Ballot for two Persons, of whom one at least shall not be an Inhabitant of the same State with themselves. And they shall make a List of all the Persons voted for, and of the Number of Votes for each, which List they shall sign and certify, and transmit sealed to the Seat of the Government of the United States, directed to the President of the Senate. The President of the Senate shall, in the Presence of the Senate and House of Representatives, open all the Certificates, and the Votes shall then be counted. The Person having the greatest Number of Votes shall be the President, if such Number be a Majority of the whole Number of Electors appointed; and if there be more than one who have such Majority, and have an equal Number of Votes, then the House of Representatives shall immediately choose by Ballot, one of them for President; and if no Person have a Majority, then from the five highest on the List the said House shall in like Manner chose the President. But in choosing the President, the Votes shall be taken by States, the Representation from each State having one Vote; A quorum for this Purpose shall consist of a Member or Members from two thirds of the States, and a Majority of all the States shall be necessary to a Choice. In

every Case, after the Choice of the President, the Person having the greatest Number of Votes of the Electors shall be the Vice President. But if there should remain two or more who have equal Votes, the Senate shall choose from them by Ballot the Vice President.

*****

Twelfth Amendment of the constitution

The Electors shall meet in their respective states, and vote by ballot for President and Vice President, one of whom, at least, shall not be an inhabitant of the same state with themselves; they shall name in their ballots the person voted for as President, and in distinct ballots the person voted for as Vice President, and they shall make distinct lists of all persons voted for as President, and of all persons voted for as Vice President, and of the number of votes for each, which lists they shall sign and certify, and transmit sealed to the seat of the government of the United States, directed to the President of the Senate;

— The President of the Senate shall, in the presence of the Senate and House of Representatives, open all the certificates and the votes shall then be counted.
— The person having the greatest number of votes for President, shall be the President, if such number be a majority of the whole number of Electors appointed; and if no person have such majority, then from the persons having the highest numbers not exceeding three on the list of those voted for as President, the House of Representatives shall choose immediately, by ballot, the President. But in choosing the President, the votes shall be taken by states, the representation from each state having one vote; a quorum for this purpose shall consist of a member or members from two-thirds of the states, and a majority of all the states shall be necessary to a choice. And if the House of

Representatives shall not choose a President whenever the right of choice shall devolve upon them, before the fourth day of March next following, then the Vice President shall act as President, as in the case of the death or other constitutional disability of the President. note 14 —The person having the greatest number of votes as Vice President, shall be the Vice President, if such number be a majority of the whole number of Electors appointed, and if no person have a majority, then from the two highest numbers on the list, the Senate shall choose the Vice President; a quorum for the purpose shall consist of two-thirds of the whole number of Senators, and a majority of the whole number shall be necessary to a choice. But no person constitutionally ineligible to the office of President shall be eligible to that of Vice President of the United States.

*****

4. The Congress may determine the Time of choosing the Electors, and the Day on which they shall give their Votes, which Day shall be the same throughout the United States.
5. No Person except a natural born Citizen, or a Citizen of the United States, at the time of the Adoption of this Constitution, shall be eligible to the Office of President; neither shall any Person be eligible to that Office who shall not have attained to the Age of thirty-five Years, and been fourteen Years a Resident within the United States.
6. In Case of the Removal of the President from Office, or of his Death, Resignation, or Inability to discharge the Powers and Duties of the said Office, the Same shall devolve on the Vice President, and the Congress may by Law provide for the Case of Removal, Death, Resignation or Inability, both of the President and Vice President, declaring what Officer shall then act as President, and such Officer shall act accordingly, until the Disability be removed, or a President shall be elected.

Twentieth Amendment of the Constitution

1. The terms of the President and Vice President shall end at noon on the 20th day of January, and the terms of Senators and Representatives at noon on the 3rd day of January, of the years in which such terms would have ended if this article had not been ratified; and the terms of their successors shall then begin.
2. The Congress shall assemble at least once every year, and such meeting shall begin at noon on the 3rd day of January, unless they shall by law appoint a different day.
3. If, at the time fixed for the beginning of the term of the President, the President elect shall have died, the Vice President elect shall become President. If a President shall not have been chosen before the time fixed for the beginning of his term, or if the President elect shall have failed to qualify, then the Vice President elect shall act as President until a President shall have qualified; and the Congress may by law provide for the case wherein neither a President elect nor a Vice President elect shall have qualified, declaring who shall then act as President, or the manner in which one who is to act shall be selected, and such person shall act accordingly until a President or Vice President shall have qualified.
4. The Congress may by law provide for the case of the death of any of the persons from whom the House of Representatives may choose a President whenever the right of choice shall have devolved upon them, and for the case of the death of any of the persons from whom the Senate may choose a Vice President whenever the right of choice shall have devolved upon them.
5. Sections 1 and 2 shall take effect on the 15th day of October following the ratification of this article.
6. This article shall be inoperative unless it shall have been ratified as an amendment to the Constitution by the legislatures of three-fourths of the several States within seven years from the date of its submission.

Twenty-Fifth Amendment of the constitution

1. In case of the removal of the President from office or of his death or resignation, the Vice President shall become President.
2. Whenever there is a vacancy in the office of the Vice President, the President shall nominate a Vice President who shall take office upon confirmation by a majority vote of both Houses of Congress.
3. Whenever the President transmits to the President pro tempore of the Senate and the Speaker of the House of Representatives his written declaration that he is unable to discharge the powers and duties of his office, and until he transmits to them a written declaration to the contrary, such powers and duties shall be discharged by the Vice President as Acting President.
4. Whenever the Vice President and a majority of either the principal officers of the executive departments or of such other body as Congress may by law provide, transmit to the President pro tempore of the Senate and the Speaker of the House of Representatives their written declaration that the President is unable to discharge the powers and duties of his office, the Vice President shall immediately assume the powers and duties of the office as Acting President.

Thereafter, when the President transmits to the President pro tempore of the Senate and the Speaker of the House of Representatives his written declaration that no inability exists, he shall resume the powers and duties of his office unless the Vice President and a majority of either the principal officers of the executive department or of such other body as Congress may by law provide, transmit within four days to the President pro tempore of the Senate and the Speaker of the House of Representatives their written declaration that the President is unable to discharge the powers and duties of his office. Thereupon Congress shall decide the issue, assembling within forty-eight hours for that purpose if not in session. If the Congress, within twenty-one days after receipt of the latter written declaration, or, if Congress is not in session, within twenty-one days after Congress is required to assemble, determines by two-thirds vote of both Houses that the President is unable to discharge the powers and duties of his office, the Vice President shall continue to discharge the same as Acting President; otherwise, the President shall resume the powers and duties of his office.

*****

7. The President shall, at stated Times, receive for his Services, a Compensation, which shall neither be increased nor diminished during the Period for which he shall have been elected, and he shall not receive within that Period any other Emolument from the United States, or any of them.
8. Before he enters on the Execution of his Office, he shall take the following Oath or Affirmation: — *"I do solemnly swear (or affirm) that I will faithfully execute the Office of President of the United States, and will to the best of my Ability, preserve, protect and defend the Constitution of the United States."*

Providing all the sections in the constitution, including the Twelfth, Twentieth, and the Twenty-Fifth Amendments that defines the office of the president and the vice president of the United States of America, is by design. Since this book is for the consumption of the layman and not necessarily for experts in constitutional laws, it is important for us to understand that the office of the president and vice president of the United States began as ceremonial positions and then to becoming the most powerful office in the land. Although the president is the leader of this great country, the power of the presidency is still the power of the people.

Perhaps, among some of the issues the founders did not anticipate is the idea of a president who loses a reelection bidding and decides to manipulate the terms of the constitution to remain in office despite every evidence that he or her lost the election. The attempted coup carried out by Donald J. Trump in 2020 election to remain in office despite losing the popular vote by more than seven million votes and losing the electoral college by a whooping seventy-four less votes than Joe Biden. Therefore, it is important for all the citizens to understand that the president is a representative of all the people, voted in by majority of the people, to work for the good of the people of United States of America. He is a leader for all and not only for those who voted him into office. The loyalty of the president is to the people and not to his party or special interest groups. As a leader, respect for the presidency is bestowed on him, and the respect and honor of the people is embodied in that position. The position of the president must inspire awe, not just from the citizens, but from the person occupying the position. From the mannerism of the president to his speech presentations, the respect and eloquence of the leader of the free world is expected.

For the first time in modern history of the United States of America, Americans all over the world felt the total dishonor meted out to this special position because of the personality of the occupant of the office. The president spent almost the whole duration of his four-year term in campaigning for his party. Week in, week out, the rant of "Lock her up!" rend through our television sets as the unconstitutional call to imprison the former secretary of state, Hillary Clinton, without any indictment, trial by jury, or conviction became the rule. To his party faithful, it was entertainment gallows, but to other Americans who probably expected better from a leader, it was the most torturing disrespect meted out to the presidency. Not only did he distort the real image of the president of the United States of America, but the language and speech making ability of an American president was also completely debased to the consternation of most citizens, if not all.

For the first time in the history of our democracy, America was presented with a president whose personality was completely contrary to the position of an American leader. Between January 20, 2017, and January 20, 2021, American citizens experienced the most distorted administration in American history: the unconstitutional banning of Muslims from Arab countries, the disrespectful reference to African and Central American countries as "Shithole countries!", the interference in the work of health scientists or weather scientists by a person whose knowledge of science and technology is less than that of an elementary school pupil, the name-calling of anyone whose opinion is contrary to the view of the president, and nepotism that reigned in the White House, to mention but a few.

The dishonor did not stop at home but found its way to foreign policies and foreign lands. Who will claim that they have forgotten the near collapse of NATO because of the "Pay to play!" approach of Donald Trump in dealing with the member nations of the greatest military alliance that was spearheaded by the United States of America to prevent the recurrence of the factors that led to the Second World War? If Americans have forgotten, the world has not! To add salt to injury, the unjustifiable withdrawal of the United States from the Paris Climatic Accord when the world's climatic condition was becoming extreme gave no credence to reasons. The unfortunate, self-centered cover-up perpetrated to deceive American citizens regarding the seriousness of the invading COVID-19 virus that led to the avoidable deaths of more than one million Americans within a space of three years of the pandemic. If you as an American citizen, no matter your sociopolitical affiliation, have forgotten the terrible loss of souls, the families, and relations of those whose loved ones perished have not forgotten. It's all due to the corrupt behavior of Donald John Trump. To be candid, the American people prefer to be told the truth and allowed the opportunity to make decisions that will affect their lives either positively or negatively instead of the cover-up scheme carried out by an autocratic personality for his self-aggrandizement.

All the incandescent display of incompetency and utter disregard to the constitution and laws of the United States of America by an American president whose oath of office demands upholding the constitution and implementing the laws of the land has finally sunken in that the congress must pass the "Presidential Behavior Act" that will specify how an American president must behave, carry out his or her duties without conflict of interest, and treat the office of the president with the respect which befits the leader of the free world. It is time to spell out the consequences for breaking leadership rules beyond just impeachment and removal from office. It is time to remove the stringent conditions that makes it almost impossible to hold the occupants of the office accountable for their illegal behavior while at the same time protecting the office from political manipulation of liars and those who intend to do harm to or defame the president.

The idea of certain members of the United States Congress spearheading an unfortunate act of abusing their position in carrying out fake investigations aimed at defaming the family of the president, simply because he or her is not from their party platform. Over and over and over again, American citizens have been bombarded with the false information of referring to the Biden's family as "a crime family," without any evidence, grand jury indictments, or criminal convictions. A family whose members never participated in the governance of this country, except one, the president. Why should a group of politicians persist in defaming the character of this family for the purpose of gaining political advantage? Maybe as voters and the owners of the government, you have allowed that to happen. If politicians lie to your face to curry your vote, it means they have no respect for you, and you must make them pay by voting them out. The direct responsibility lies with the districts they represent to do the necessary thing. The other districts must put on political pressure to make sure that justice is done. American democracy can only excel with truth as the foundation. Without truth, chaos sets in, and democracy turns autocratic.

Any presidential candidate who promises to fight for the people or make changes to the ways the White House operates must state exactly how he or she intends to carry that out. The voters must demand specificities in their promises and monitor their achievements when voted in. If they promise making changes to the ways and manners of doing business in the presidency without stating the legality and constitutional support of their proposals, we the people should know that deception is in the making and must separate from such candidates. A candidate whose intention is to break the constitution to impose his will on the people must not be allowed to go near the presidency by any district, party affiliates, state, domain, constituency, or any group through voting. The main responsibility of the president is to uphold the constitution and enforce the laws of the country. He or she is the chief law enforcement officer of the nation and must be dedicated to the duty of law enforcement without fear or favor. America is a nation ruled by law and not by personalities. It follows "the rule of law" and not that of persons for this is what democracy is all about. We cannot as a nation allow this sociopolitical wilderness to continue its expansion because of the people's ignorance or misconceptions of the duties of the president of the United States of America. We the people must protect and promote our rights and democracy beyond our sociopolitical affiliations. We must see through the lies and manipulations of the politicians and form a strong bipartisan and multicultural defense against this political disease.

The People's Court, the Supreme Court

Until recently, the functions of the Supreme Court of the United States of America were mostly carried out based on the public confidence that the court is competent, judicious, and fair in deciding cases that involves all citizens. The present court tends to take away the rights of Americans instead of upholding their constitutional rights. I believe as do most Americans that the court had gone rogue, deviating from its major responsibilities as specified in the constitution.

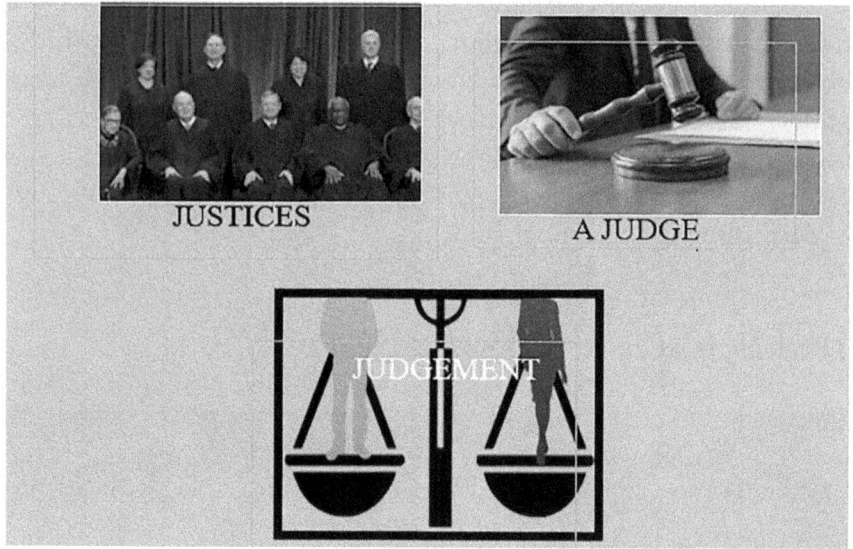

Considering some of the conflicting views that have besieged the makeup of the Supreme Court in the past, the present conservative majority justices in the court have taken the direction of imposing their personal, religious, and political opinions in making decisions that contrast with defending the constitution. Let's not forget that the constitution is defined as "the supreme law of the land." Hence, the court is the custodian of this sacred document, making it "the Supreme Court of the United States of America." Although some of the justices in the court tend not to understand their functions and responsibilities, deciding to serve as judges instead of justices, we the people need to know the distinction between the two terms to determine the competency and fairness of its makeup.

As concisely described, "Justice and judge are two words that are often used interchangeably, but they have very different meanings. Justice refers to the ideal of fairness and equality. Everyone is entitled to justice, and it is society's responsibility to ensure that everyone receives it. Judge, on the other hand, refers to a person who presides over a legal case. Judges are responsible for ensuring that the law is followed and that the rights of all parties are respected. To be a judge, one must have extensive training in the law. Justice and judge are critical concepts in our society, but they serve different purposes. Justice is something that we all deserve while judges are responsible for upholding the law." Therefore, we must understand that justice is blind to race, rank, or creed when making decisions. On the other hand, a judge is not blind and must consider all the facts and evidence that may intertwine with the factors mentioned to decide a case.

Considering the importance of the court system in our democratic republic, Article III, Section 1 through 3 of the constitution established the judicial pillar of the United States government that completes the triangular check and balances of power within the structure of our governance.

Article III, Section 1

"The judicial Power of the United States shall be vested in one Supreme Court, and in such inferior Courts as the Congress may from time to time ordain and establish. The Judges, both supreme and inferior Courts, shall hold their Offices during good Behavior, and shall, at stated Times, receive for their Services, a Compensation, which shall not be diminished during their Continuance in Office."

Article III, Section 2

1. The judicial Power shall extend to all Cases, in Law and Equity, arising under this Constitution, the Laws of the United States, and Treaties made, or which shall be made, under their Authority;—to all Cases affecting Ambassadors, other public Ministers and Consuls;—to all Cases of admiralty and maritime Jurisdiction;—to Controversies to

which the United States shall be a Party;—to Controversies between two or more States;—between a State and Citizens of another State;—between Citizens of different States, —between Citizens of the same State claiming Lands under Grants of different States, and between a State, or the Citizens thereof, and foreign States, Citizens or Subjects.

2. In all Cases affecting Ambassadors, other public Ministers, and Consuls, and those in which a State shall be Party, the supreme Court shall have original Jurisdiction. In all the other Cases before mentioned, the supreme Court shall have appellate Jurisdiction, both as to Law and Fact, with such Exceptions, and under such Regulations as the Congress shall make.

3. The Trial of all Crimes, except in Cases of Impeachment, shall be by Jury; and such Trial shall be held in the State where the said Crimes shall have been committed; but when not committed within any State, the Trial shall be at such Place or Places as the Congress may by Law have directed.

The Eleventh Amendment affected Article III, Section 2, Clause 1

Eleventh Amendment

"The Judicial power of the United States shall not be construed to extend to any suit in law or equity, commenced or prosecuted against one of the United States by Citizens of another State, or by Citizens or Subjects of any Foreign State."

This amendment automatically shields the states from prosecution by citizens of another state or citizens of another country in a federal court. This allows a partial sovereignty of the states, as well as the federal government. However, there are four accepted exceptions to the ban on federal courts hearing these types of cases:

1. Lawsuits can be brought in a federal court against municipalities, cities, and counties within a state.

Finding Oasis Within the Wilderness of our Sociopolitical Ideologies

2. If a state gives its consent, then a lawsuit against it can be heard in a federal court.
3. Where a state itself breaches federal law, it cannot be sued. However, a state official can be ordered to abide by federal law in his or her own name.
4. It is possible for Congress to suspend or remove a state's immunity from being sued in a federal court. Congress must be seen to be clear in its reasons for taking this step.

Article III, Section 3

1. Treason against the United States shall consist only in levying War against them, or in adhering to their Enemies, giving them Aid and Comfort. No Person shall be convicted of Treason unless on the Testimony of two Witnesses to the same overt Act, or on Confession in open Court.
2. The Congress shall have Power to declare the Punishment of Treason, but no Attainder of Treason shall work Corruption of Blood, or Forfeiture except during the Life of the Person attained.

The Supreme Court is the highest court in the land with the responsibility of defending the constitution of the United States of America. It was established to protect the rights of the citizens of the United States of America and to protect the certificate of incorporation of the democratic structure of the American government, including the authority of the states to exist within the union. A justice of the Supreme Court is not a judge but a protector and defender of the tenets and principles of the constitution. Their job is not to judge cases but to compare cases from the lower courts with the constitution and justify the constitutionality of their decisions and make amends. In this situation, personal opinions of the justices do not matter, religious beliefs are inconsequential, cultural affiliations has no effects, and personal ideologies or philosophical lineage does not matter; it is the tenet and only the tenet of the constitution that matters. Every written opinion of any Supreme Court justice is to justify the constitution and not to break it, to justify the rights of the people as stated in the Bill of Rights, and not to step on or take such rights away.

The present conservative majority in the Supreme Court have chosen to decide cases, not by the tenets of the constitution, but by their cultural and religious beliefs. The constitutional rights of the people to do or not to do religion have been literally smashed by the six conservative justices of the court. *Roe v. Wade* decision that upheld the right of every American citizen to decide to do abortion or not to do abortion was literally transferred to the states to decide. Here the states have no constitutional right to make such decisions, but the rogue conservative justices decided to adjudicate their constitutional responsibility to the states. They know that as the custodians of the people's rights, the defense of *Roe v. Wade* is their constitutional responsibility. The question is, why must the right of the people to do religion or not to do religion be decided by the states? Why must the creature of the constitution, in this case the states, be the sole decider of the constitutional tenets that created them? If the right of any other American citizen is threatened or tampered with, my right is equally at risk. If the rights of women to decide to give birth or not to give birth is obstructed because of the religious beliefs of Evangelical Christian justices in the court, then my right to existence has been trampled, your right to freedom of speech and movement is being gradually eroded. Therefore, we the people must vote out the senators in the Congress that spearheaded the makeup of the court and insist on making changes that will root out the corrupt justices and restore the respect and honor that the court demands.

If the rights of every citizen of this great country now depends on who is in the court, what philosophical ideologies they imbibe, and what religious sentiments they tend to express, then democracy as an idea that made this nation unique and successful is now in real jeopardy. If any group, religious or cultural, believes that they made America great because of their cultural and religious sentiments, then their understanding of the foundation and development of the United States of America is completely distorted and must

Finding Oasis Within the Wilderness of our Sociopolitical Ideologies

be exposed and eliminated. Unfortunately, the Supreme Court has given itself the power that they do not have.

The conservative majority in the court have accorded themselves the power of majority which belongs squarely to the people of United States of America. The will of the majority is now being handled, determined, and squashed by a small unelected group of people who claim to be justices but in the real sense are corrupt judges. They believe that their life appointment in the court makes them untouchable. They believe that with the power of majority, which is not a factor in deciding any Supreme Court case, they can take the rights of Americans away without a second thought. Let's be very clear here, every bad decision by this court is aimed at all the people. Do not for once think that the abrogation of *Roe v. Wade* affects only Democrats or Independents, it affects Republicans as well.

Do not be comfortable that the tampering on the Voting Rights Act affects the opposition party only; your party platform is equally affected. The effect of gerrymandering affects every American community equally no matter their party or sociopolitical affiliation. The Voting Rights Act was passed to protect the rights of all Americans to be involved in the process of electing their leaders, but the extreme-right authoritarians who for years have been working to turn this great nation from a democracy to an autocracy for their own selfish interests have finally infected the Supreme Court with their corruption.

It is time for the people to fight back, Democrats, Republicans, Independents, or Progressives, it does not matter. What matters here is that the people must reclaim the power that belongs to them. It is time hit the pools as one people to vote out the elements that spearheaded this corruption, whether they are Republicans, Democrats, Independents, or Progressives, it's of no consequence. For once, all the people must be alert to the eroding wilderness that is gradually destroying the principles of our democracy. It is a gradual process because some Americans are deceived to think that the destroyers are fighting for them while in the real sense they are destroying our liberty, freedom, and right to equal justice and fairness.

CHAPTER 4

Expanding the Oasis against Encroaching Wilderness: The Bill of Rights

The picture of what we are looking at here is that of nature for which humans are an integral and important part. The wilderness, as we had already defined or described, is the "wild," uninhabitable part of our geographical world that is conducive to wild animals and less useful vegetation but unconducive to humans and domesticated animals. In a spiritual sense, it represents chaos, conflict, confusion, incivility, lack of progress, hate, lawlessness, and in a deeper understanding an inspirational desert that destroys a nation. On the other hand, an oasis symbolizes divine promise of liberty, freedom, equality, justice for all under the law, cultural harmony and peace, fairness in distribution of resources, inspirational growth as we dream and have our dreams realized, and the love for our country because our country loves us.

If the desire of all American citizens is not an oasis of life, what is? As it is written, "But he also can turn a barren wilderness into an oasis with water! He can make springs flow into desert lands." As water is to the physical and biological survival of all life on earth, so is faith to our spiritual existence. Faith is the key to receiving the promise and opening the door to our blessings as a nation. As beautifully portrayed by Tracy Williamson in the picture shown, we can transform individual wilderness, as well as community or country wilderness, into an oasis of life if we do the right things as the condition of God's promise requires.

It is based on the command that we love our fellow men as we love ourselves, even those who hates us. "If ye love me, keep my commandments" (John 14:15). Our love for God is confirmed by our love for our neighbors, and our love for our neighbors confirms our love for God. Loving our neighbors is as simple as upholding their rights as divinely given, and loving ourselves is maintaining our rights to life, food, shelter, security, good health, safety, and prosperity as it is naturally inputted to us. Therefore, we must wish for them to have the same privileges as we do, even working hard to provide for others when it is possible and when it is nearly impossible.

The Bill of Rights

The first ten amendments of the constitution are fondly referred to as "the Bill of Rights." They are the rights of all Americans specified in the constitution to be upheld, implemented, and always protected by the government in all situations. It is important to understand that the constitution did not confer rights on the people but identifies and protects them. As Democratic-Republicans, we are to respect the rights of all other Americans as we expect them to respect the same rights that we are entitled to. In a more general perception, our civil rights stems from our human rights, and by implication, they cover humanity as freedom of choice from God.

First Amendment

"Congress shall make no law respecting an establishment of religion or prohibiting the free exercise thereof; or abridging the freedom of speech, or of the press; or the right of the people peaceably to assemble, and to petition the Government for a redress of grievances."

Second Amendment

"A well-regulated Militia, being necessary to the security of a free State, the right of the people to keep and bear Arms, shall not be infringed."

Third Amendment

"No Soldier shall, in time of peace be quartered in any house, without the consent of the Owner, nor in time of war, but in a manner to be prescribed by law."

Fourth Amendment

"The right of the people to be secure in their persons, houses, papers, and effects, against unreasonable searches and seizures, shall not be violated, and no Warrants shall issue, but upon probable cause, supported by Oath or affirmation, and particularly describing the place to be searched, and the persons or things to be seized."

Fifth Amendment

"No person shall be held to answer for a capital, or otherwise infamous crime, unless on a presentment or indictment of a Grand Jury, except in cases arising in the land or naval forces, or in the Militia, when in actual service in time of War or public danger; nor shall any person be subject for the same offence to be twice put in jeopardy of life or limb; nor shall be compelled in any criminal case to be a witness against himself, nor be deprived of life, liberty, or property, without due process of law; nor shall private property be taken for public use, without just compensation."

Sixth Amendment

"In all criminal prosecutions, the accused shall enjoy the right to a speedy and public trial, by an impartial jury of the State and district wherein the crime shall have been committed, which district shall have been previously ascertained by law, and to be informed of the nature and cause of the accusation; to be confronted with the witnesses against him; to have compulsory process for obtaining witnesses in his favor, and to have the Assistance of Counsel for his defense."

Seventh Amendment

"In Suits at common law, where the value in controversy shall exceed twenty dollars, the right of trial by jury shall be preserved, and no fact tried by a jury, shall be otherwise re-examined in any Court of the United States, then (Except) according to the rules of the common law."

Eighth Amendment

"Excessive bail shall not be required, nor excessive fines imposed, nor cruel and unusual punishments inflicted."

Ninth Amendment

"The enumeration in the Constitution, of certain rights, shall not be construed to deny or disparage others retained by the people."

Tenth Amendment

"The powers not delegated to the United States by the Constitution, nor prohibited by it to the States, are reserved to the States respectively, or to the people."

All for One and One for All!

The First Amendment is basically the freedom of choice that every citizen is entitled to exercise or refrain from. We as citizens do have the right to do or not to do religion, believe in a divine deity, or doubt the existence of such a being, choose who to marry or not to marry at all, and decide how to treat our bodies based on our beliefs or preferences. Our total existence is based on our religious philosophies or nonreligious beliefs. The right to life is the basis of creation of man and other creatures. As commanded by the Creator, "Thou shall not kill!" confirms the right of every human being to life, except in actual, truthful, and factual situations of self-defense where one's life is at stake. If you under any circumstances, pretends self-defense as to take a life, you are a murderer before God and before man.

Each and every one has the right to life and all that are needed to be alive: food, shelter, nurture, education and information, protection and health, freedom of movement, freedom of speech, emotional support, and fairness in justice, etcetera. Our freedom of speech does not allow us to incite violence against our fellow citizens, dehumanize anyone by our rhetoric, or threaten harm orally or by symbolic expressions. "Where one's right stops, another's begins!" The First Amendment confirms your right as a citizen and a human being, as well as protecting the rights of others from you. "All for one and one for all!" The call to arms by the musketeers means to look out for one and another as it is written and commanded by God "Therefore all things whatsoever ye wish that men should do to you, do ye even so to them: for this is the law and the prophets" (Matt. 7:12). Our rights are intertwined with the rights of all others; where one's right is broken, all other rights are broken.

Relative to our rights to freedom of speech and expression is the projection to freedom of the press. The press is the people's "watchdog" that projects the voice of the people and alerts them when their rights are threatened or violated. Like the dog who barks to alert its owner of trespassers, pending dangers, or the presence of arriving members of the household or visitors, the press searches for and publishes information or news to the beneficiaries—the people! Also, like the dog who is a friendly member of the family, the press is expected to be a friendly and truthful institution that serves the people of the United States of America and the world at large. Unfortunately, some elements of the society refer to the press as "enemy of the people" maybe because they expose the hidden atrocities committed by these dubious elements or exists as an undercover detective ready to pounce on misdeeds and corruption of public officials or private citizens. Sometimes, bad press may be detrimental to people, like some dogs who bark at the wrong tree or at anything that passes by without any cause. However, we must not allow anyone to dent the image of this institution, whether as a bad reporter or as a derogatory abuser. We must condemn the abusive use of the press to intrude into the privacy of innocent citizens or initiate character assassination of people with false information.

In addition, the First Amendment confirms the people's right to assemble and peacefully protest the government, any public or private institution for redress of grievances for any act of abuse or injustice. However, any assembly to commit crimes, carry out insurrection against the government, conspire to defraud the people, collude with foreign powers against the United States, or commit acts of terrorism against any one is not covered in this amendment. Again not covered in this amendment! If any single individual or group commits these atrocities against any one citizen or the government have done so against the people of the United States of America!

The republic belongs to the people, and the government is the people's business! Although most of the factors that are covered by the First Amendment are not straightforwardly stated in the statement, the understanding is that the free movement of all Americans to do business, gather for religious purposes, gather for political objectives, walk on any American street, drive on any American road, attain any school, live in any part of the country without permission, be whoever they want to be, and decide their health and life conditions is fully covered under this amendment.

An Oasis of Life, Not the Wilderness of Death

The Second Amendment of the Constitution of the United States of America have been so misinterpreted, misconstrued, and misquoted at every turn by some whose main intensions are to abuse this status. "A well-regulated Militia, being necessary to the security of a free State, the right of the people to keep and bear Arms, shall not be infringed." This was passed at the time when America did not have standardized security apparatuses. On June 21, 1788, the constitution became the official framework of the government, then on December 15, 1791, the Bill of Rights was ratified and passed as the coded rights of all citizens. Based on the timeline of the history of the United States Military, the US Army was formed by the Congress on June 3, 1784, and ten years later, on March 27, 1794, the US Navy was established. Four years after that, on July 11, 1798, the US Marine Corp was formed. Despite these military branches being created, the actual on-the-ground existence took many years to accomplish.

Consequently, the states' rights to form militia for emergency purposes remained for many years after due to itinerary and troops deployment constraints. Ever before the first passenger steam-powered locomotive train became a popular means of transportation, traveling by horses and stagecoaches were the only means of transporting people and goods. Therefore, the laborious implications of deploying soldiers took many days or several weeks to months apart, justifying states' rights to organize their own security to protect lives and properties. Situations and conditions at the present time, with the great advancement in science and technology, are quite contrary to those in the early part of our history as a nation. Today, American military is the best in the world, mobile enough to be deployed in a matter of hours, not days. Every city has police departments that can easily respond to emergencies in a matter of minutes, with precision derived from standard training that prepares cops to quickly intervene in any life-threatening situation.

Consequent to the standardization of the military branches in the United States, every state has at least a National Guard Unit stationed in the state to be called upon by the governor of the state to protect life and properties in cases that police departments could not handle. Although each state is responsible in administering these units, the training and regulation of all units and branches is centralized from the national headquarters. Therefore, the aspect of the Second Amendment that gives states the right to form regulated militias is already taken care of and does not require any private militias to be raised by the citizens, except in times of war.

Unfortunately, based on misinterpretation of the constitution or through abuse of rights, private militias such as the Oath Keepers, the 3-Percenters, the Proud Boys, Michigan Militia, the Ohio Defense Force, Montana Militia, etcetera, have in many instances been used to terrorize innocent citizens, ferment fights and riots, all in the name of protecting their Second Amendment rights. These are right-wing White supremacist groups whose ulterior motives are based on introducing autocracy within our democracy, overthrowing democratically elected governments that they don't approve of, institute a national religion of "White Christianity," and control both state and federal governments.

According to Wikipedia (December 2022), "The movement is composed largely of veterans, libertarians, and Second Amendment advocates who share a common belief in individual liberties and civil responsibilities, according to their interpretation of the US Constitution, as well as disdain for what are perceived to be abusive, usurping, or tyrannical federal government decisions and actions, and a set of ideals associated with the values of the militia they see embodied in the Constitution. From the inception of the modern movement there has been controversy over whether the movement was an important part of a complete response to many important threats, or a threat."

Behold a country where guns are easy to come by as are other commodities that are purchased from local stores. The terror displayed at the corners of our streets where people just stand by with heavy weapons of war in times of peace cannot be imagined by others who don't have to go through these scenes. No one should be castigated for feeling unsafe in situations such as these because they are unsafe. The Second Amendment states that American citizens have the right to keep and bear arms, and their rights must not be infringed upon by the government. Perhaps, if we really paid attention to the word "arms," maybe we would have understood that it goes beyond

Finding Oasis Within the Wilderness of our Sociopolitical Ideologies

just guns to other weapons: knifes, axes, harpoons, spears, bow and arrows, javelins, daggers, swords, to mention but a few. Picture the scenes where everyone, young and old, carrying weapons publicly displayed as they go about their businesses, in and out of any building, including hospitals and worship buildings. Maybe, just maybe, we could understand the feeling of nostalgia, fear, and discomfort the imagery arouses in us that will begin the process of amending the Second Amendment.

This wilderness of chaos, brutality, death, fear, lawlessness, and ultra disregard for human life has unbelievably permeated our society such that we can begin to think that abuse of this right by some people is now a stink of death and destruction rather than the freedom of choice and liberty. If we the people do not see the fraud perpetuated by a small part of our society who benefits from flooding our streets with massive weapons or killing machines, such as AR-15, AK-45, automatic handguns, etcetera, then our society have become enslaved by the minority groups who now rule in place of the majority.

We may ask the simple question, "Is the First Amendment not greater than the Second Amendment?" or "Is the major purpose of the Second Amendment not to protect the First Amendment?" We cannot begin to imagine the atrocities and evil that had been unleashed on the people by a few who abuse the second amendment right. According to John Hopkins Center for Gun Violence Solutions, "Every year, nearly 40,000 Americans are killed by guns, including:

- more than 23,000 who die by firearm suicide;
- fourteen thousand who die by firearm homicide;
- more than 500 who die by legal intervention;
- nearly 500 who die by unintentional firearm injuries;
- more than 300 who die by undetermined intent; and
- this equates to more than 100-gun deaths every single day."

This statistical imagery does not include gun deaths caused by mass shootings in schools, grocery stores, movie theaters, concert venues, churches, mosques, synagogues, temples, on the streets, nightclubs, and other people's save spaces. The massive killings of innocent students, whether in college campuses, elementary schools, middle schools, or in high schools is so abhorring that we have become numbed to the utter devastating effects of these events. Wikipedia documents the undesirable records at https://en.wikipedia.org/wiki/List_of_school_shootings_in_the_United_States_(2000%E2%80%93present).

As a nation, we must do the right thing, amend the Second Amendment to protect the lives of innocent citizens being seized and destroyed by evil men and women. As a country ruled by laws, we must insist that those who are responsible for implementing the laws that protect the lives of the people must execute their responsibilities without fear or favors of or for any persons or groups. It is written, "Therefore, anyone who knows what is right but fails to do it is guilty of sin" (James 4:17 ESV). The families of these murderers, who knew how dangerous their family members were, and are still but fail to alert the authorities or find help for them, are equally as guilty as the perpetrators. They are guilty of being passive. The authorities who were alerted or have records of the killers' history of gun violence or domestic violence and choses to be lackadaisical in preventing these deadly occurrences are equally to be blamed for the death of each innocent and unsuspecting citizen whose lives were taken without the chance to fight for them. The lawmakers who refuse to pass laws that bans assault weapons, restrict children from having access to guns, allow background checks of would-be owners of guns, prevent criminals from peddling with illegal gun sales or abuse, or stopping domestic terrorism by people who claim the Second Amendment right with ulterior motives are smack in the middle of this wilderness of death. They are equally responsible, directly or indirectly, for these crimes.

It may be deceitful to think that the problem is not yours because the events did not involve you directly. But you should know that we are one people; where one suffers, we all suffer. Where one's human or constitutional rights to life are breached, all our rights are trampled upon as well. As it is written, "Be not deceived; God is not mocked: for whatsoever a man soweth, that shall he also reap" (Gal. 6:7 KJV). If you sow hate, you reap intolerance. If you persist in misinterpreting the constitution for your own selfish benefits, you reap lawlessness and chaos. If you are comfortable in resisting changes to gun laws because of your "quid pro quo" relationship with gun lobbyists like the NRA, you reap deaths and sorrow for the American people. Be not deceived, one day maybe you or your relatives will get caught in this net of violence. What would you do? Condemn it or accept it? Decide to change the laws or keep them? Let your answer remain intrinsic if you may, but your reward will always be extrinsic for all to behold.

The Fight to Keep Our Democracy Depends on Us

President Ronald Reagan once stated, "Democracy is worth dying for, because it's the most deeply honorable form of government ever devised by man." It is a declaration that holds every Democratic-Republican accountable in preserving, advancing, and expanding our democratic influence across the world. From the infancy of this republic, the struggle to understand democracy and how to make it work for all went in a roller-coaster progressive direction. The struggle led to the civil war, a very devastating period of American history. Democracy reasserted its form in the people's understanding: if we must be free at all, everyone must be freed. If we must be liberated from the influences of autocracy, every single citizen must be liberated from slavery and restrictions based on their backgrounds, no matter what they may be. If we must enjoy our national prosperity, then every citizen must be given equal opportunity to pursue their happiness without hindrance or deprivation.

To fight for democracy is to fight for the people, all the people, 100 percent of them. Benjamin Franklin famously stated that democracy is "an equal dispensation of protection, rights, privileges, and advantages" that everyone "is entitled to and ought to enjoy." However, it is very important for us to understand the nature of this fight before we embark on it. It is a fight that is deeply imbedded in the very soul of man, the deep-rooted self-centeredness that makes the idea of sharing repulsive to those who wants it all. B. R. Ambedkar simply expressed this by saying, "Political democracy cannot last unless there lies at the base, its social democracy. What does social democracy mean? It means a way of life which recognizes liberty, equality, and fraternity as the principles of life." The politicians have split democracy apart for their self-serving indulgences. Though it is government of the people (social democracy), by the people (political democracy), for the people (economic, welfare, and security democracy), they tend to focus more on political democracy that puts them in office and avoid accountability while working for special interests. Therefore, our fight is recoupling these parts back into one Democratic-Republic.

Also we must understand that this fight is against unseen enemies imbedded in the hearts of men and women, race, or ethnicity, notwithstanding social status inconsequential and finances or achievements not important. It is written, "For we wrestle not against flesh and blood, but against principalities, against powers, against the rulers of the darkness of this world, against spiritual wickedness in high places" (Eph. 6:12). Which high place is closer to us than our minds? For all the sins or crimes committed by anyone begins from the mind. "At the fullness of the heart, the mouth speaks." A person who makes racial slurs against someone else had thought about it before blurting it out. An evil mass murderer plans his atrocities before executing them. A corrupt politician or public official may have thought about quid pro quo before carrying out the transaction. In most cases, we hear people say "I did not mean to do that!" or "I did not mean to say that!" Yes, you thought about it, but did not weigh the consequences or control your thinking. Yes, you had a motive; ulterior or otherwise, it's yours.

In another instance, a high place could be a group of people meeting to make decisions on the generality of the public, positive or negative. Political high places may include governor's mansions, state legislatures, presidential mansion, the Congress, the Supreme Court, lower courthouses, city halls, county offices, etc. Also economic, commercial, and institutional high places, such as corporations' management boards, educational institution boards, professional association offices, licensing offices, standard bureaus, and so on, may become battle fields for justice. We wrestle against occupiers of rulership or authorities of these high places that resort to injustice, cruelty, discrimination, corruption, and inflicting despondency against the people.

Though most people interpret "principality" in relation to spirituality, the Greeks who were the first to use the word describes its meaning as "magisterial power or rule. The word for powers in Greek also means authority, jurisdiction, power, right, and strength. Principality exhibits a hold, power, or authority over his subjects." The root word is "prince" which depicts a male member of a monarchy or a would-be ruler with authority to decide issues. In contrast, democracy does not invest such absolute power on any one individual, and when people chose to usurp their positions in that way, autocracy sets in and must be resisted at all costs. If we let political corruption ignite itself, it will burn like wildfire without control, with the ripple effects reaching almost all the fabrics of our society and beyond our imagination.

Although this battle is not a physical confrontation, it does require a special type of armor that will help us defeat the enemies of democracy. It is written, "Wherefore take unto you the whole armor of God, that ye may be able to withstand in the evil day, and having done all, to stand. Stand therefore, having your loins girt about with truth, and having on the breastplate of righteousness; And your feet shod with the preparation of the gospel of peace; Above all, taking the shield of faith, wherewith ye shall be able to quench all the fiery darts of the wicked. And take the helmet of salvation, and the sword of the Spirit, which is the word of God" (Eph. 6:13–17).

With the passage stated above, we must understand that the importance of armor in any battle is for defense and offense. The defensive armor protects us from the enemy's strikes or attacks, and the offensive ones are for us to attack the enemy with skills and courage necessary to destroy their defenses. Although one requires enormous training and practice to master, the other requires carefulness in strapping them on to allow free movement in battle. Overall, we need both to survive and to win. Similarly, fighting for democracy is fighting a spiritual warfare and requires the same vigilance and intensity to succeed.

To illustrate the idea of girting your loins with the truth, let us relate to a situation where you forgot to strap on your belt and then realized that your pant was falling off, either you go back to fetch the belt or continue with the uncomfortable situation of pulling up your pant at every instance. To be an effective fighter for democracy, you must search for and know the truth imbedded in the constitution and laws of the United States of America. Let your knowledge of your rights and the rights of other citizens under the Bill of Rights be the belt that gives you the confidence to stand. Know the truth, tell the truth, uphold the truth, and the truth shall set you free. If your girdle is based on facts, evidence, precise knowledge, honesty, sincerity, and fairness, then your fight for your rights will be no different from your fight to uphold other citizens' rights. The beauty of it all lies in "Do unto others, what you wish them to do unto you!"

Our chests and rib bones are meant to protect some of the vital organs in our body, such as the heart, liver, lungs, etcetera. Therefore, to put on the breastplate of righteousness is to put on virtue. "The quality or state of being morally right and good. The quality or state of being just or rightful. Justice; goodness; respectability; fairness; uprightness; honor; virtue; justness." According to Proverbs 14:34, "Righteousness exalted a nation: but sin is a reproach to any people." We can as well state that "lawfulness exalts a nation, but lawlessness destroys its existence." Upholding our constitution and laws is a direct way of fighting for democracy and advancing our civilization, which is based on us always doing the right thing. If more people do the right thing in our workplaces, schools and institutions, governmental systems, public services, businesses, and in every economic, social, scientific, and technical endeavors, criminals will not have any opportunity to commit crimes against the people because you and I would always stand in the gap as a sure line of defense for our democracy.

Permit me to say that an immobile soldier is one whose duration of survival on the battlefield is limited. "And your feet shod with the preparation of the gospel of peace." Warriors spend more time practicing footwork and stealth for the purpose of willing their weapons to perfection, avoiding the enemy's attacks by dogging and maneuvering, and executing the commander's instructions in precision. In political battles, it means using all the peaceful tools available to confront injustice within the system: Court cases, protests, media, educating the people, civil activism, debating issues relative to the system, standing up for all the people, campaigning for justice, fairness, etcetera. Remember "All for one, and one for all!" means that we take care of each other, respect each other's rights, and are ready to always defend the less-fortunate members of our society.

In addition, the shield is the second-most important weapon in a warrior's arsenal. It is a defensive weapon but has been used as an offensive tool by adaptive and very skilled fighters. The ancient Roman military mastered the art of using the shield to their tactical advantage over the enemy by setting walls of shields for defensive compartments that protect against javelins and fiery arrows. Also the fierce Viking warriors would not go to war without their tough iron-clad circular shields. They understood the advantage of their famous "shield wall!" precision in warding off enemies' attacking calvaries. In both cases, the walls must be built faithfully with precision and speed by all the units to be effective in battle. So are we commanded to use the shield of faith in spiritual and political warfare against injustice and wickedness? "Above all, taking the shield of faith, wherewith ye shall be able to quench all the fiery darts of the wicked." Your faith in doing the right thing, no matter if heaven falls, is your shield against intimidation, harassment, resistance, threats, physical attacks, even political jail terms.

If you are a poll worker, your faith in an accurate and fair election system should be your defense against election deniers and those who try to cheat in the polls. If you are a judge, let the shield of fairness, equal justice, and decision-making based on facts and evidence be your protection against all the pressures from the high places to misjudge any case to their advantage. No matter your position in the people's business, be faithful, sincere, honest, reliable, and truthful in all your responsibilities. Do not be swayed by the fiery darts of the enemies' corrupt intents but quench them by faith.

Despite the helmet being defensive or protective armor and the sword an offensive weapon, both are wielded together for some reason. "And take the helmet of salvation, and the sword of the Spirit, which is the word of God." The helmet protects against head injuries, concussion, disorientation from blows, and sudden deactivation of any fighting man. It protects the brain which is the central control system of the body: nerve controls, speed or pace controls, skill sets storage and usage, memory and remembering, awareness and perception, strength and courage, bravery and perseverance, and determination with focus, without which the sword is useless. We fight from inside to outside, what we think within is displayed without, how we feel within determines how we execute our actions, and what we believe in incites our faithfulness to our mission. Therefore, the sword is wielded with knowledge and knowledge by the word of God.

An American citizen that believes in the republic and democracy as the system of governance that drives the order, existence, and advancement of our civilization is one who either by birth or naturalization is sworn to uphold the constitution and laws of the land and defend the nation against all enemies, foreign and domestic. Foreign enemies we know, but domestic ones are difficult to detect. They may be right in front of us or live in our neighborhood or work in the same workplace as we do, and unfortunately could be members of our close families. However, "by their fruits you will know them!" It is the sword of righteousness that cuts through evil, and it is a double-edge sword. One edge destroys the enemy, the other sharpens the wielder, without which the whole experience becomes hypocritical. We fight evil with goodness! You cannot fight against corruption if you are corrupt. Therefore, the sword of the spirit is the character of God reflected in us as his image, personified by his Word. Indeed, we must swing the sword of morality against immorality and baseness, honesty against dishonesty, kindness against cruelty, truth over lies, openness over cover-ups, sincerity against manipulation, fairness against bias, justice against injustice, and patriotism against sectionalism. The battleground for these fights is within our immediate communities and neighborhoods and requires us to treat our fellow men with respect, kindness, compassion, concern, and fairness.

Neighbors and Neighborhoods within Our Oasis of Life

A lot of people may have difficulties identifying who is who in their immediate vicinity, let alone in much wider communities. It could be that they show no interest in their neighborhoods or they lack the social skills needed to relate to other neighbors. People of different worth's of life, celebrities, famous individuals, wealthy and powerful, highly educated and less educated, fortunate and less-fortunate ones, highly skilled or less skilled individuals, widely traveled or not much of traveling done, have different views of who a neighbor is and what a neighborhood means. Mike Leach, an American coach, once said, "Tracked a raccoon one time in the snow. I was in the neighborhood, and I was just curious where this raccoon lived. There are some fresh raccoon tracks. He'd been digging at somebody's garbage." Well, Mr. Leach knows exactly what he was referring

John Aris Eleleme

to: a neighborhood is where we live, work, and carry out our routine activities, even the act of digging into somebody's garbage for food. The raccoon lives by him and is his immediate neighbor, whether he likes it or not. The famous *Sesame Street* television's song, "A friend is a person in your neighborhood… The person that you see or meet is he!" Whether it is good, bad, or ugly, it's our neighborhood and our neighbors who are other living things, human or nonhuman, that pit tents within the community.

The famous Mexican poet, Luis Alberto Urrea, declared, "There is beauty in our roots. Sometimes we think our roots are shameful, and people tell you that you're no good or your ancestors are no good or that you come from a neighborhood of no hope and terrible crime. But it's about the beauty of those places, and I carry that with me." Nobody knows our neighborhood better than we that grew up or raised within their borders and boundaries. Most people, if not all, have acquired certain levels of fondness for their childhood communities that bring smiles to their faces when remembered. But it is the unpleasant experiences they tend to remember with disgust and disappointment. Although we may hold on to the fondness of our history or bear the scars of unjust treatment, our sense of justice must inspire each of us to fight for the next generations to inherit a better neighborhood and a better nation.

The idea of leaving our neighborhood better than we found them is beautifully expressed by one of the greatest American poets, Maya Angelou, on quote, "I have great respect for the past. If you don't know where you've come from, you don't know where you're going. I have respect for the past, but I'm a person of the moment. I'm here, and I do my best to be completely centered at the place I'm at, then I go forward to the next place." Read more at https://www.brainyquote.com/authors/maya-angelou-quotes.

Unfortunately, economic, social, educational, and political injustice inflicted upon many low-income, minority, and culturally disadvantaged communities still display the scars of these misfortune and barbarism. Every community, neighborhood, family, and individual within the American society do have the rights under the constitution and human society to be fairly treated, to dream and have their dreams realized, to live and thrive in every endeavor of their choice, and to be a respectable and respected member of the society.

Let us understand and be fully aware that the injustice perpetrated against certain communities, neighborhoods, ethnicities, and races were systematically executed decades, even centuries ago. The systemic injustice may continue unless it is disrupted, changed, or eliminated for the sake of all Americans. Resources are distributed not based on population but on who lives in the communities. We have noticed that the infrastructure in some cities is different from the ones in others within the same county. You may ask, how come? Then followed by, why so? Who decides who gets what?

Someone at the helm of the setup unilaterally decides that some communities are more privileged than others. This person or persons are hidden from you because they operate behind the curtain. Until someone like you steps up to fight for the mistreated communities, the injustice may continue for years unending.

A group of wealthy individuals who collude to bring best resources to their communities to the alienation of other communities because they have the power to do whatever they want without any challenge. Until we begin to collaborate with each other to challenge the status quo, the bias and unfair situation will persist. Remember, this fight cannot be won by individual efforts alone but by group's combined action and consistent efforts.

Unjust laws that were passed decades ago to suppress the progress of certain minorities have endured till now. Any attempt to abrogate these laws is met with total resistance by some people whose sense of justice is adulterated. We must be consistent with our efforts to overcome the resistance with all the weapons in our political arsenal. We must always remember that injustice found anywhere is injustice committed everywhere. Discriminating laws enacted many years ago to control the minority are truly against the constitutional and moral rights of all Americans and non-Americans alike. If you enact any law to take my rights away, the same laws directly take your rights away when you finally become the minority. In our democracy, it is the right of every citizen to choose their leaders, and any law enacted to deprive any citizen of such rights is against the constitutional and human rights of the people. It is the power of the people that whoever is selected through voting by most of the voters ascends any political or public office they contested for and won.

In democracy, most of the votes elect any officer, not the minority. If the minority try in any way to impose their will on the rest of the people, it becomes an autocracy and no more democracy. No matter your party affiliation, political ideology, sociocultural beliefs, or your statutory position in the society, it is the responsibility of all Americans to defend the constitution and democratic principles of our country. If the enemies of American democracy stems from your party, fight them. Whether the enemy is a member of your family, relation, friend, or community member, your charge to defend the constitution and our democracy cannot be trifled.

Some communities are cheated off their rights to resources because of ignorance or lack of information. The perpetrators would want it to remain so as to continue their corrupt practices. Therefore, information dissemination must be improved to cover every community by either governmental agencies or nongovernmental organizations. The people must identify the specific individuals who do the dirty job of suppressing information from communities and vote them out of power. If we get rid of the sources, then the system could be sanitized.

Corrupt politicians give unfortunate reasons why certain projects should be established in certain communities and not in others. These reasons are assumed to be very important to the success of the projects based on the economic status of the neighborhood. There is no truth in this assertion than a manipulative opinion, which is intended to deprive certain neighborhoods of the opportunity to thrive and crown others with privileges they do not merit. The antidote to this is electing representatives that care about their districts and would do all it takes to fight for them. Do not vote for parties, but for people of integrity, honor, sincerity, and moral uprightness to work for the community or district. Do not be deceived by politicians who are fraudsters; they make impossible promises and fulfill none. By their fruits, you shall know them: they defame other candidates to curry your favor, they make statements without facts or evidence, they do any to cover up their crimes or hidden secrets from you, they blame everybody else for their mistakes and take no responsibility, and they show no compassion to you as a community and careless about the difficulties your community is experiencing. A presidential candidate or any politician who shows no emotion when an innocent member of the community is gunned down by an irate bigot is the wrong person for your vote. A candidate who is careless about your innocent children being killed while in school is surely a perpetrator in that action, and giving him or her the key to the government house is like making a bargain with the devil. If these people are members of your preferred political platform, vote for the opposition to serve in the office.

Staking the wrong peg in the wrong hole could be the devastating result of voting for people for other reasons except by merits. A weak representative may not be capable of withstanding the pressure from others to abandon the interests of his or her constituency. A corrupt politician would not mind selling out the constituency for personal benefit. Also an uninformed representative may end up contributing to passing bills that are not beneficial to his constituents due to ignorance. Worst still, a representative without character of truth may end up voting against his or constituency's benefits because some party leaders demand that party members must not vote in a bipartisan proposal due to their party fights against other parties. We the people must vet all candidates before casting our votes for them.

The fire that should be burning in every heart is that of fighting for all the people and not for some of the people. Democracy is for "we the people"; access to resources must be given to all the people, and benefit of resources must be fairly distributed to all the people and all the communities. The Lord in Matthew 7:12 says, "So whatever you wish that others would do to you, do also to them, for this is the law and the prophets." If you wish your community to have the best resources, do the same for others. Do not be a resister to others sharing in the wealth of this great nation, be the defender and champion of all Americans no matter how small your contributions may be or the race, ethnicity, economic status, educational achievement of those you are fighting for. As you fight for others, you are fighting for yourself.

CHAPTER 5

Wilderness of Misinformation and Disinformation

In a communication and information class, a lecturer carried out a simple demonstration of how the terms communication, misinformation, and misconception can easily manifest in our daily activities. His strategy for the lesson was to begin his lecture with a real-life situation and specifically with a scenario the students can immediately appreciate. The teacher whispered the statement "Send reinforcement to the front of the class!" in the ears of the first student in the first row, from the left-hand side of the classroom. The first student then whispers the same statement to the next student, and the next to the next until the last student receives the information. Well, the statement was completely altered by the time it got to the last student in the class and became "Send by force all the men to the front of the class." These communication bleeps take place in our daily information dissemination or information consumption. Therefore, this chapter is to describe the pitfalls and how we the people who believe in the republic and democracy can avoid being deceived by them.

The rate at which misinformation and disinformation, including propaganda, have berated our society with so much misconception and poor perception of situations, events, and decision-making is almost at the point of spiraling this great nation into information

Finding Oasis Within the Wilderness of our Sociopolitical Ideologies

"Dark Age." The unfortunate part of it is that some unpatriotic individuals are making great profits from this created wilderness. They care less about whom they hurt and feel nothing for the national survival of the United States of America. Without doubt, a lot of people have been caught in this destructive web of lies that has created divisiveness among individuals, communities, constituencies, states, and families. If this perilous situation continues, the greatest nation in history may finally come to an end.

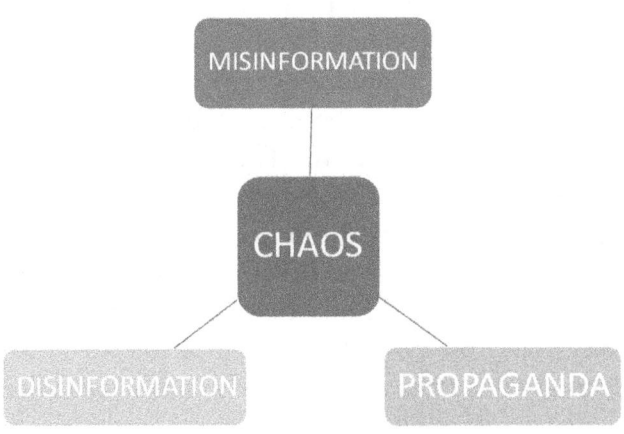

Communication: Give Some! Take Some!

According to Rollo May, "Communication leads to community, that is, to understanding, intimacy and mutual valuing." This strikes a very high note on the importance of communication in our daily lives. Rollo May is often associated with humanistic psychology and existentialist philosophy, alongside Viktor Frankl. Until his death in 1994, he was a major proponent of existential psychotherapy. His studies on stages of development, and his influential book, *Love and Will*, gives a good insight on how communication and other factor play critical roles in this theory that over time humans go through a series of developmental stages regarding behaviors, personality, and feelings about their own existence. But what is communication? How does it influence all that we do?

The word communication is derived from the Latin word *communis*, which means common sense. Yes, common sense! Some may at this point be thinking of the mental state of an individual. But the real meaning is common knowledge held by people involved in the process. It is a back-and-forth interaction between two or more people transmitting facts, ideas, opinions, feelings, attitudes, or beliefs in verbal means, such as conversations, writings, debating, electronic devices, etc. Also through nonverbal means, such as pictures, symbols, body language, facial expressions, hand gestures, signs, or touches. In communication, there is a sender of information and a receiver of information, then the receiver becomes the sender of information, and the sender becomes the receiver. The process continues if there is more information to be exchanged or transferred.

Categorically, words play the most important aspect of communication despite the popularity of other means of communication. A famous author and rabbi, Yehuda Berg, once declared that "words are singularly the most powerful force available to humanity. We can choose to use this force constructively with words of encouragement, or destructively using words of despair. Words have energy and power with the ability to help, to heal, to hinder, to hurt, to harm, to humiliate and to humble." Therefore, what we say, to whom we say them to, how we say them, and when we say them matters a lot in any communication process than we care to admit. It is written, "But I say unto you, that every idle word that men shall speak, they shall give account thereof in the day of judgment" (Matt. 12:36). We are truly responsible for our words and the effects they have on other people; it does not matter what medium we may use: texting, Internet website, posters, television, public speaking, social media, podcasting, or radio broadcasting. As Democratic-Republicans, we must be ready and willing to fight against misinformation, disinformation, conspiracy theories, and lies in all their ramifications.

As the scriptural reference stated, "Every idle word that men shall speak is subject to divine judgment." Idle words may include written or spoken podcast meant to socially or politically deceive or confuse any individual in opposition to an actual thought process or sense of direction. It may involve radio and television propaganda meant to control the thinking pattern of the masses. In our present dispensation, people have established radio and television stations just for the purpose of countering the opposition with truth or falsehood. In most cases, their desire to generate followership has led to them twisting the truth to their own damnation. Let's consider a family traveling from point A to point B, about one hundred miles apart. They boarded their 1962 Ford Falcon on their way to a family reunion. The whole event took place in 1965, a period when the Internet, Google, MapQuest, and other comforts that we enjoy today were not invented yet. You can imagine the difficulties in preparing for and accomplishing such a journey; any slightest misinformation spells disaster.

After covering thirty miles, the family came to a crossroad. Without knowing that the wind had moved the crossed signpost slightly off course a night before, they turned into the wrong road. However, after covering another thirty miles, they realized they were going the wrong direction and needed to recourse back to the right direction. Unfortunately, a hundred-mile journey took 160 miles to accomplish because of the little twist in direction. This is exactly what misinformation can do as we ravage through our daily lives, unsuspecting of the information obstacles thrown our way by people whose aims are to do us harm by deception. As these people create and execute their various strategies of deception, it is important that we must be always alerted to detecting this falsehood and avoid falling into the "rabbit holes" prepared specifically for the unsuspecting members of our society. We cannot afford to give the propagandist, the mis-informer, or dis-informer the loophole to create such devastating wilderness that could bring enormous confusion and chaos to our various communities. Therefore, I enjoin you to pay a little more attention to this section as we discuss the pitfalls we may encounter in this wilderness.

John Aris Eleleme

Wilderness of Misinformation and Lies

What is happening today in our country in terms of misinformation and lies is now out of control and very damaging to society in every way possible. Anyone with a computer, access to the Internet, and skills of making information go viral can easily misinform or deceive other people who may be unaware or too trusting. The situation is now a wilderness of misinformation, full of lies and deception. Misinformation is providing wrong information, misleading information, manipulating advice, misdirection of instructions, or unavoidable error in messaging no matter the intent of who is doing the dissemination. Information is supposed to be the transportation for the truth, facts, and knowledge needed for our daily life functions within our society. On the other hand, misinformation can lead to drastic consequences: wrong traffic signs lead to accidents, wrong direction on a medication slip may lead to overdosing and death, misrepresentation of a candidate's profile will surely lead to misjudgment in selection, and wrong time on an invitation card will create confusion among the invitees, etc.

The worst type of misinformation is one that is done on a massive scale. It may be easier to detect and correct misinformation within a workplace, an organization, a school, or an institution of population less than one thousand people. Unfortunately, large populations that may be of the size of a state, a nation, or a region of the world would create devastating effects on an uncontrollable scale. Wrong messages tend to go viral on the Internet than the correct ones. People tend to be attracted to errors, misinformation, misconceptions, or perverted ideas that seem to confirm their beliefs rather than the truth. To our greatest dismay, religious, political, and cultural differences are the factors that contribute to the wilderness of misinformation in our ecosystem. The power of spread is magnified to astronomical levels when famous persons or news organizations are the source of the adulterated information.

The forty-fifth president of the United States of America, Donald J. Trump, between 2019 and 2021, created chaos among the citizens by misinforming the people on the use of hydroxychloroquine as a cure to COVID-19 viral infections. As a result, many Americans loss their lives by overdosing on this drug that is meant for preventing malaria fever, as well as the treatment of rheumatoid arthritis, lupus, and porphyria cutanea tarda. Although he had initiated so many misinforming messages from the bully pulpit aimed at deceiving his followers to his own advantage, the worst of them all was that of January 6, 2021. A day we may conclude that it is one in infamy: his doubled-down lies that he won the 2020 presidential election instead of the current president, Joseph Biden. In his self-centered greed, he incited insurrection against the United States government, a government that he was technically the head of the executive branch at the time. For the first time in the history of the United States of America, a United States president engineered a deadly attack on the United State Congress, the people's house, by a mob of his teaming supporters loyal only to him. They were not patriots to the United States of America, they were not defenders of the American democracy, but instead they were the domestic enemies to our system of government, whether they knew it or not. He broke the oath that he swore on January 20, 2017, to "Defend the United States of America, against all enemies, foreign and domestic!"

For many decades in our modern history, Americans have invested confidence in the presidency to provide the right information to the people in times of crises, natural disasters, intense national mourning, or war. No matter who the president is or from which party the person was elected to office, the president is the leader to all Americans. We can understand why information from the "bully pulpit" is held to high esteem, and for anyone occupying the position providing misleading information to the people is abhorrently dubious. You cannot uphold the constitution and laws of the land by misinforming or disinforming the people. You cannot profess to protecting the republic by being treacherous to the welfare and safety of the American people. Therefore, everyone that did not challenge the unprecedented behavior, or conspired for any reason to cover up the activities are equally responsible for the results.

In another instance, a gubernatorial candidate in the state of Virginia misinforming the electorates on a topic such as "critical race theory" and "woke theory" and winning an election because of the deception should be very concerning to all Americans. Critical race theory, a coursework taught in law schools only, is meant for lawyers and legal professionals as a wedge against deciding cases with racial bias. In essence, it is a philosophy that prepares attorneys and judges to critically consider cases by merits, facts, and evidence without any cultural or racial bias. This theory in its academic entirety is not taught in K-12 schools, never had. However, a similar but secondary school-friendly version is taught as a social studies topic, "Diversity, Tolerance, and Ethnic Harmony." Parents who attacked various school boards across the country over this issue were not just misinformed but disinformed as well. Ignorance is not an excuse, we must fact-check every information before we act on them. To avoid the negative consequences of misinformation and disinformation and stop the encroaching wilderness of lies, we must unleash the oasis of truth, confirmation of facts, and sincerity of evaluating evidence before making decisions.

For the last four to five years (2017–2022) of American democracy, misinformation and disinformation, perversion and distortion of facts, rumors and conspiracy theories had ruled our communication space. The speed and cover-up strategies based on technology have made it virtually impossible to distinguish between falsehood and truthfulness. It is because actual truth tellers have withdrawn from the battlefield further away from expanding their capacity to counter the lies and preserve our democracy. Plato, the legendary Greek philosopher, stated, "One of the penalties for refusing to participate in politics is that you end up being governed by your inferiors." And politics in our modern world is beyond just running for a public office; it includes all that is needed or required to preserve and improve our civilization. Politics is the process of making policies, laws, and standards for public office performance and societal living. Truth plays the most important part in all these factors. So either we fight against misinformation and lies together, or we become enslaved by chains of lies from liars and cover uppers.

Most misinforming messages are released in drips and not in waves. They steal from the unsuspecting public with stealth and an appearance of normality that could deceive even the highly intellectuals of society; for example, "democrats are pedophiles, child abusers, and Satan worshippers." Without doubt, you know there is no atom of truth in that statement. Also you should know that a statement such as "Republicans are only focused on cultural grievances than working for the people!" is not true. Majority of republicans believe in our democracy despite the poor judgment of few. However, the effect such statements generate can be very devastating since we don't think or believe the same things. People who came from societies that experienced situations like these would immediately believe it, and their political decisions may be distorted by the misinformation. The best possible defense against these must be to identify the source immediately, in most cases politicians who resolve to vilifying their opponents to win elections, counter the falsehood with the truth by probing the liar for facts or evidence. If they cannot provide any proof, call them out, not once but as many times as possible and through any means necessary. Make your findings go viral, touch as many receiving platforms as possible, and do not relent until the people see the injustice and resolve to punish them by voting against their bids for the elected positions they are contesting. This can only be done if we can look beyond the media as the only watchdog for the people. We must all become watchdogs for our country no matter what economic, political, and social status that describes us.

In retrospect, we have more on the side of truth than those who have chosen to spread lies through the Internet, cable networks, conservative radio stations, liberal platforms, deceptive podcasting, and so on and so forth. If you believe in American democracy and want to keep it, you must get in the fight to run misinformation, disinformation, manipulation of the populace, lying, cover-ups, and false indoctrination out of our social and political information space. We have no safe place called neutral; either you promote truth and decency or you fall prey to falsehood and degeneration. As it was in the olden days, so it is today; the only differences lie in the nature and means of misinformation, the speed at which messages are broadcast, and the ease of access to sources tend to magnify the problems many folds. Information manipulators are still at work today and possess more tools in their arsenals to deceive many. We the people must remain vigilant so as not to fall into their deceptive nets.

Besides claiming security and truthfulness by several media and news sources, the elements of misconception and cultural affiliations have in no small part influenced their news and information dissemination. So far as human beings are in pole positions of the information space, the tendency to be influenced by cultural and religious sentiments remains high. A good judge of character weighs all sides before making conclusions. An unbiased investigation requires the sincerity and truthfulness of looking at all the information, assessing it, evaluating every input, and comparing all facts before making conclusions. The same standards of responsibility are required from each one of us. It is important to compare the news from MSNBC and FOX News before consuming it; evaluate information from CNN and MAX NEWS before making your conclusions; and assess information from *social media* by comparing their sources, credibility, and reliability before accepting and retweeting such information into virality.

As stated by Edward Osborne Wilson, an American biologist, naturalist, and writer, "We are drowning in information while starving for wisdom. The world henceforth will be run by synthesizers, people able to put together the right information at the right time, think critically about it, and make important choices wisely." Yes, Professor Wilson who passed away last year, December 2021, hit the nail right on the head, we are drowning in information so much as they come at us from all directions. The information space is so overwhelming that we must not expect other people to organize them for us; we must do it ourselves or perish underneath its weight.

The zenith of every human being's mental, psychological, emotional, and physical activity is to reach wisdom. Knowledge without wisdom leads to an unprogressive society. "Data is not information, information is not knowledge, knowledge is not understanding, understanding is not wisdom" (Clifford Stoll). As citizens of this great country, we experience data being thrown at us daily: "21 people were killed by a gunman; 19 children and 2 teachers in an Uvalde School Shooting on May 24, 2022." If the news stops at just numerical representation of the event, it is not information. When we are confronted with images of the those murdered, who the gunman was, what kind of weapon used, lackadaisical behavior of law enforcement officers at the scene of crime, etcetera, then we have information in our hands that may lead to our knowledge of what happened. Knowledge is how we feel about the information we got, asking questions that will help us to understand all the actors involved. Why did the gunman choose to commit this evil in this school? Why the specific classes? Who granted him the permission to purchase the killing machine (AR-15) he used, and how did he go through the cracks without any check on his background? With many probing questions, we may acquire the knowledge needed for us to understand the whole scenario. Understanding is not knowledge, but feeling what the victims felt before their deaths, feeling what their parents and relations felt after the incident, and trying your best to get into the minds of the coverers to understand why they are trying everything possible to withhold information from you and me, who they were trying to protect, and who are the hidden syndicates behind this tragedy.

Here comes wisdom! It is the application of knowledge and understanding in finding solutions to impeding problems or resolving the existing ones. Unless you believe that changes should be made to solve only problems that patterns to your needs and not others, then all the indigenes of the State of Texas should have been unanimous in voting out the governor whose decision to allow the proliferation of guns in the state led to this and other gun-related tragedies. State legislators whose financial affiliation to NRA has directly infringed on their willingness to enact laws that will ban assault weapons, close the loopholes on background checks, and abrogate the open-carry laws of the state should have been voted out of office. Unfortunately, most of the people of Texas tend to worry about maintaining their cultural and religious sentiments than protecting the lives of all the people. What is happening in Texas is also happening in other states, with higher or lower rates per day. In truth, we need the spring of wisdom from our oasis of life to understand that life weighs more than wealth and cultural attachments. To know that our lives are intertwined in all respects, we must treat every human being as important and deserving of life.

"For God so loved the world, that he gave his only begotten Son, that whosoever believeth in him should not perish, but have everlasting life" (John 3:16). We cannot claim to love God if we don't care about the lives of our fellow men! The scriptures have shown us that our existence is from him that created all men (human being), and as each of us is connected to him, we are also connected to each other. "If a man says, I love God, and hated his brother, he is a liar: for he that loveth not his brother whom he hath seen, how can he love God whom he hath not seen?" (1 John 4:20) Therefore he declared, "If ye love me, keep my commandments" (John 14:15), and his commandments includes "Thou shall not kill!"

As stated, we are all connected. Whatever happens to one of us happens to all of us. In many instances people tend to remain neutral in many social, political, cultural, and economic issues unless they are involved directly. Remember, problems travel in waves; if the waves don't get to you now, it will any other time. People who have of recent loss their family members or relations due to gun violence did not imagine that they would fall into the same situation, but the wave rolled right to their harbor. Consequently, the ever-increasing statistics of gun violence, domestic or massive occurrences, continue to deaden our moral sensibilities against this terrible crime. You may not be religious, but each one of us is spiritual in nature, and within our DNA lies the code that reminds us always that we were created in the image of God. We can express our sense of loss when someone is killed or murdered; we may display outwardly the anger against the perpetrators or suppress them to avoid relative violence. However, it is our civil responsibility to call for justice and to sorrow for the blood of the innocent and to use all means necessary to put an end to this evil.

The politician who blames gun violence on mental illness and not on the proliferation of assault weapons is equally guilty but of the crime of omission. Isaiah 59:1–4 declares, "Behold, the Lord's hand is not shortened, that it cannot save; neither his ear heavy, that it cannot hear: but your iniquities have separated between you and your God, and your sins have hidden his face from you, that he will not hear. For your hands are defiled with blood, and your fingers with iniquity; your lips have spoken lies, your tongue hath muttered perverseness. None calleth for justice, nor any pleaded for truth: they trust in vanity, and speak lies; they conceive mischief, and bring forth iniquity."

A White nationalist who decided to enter a place of worship and murder the worshippers because he hates them due to their skin color has defiled his hands with the blood of the innocent. They were innocent because they did not know what they were accused of or were they arraigned in the court before the jury of their peers. Up and until the moment that life was snoozed out of them, they were innocent before man and before God. The curse of violence and the evil of shading innocent blood on our streets and homes can only be availed by our commitment to banning of assault weapons, not allowing guns to get into the hands of criminals by law, establishing strict background checks before allowing people to acquire a gun, and legally requiring gun owners to undergo serious training on gun safety and gun handling before licensing.

In truth, your Second Amendment right does not give you any freedom to take the First Amendment right, the right to life, of anyone away. Not only will the law come after you, but you will also be damned for eternity. From the dawn of time, man's right to protect and take care of himself started from his right to life which came from the very breath of life that God breath into his nostrils. This is the first and most important freedom God gave to man directly. Therefore, no man has any right to deprive another man the right to life without cause. It is hypocritical for anyone to simply blame the various gun violence on mental illness when in retrospect you hide a butter knife from emotionally disturbed individuals and then allow such individuals access to military-styled weapons. This is where and when the same curses that the Lord heaped upon the Pharisees, Sadducees, and scribes are declared on the behaviors of today's gun lobbyists: "Wore unto you hypocrites, for you strain over swallowing a small mouse, but are very quick in swallowing a big cow!" You choose to hide a butter knife from the killers but allow them free access to killing machines. You choose to secure a corrupt politician who grants gun lobbyists their will but leave innocent schoolchildren defenseless. To you the hypocrite, the life of an American citizen is worth nothing, even when the life of one sinner like you demanded the shading of the blood of the innocent Son of God.

The various states' legislatures and legislators who care less about the lives lost in their various states due to gun violence but stake their own lives in stopping those who want to do the right thing in banning assault weapons and curtailing the proliferation of gun violence have chosen to fight on the wrong side of history to the consternation of the whole world. Remember, "Whatsoever a man sows, that shall he also reap!"

The Jungle of Disinformation, Conspiracy Theories, and Manipulation

To any layperson, misinformation and disinformation may be regarded as one and the same thing. Despite this layman perception, the difference between the two terms is thin but unique. "Disinformation is the deliberate and purposeful distribution of false information. The term is generally used to describe an organized campaign to deceptively distribute untrue material intended to influence public opinion" (Robert McNamara, ThoughtCo.com). Here information is manipulated to deceive, influence public opinion, or initiate cover-ups. In most cases, the focus message is either outrightly false, partially true, or severely misinterpreted with the purpose of misleading the consumer of the information. Since the information manipulator's intention is to impress on the mind of the consumer of the information, the next level of his or her strategy is to turn up the volume and the reach of the false information. The rate of false messages rises to an astronomical level, and the medium of distribution is expanded adversely: radio, television, newspapers, texting, videos, web manipulation, social media distortion, ideologue podcast, etcetera.

Finding Oasis Within the Wilderness of our Sociopolitical Ideologies

Unfortunately, the disinformation is propagated into propaganda used by certain sources to subjugate the people to social-information controls. "To have young or issue; to be produced or multiplied by generation, or by new shoots or plants; as, rabbits propagate rapidly. To take effect on all relevant devices in a network. It takes 24 hours for password changes to propagate throughout the system. To cause to take effect on all relevant devices in a network" (www.thefreedictionary.com/propagate). When insects, bugs, or rodents propagate, we refer to it as infestation; when human population increases beyond the available resources, we call it overpopulation; and when false information spreads like wildfire across all spectra of the information space, we have propaganda. That is right, propaganda! It is a disinformation infestation; like bugs, it is undesirable, uncomfortable to have around, and a nuisance beyond words.

Propaganda!

Adolf Hitler applied propaganda against Western civilization to a devastating effect. The continuous lies and false claims that the Germans or Ariane race were superior to other Europeans and the rest of the world and that they must rule the world for this reason activated the propaganda machine of the Nazis that mesmerized the people of Germany until they begin to believe Hitler, became sympathetic to his cause, and supported his atrocities in WWII. The disinformation that the Jews were responsible for all the evil in Germany and across the world provided Adolf Hitler the covers he needed to systematically murder more than six million Jews by incineration. Today, the Holocaust, as the incident is famously known, still daunt the world for man's cruelty against humanity. Unfortunately, the evil continues as some, either by ignorance or intentionally, are ravaging the world of communication with the falsehood that the Holocaust did not happen. If you are among the perpetrators of this falsehood, God's spiritual and divine rebuke is on you today as it was on the ancient people of Israel. "For your hands are defiled with blood, and your fingers with iniquity; your lips have spoken lies, your tongue hath muttered perverseness. None calleth for justice, nor any pleaded for truth: they trust in vanity, and speak lies; they conceive mischief, and bring forth iniquity."

A former president of the United States of America who lied to the people that the 2020 presidential election was stolen from him without any fact or prove—leading an insurrection against his own government that led to loss of lives, injuries, wanton destruction of government properties, and complete disregard to the constitution that he swore to uphold—may have the notion that he has escaped the consequences of his action. No matter what anyone thinks, his hands are defiled with blood of those he led to death. All the people who conspired with him to commit these atrocities, "Your lips have spoken lies, your tongue hath muttered perverseness." And you laid nets of hateful perversion privately for the innocent to fall in. Be not deceived, God cannot be mocked. For whatsoever a man sowed, he shall also reap.

Many have fallen into the pits of lies, rumormongering, propagated falsehood, and reshaping our social, political, and religious values in the image of the impostor, not the image of God of truth. When you tweet or retweets misinformation, knowingly or ignorantly, you make yourself a part of the propaganda machine of the wicked. Some people turn away from this state of mind when they realize that it is wrong, but some become consistent in their efforts to deceive the masses for their self-centered interests. The scripture condemns the second set more vehemently. "You are of your father the devil, and your will is to do your father's desires. He was a murderer from the beginning, and does not stand in the truth, because there is no truth in him. When he lies, he speaks out of his own character, for he is a liar and the father of lies" (John 8:44). He deceived Adam and Eve, our first parents, by appealing to their desires with the possibility of becoming gods and knowing what is good or evil, with power to change them at will. He, the devil, is a master of lies, deception, misinformation, disinformation, and manipulation from the dawn of time. His workings on earth have magnified many folds. He hides his true motives behind perversion of the truth that even the very elect will fall prey to his antics.

The subtility model displayed in the garden of Eden is the same template for today's deception and propaganda. If we review the dialogue between him and the woman, Eve, we may understand his modus operandi. "Now the serpent was more subtle than any beast of the field which the Lord God had made. And he said unto the woman, 'Yea, hath God said, Ye shall not eat of every tree of the garden?'" His probe was to confirm what Eve already knew. "And the woman said unto the serpent, 'We may eat of the fruit of the trees of the garden: But of the fruit of the tree, which is in the midst of the garden, God hath said, Ye shall not eat of it, neither shall ye touch it, lest ye die.'" The serpent then built his disinformation from the woman's prior knowledge, "And the serpent said unto the woman, 'Ye shall not surely die,'" creating doubt in the woman's mind and inciting her curiosity to find out why her Father and Creator should lie to her. As a master of deception, the devil proceeded with emphasis, "For God doth know that in the day ye eat thereof, then your eyes shall be opened, and ye shall be as gods, knowing good and evil." He laid in the woman's mind false allegation, accusation, and misrepresentation of God's character. He represented God as a false god and not the perfect father that created man and the whole universe. But it is written, "I am the way, the truth, and the life." The devil's lies did not change God's character but perverted him in the mind of his created being. Unfortunately, Eve bought every deception, manipulation, or falsehood the devil sold out to her, and she then transmitted the disinformation to Adam, her husband, "And when the woman saw that the tree was good for food, and that it was pleasant to the eyes, and a tree to be desired to make one wise, she took of the fruit thereof, and did eat, and gave also unto her husband with her; and he did eat" (Gen. 3:6).

Disinformation and propaganda are ignited through the media but spreads like wildfire through person-to-person dissemination. The danger lies within family units and magnifies through social, religious, and workplace units. We tend to trust our families, relations, and friends as sources of information even when we doubt the validity and reliability of such messages. Eve transmitted the disinformation to Adam who accepted it because it came from his wife, not necessarily confirming the truism of the message. Right from the beginning of the world, disinformation and propaganda have been used to target unsuspecting individuals, groups, cultures, or ethnicities. It started in the garden, Eden, and spread throughout the history of this world until now.

We may be familiar with the story of Joseph and his brothers, sold into slavery, and proceeded with the lies of him being killed by a wild beast. The deception which was engineered by Jacob and his mother to steal his brother, Esau's birthright. The manipulation carried out by David to kill Uriah after sleeping with his wife Bathsheba, a grievous sin that ravaged his family and threatened his nation. Let's not forget the disinformation, allegations, and accusations labeled against Jesus Christ by the high priest and the Sanhedrin: he claimed to be the King of the Jews, the Son of God, and able to forgive sins, they rant. He is all that he claimed, but the intention of the accusers was to brand him a liar and a traitor, to destroy him. They tweaked his statement against him, "When you destroy this temple, I will build it again in three days" (Matt. 27:39–40). The serpent was at work again, inciting the people against him: "And those who passed by derided him, wagging their heads, and saying, 'You who would destroy the temple and build it in three days, save yourself! If you are the Son of God, come down from the cross.'" In contrast to their understanding, Jesus's statement was a metaphor, referring to his death and resurrection in three days. Hidden from the crafty serpent, who is the devil, was the will of God that his Son must die to save the whole world from their sins. Satan magnified his propaganda to have the people demand that Jesus be crucified, believing that if the Son of God is killed, the battle would be won by him. He remained ignorant of God's will up and until the savior's last words, "Father, forgive them, for they know not what they do."

Countering Bad Rhetoric with the Truth

In this section, we would discuss the aspect of misinformation, disinformation, and propaganda that affects people in a variety of ways. We had in one way or the other experienced verbal attacks, false rhetoric, false allegation, false accusation, and character assassination or defamation, and being left in the cold, not knowing how to combat the sources. You are not alone in this situation. So many people have been bullied, verbally assaulted, stalked relentlessly online, and threatened for their beliefs without end. However, we can only overcome these unfortunate situations by joining efforts and resources to fight the perpetrators on our own terms and not theirs.

Consequently, the exploding knowledge of science and technology thus provides comfort, easy access to information, and mass dissemination of information in record times. But the unforeseen aspects of these advantages have come to bite us so devastatingly beyond measures. Abuse of technology by certain people to do harm to others is the single greatest disadvantage of social media. They hide behind the strokes of their keyboards, away from the guess of their victims, and in the shadows of their private dwellings to harass and defame the characters of those they hate and disagree with. This is not new to world history but magnified by our modern inventions. In 2 Peter 3:1–6, it puts this in perspectives, "This second epistle, beloved, I now write unto you; in both which I stir up your pure minds by way of remembrance: That ye may be mindful of the words which were spoken before by the holy prophets, and of the commandment of us the apostles of the Lord and Savior: Knowing this first, that there shall come in the last days scoffers, walking after their own lusts, And saying, Where is the promise of his coming? For since the fathers fell asleep, all things continue as they were from the beginning of the creation. For this they willingly are ignorant of, that by the word of God the heavens were of old, and the earth standing out of the water and in the water: Whereby the world that then was, being overflowed with water, perished." Yes, scoffers, scorners, attackers of the truth, abusers of those who are bearers of truth, and people who resist general societal progress, the list is endless. "Walking after their own lusts," disinforming the masses to satisfy their greed. "For this they willingly are ignorant of, that by the word of God the heavens were of old, and the earth standing out of the water and in the water," they intentionally ignore the power of words that may create or destroy, inspire, or deflect, incites war, or bring peace. They enjoy the hurtful effects their words or rhetoric generate on other people and will use every loophole to maintain or exacerbate the sufferings.

The idea of ignoring the perpetrators is not advisable. Silence is not an option in this case, but a quick response with facts and the right information must be your first push back. By responding immediately, you have drawn the first counterpunch, which is to deflect the attack from going viral. On the other hand, if you chose to remain silent, consumers of social media would unjustly accept the disinformation as the truth; once your defamed character goes viral, it is virtually impossible to recover. "A lie gets halfway around the world before the truth has a chance to get its pants on" (Winston Churchill). Therefore, for the truth to have a chance at countering falsehood, it must be released immediately before a lie even prepares to lunch. If you are a public official or a journalist, anticipation of misinformation must be your defense shield in stopping disinformation. In most cases the perpetrators are deflected when they know that the truth is already out.

Another way to defeat liars and conspiracy theorists is to push the truth with logical persuasion and evidential contrast to falsehood. Consider this, "Q-Anon Followers Think JFK Jr. Is Coming Back on the 4th of July. He's an avid Trump supporter and has been hiding in Pennsylvania for two decades, according to some people on Twitter who don't seem to realize he's dead" (Reported by EJ Dickson, July 3, 2019, *Rolling Stone*). The truth is that John F. Kennedy Jr. died in a tragic plane crash in July 1999 at the age of thirty-eight. His wife, Caroline Bessette, and his sister-in-law, Lauren, lost their lives as well. The irony is why would anyone create an alternate reality for the grieving family through a conspiracy theory? Your guess is as good as mine.

In addition to the defamation of character saga they are trying to create, it is the inner desire for self-aggrandizement that is their true motivation. The conspiracy theorist is a rumormonger who spreads rumor to prove his or her self-worth no matter who their victims are or may be. They crave attention and want people to flock to them for more—the number of people that subscribes to their "YouTube" channels, massive number of retweets of their insane posts, and thousands of birds of the same feathers that would gladden them with thumbs-up. To deflect their insanity, retweet their posts with the truth attached: facts, true images, reference materials, real photos, actual videos, and logical arguments. According to Socrates, "False words are not only evil in themselves, but they infect the soul with evil," and the more hearts are influenced by falsehood, the more people degenerate into insincerity and morality wilderness. In fact, the motive of a false conspiracy theorist is to sow dissent, conflict, and antipathy against what they don't agree with then take advantage of the chaos to achieve their selfish desires. Their purpose is to corrupt the thinking and feelings of the masses and win their loyalty with deceptive ideologies.

Conspiracy theory, as a matter of fact, is rumormongering. It is not a different concept today from what it was two thousand years ago. The same rebuke meted out to their practitioners then is the same today and forever. "No liar, or rumormonger shall enter the kingdom of heaven." The same goes for the coconspirator and co-bearer of false information or anyone that passes on false messages (gossiper). When you sit behind your computer keyboard and tweet or retweet unverified, unconfirmed, and nonfactual posts, you are doing an "electronic gossip" or "media rumormongering." It becomes a wilderness of deception, manipulation, and mental and emotional corruption, sowing doubts in the minds of the unsuspecting consumers, misleading the uninformed, sowing dissention, and creating sociocultural crises beyond measures. The effects of rumormongering and conspiracy theorizing can destroy nations, civilizations, cultures, and people. Conflicts between individuals or groups, war between nations, cultural degeneration of people and their civilization, and genocide of one ethnic group by another are the worst historic results of disinformation and propaganda.

As we have come to understand, it is better to repel the starting of rumors than stopping the spread. "Without wood, a fire will go out, and without gossip, quarreling will stop" (Prov. 26:20 NCV). The first counterpunch is not to be a medium of spread for falsehood; don't retweet or repost information that you have not confirmed to be true. Even if the information is true and you know that spreading it may cause harm to someone, refrain from making it go viral. "We cannot stop all rumors, but we can refuse to participate in them. We can break the 'telephone' chain and refuse to pass it on. When we hear slanderous news, we should go to the source and check it out. If we are not part of the solution, and the person we are telling is not part of the solution, then the news is not ours to propagate" (www.gotquestions.org). If we refrain ourselves from forwarding false information to other people, even though our intention may be noble in pointing out that it is false, then the fire of propaganda would be starved of fuel for burning. Like the pyramid of ascension, when a branch is broken, the tread stops, the lineage is discontinued, and the exponential viral lunch is prevented.

Another aspect of the fight against disinformation lies in algorithm confrontation. This aspect is particularly applicable to information technology experts through software programs that can disseminate the truth faster than falsehood. It is important for more people who believe that the truth matters to form active citizens information protection groups to combat the massive disinformation generated by people who benefit from it. Not only when it is convenient but always. The right to freedom of speech is not the same as the right to free speech. You may wonder, "What is the difference?" Freedom of speech allows all the citizens to express themselves using any form of speech: oral, written, signs and posts, cartoons and murals, television, radio, information space, websites, etc. On the other hand, free

Finding Oasis Within the Wilderness of our Sociopolitical Ideologies

speech means freedom to give your opinion, make your statement, present your counter version of other viewpoints, and debate ideas or ideologies with facts. However, no right is absolute in its application; boundaries exist, limitations apply, and confrontation will surface when they are violated. Your freedom of speech and free speech are conditioned with truth, facts, and evidence of proof. As it is written, "Then said Jesus to those Jews which believed on him, if ye continue in my word, then are ye my disciples, indeed; And ye shall know the truth, and the truth shall make you free" (John 8:31–32), it requires us to tell the truth, search for the truth, confirm the truth, abide by the truth, and live by the truth to be free. Therefore, it is our civic responsibility and citizenship to protect our information space from abusers of free speech and our freedom of speech.

Unfortunately, our sense of right and wrong may have been sullied that people don't feel the anger against lies, misinformation, and disinformation anymore. The worst implication is that politicians believe that when they lie to their political base incessantly, they will come to believe them and support their ambitions without question. For example, "If we lose this presidential election, it will be because the democrats cheated!" Whoa, this is like saying that a team can only lose the NBA final game 7 if the referee and the opposing team cheat. The same perpetrator loss the election by losing the swing states, Pennsylvania, Wisconsin, Georgia, and Arizona, with good margins; they called for recounts that yielded the same results, filed about sixty-one court cases of protests, losing sixty but one. Similarly, in an NBA game, if a call is challenged, the assistant referees and the referee call for a video replay to determine if there was any error in the call. If there was an error, the call is rescinded, and if there was none the call is maintained.

Comparatively, both situations are covered by free speech and are within their rights to invoke them. But the politician had abused that right by telling lies that were debunked by various election bodies and the court system. He then went further to propagate the lies, convincing the uninformed, deceiving the unsuspecting ones, and inciting insurrection against his own government. He knew that his proclamations were lies and he made them anyway. He understood the implications of his actions but initiated them without any guilt. I believe as well as you do that the United States of America is a nation ruled by laws and not persons. In our legal system, no one is above the law, including the president. Therefore, he must be held accountable for his actions, just as those who were misled by him are being held accountable for their actions as well. If he is allowed to go free as some people are insinuating, then we as a nation will be perpetrating injustice and hypocrisy. No one is above the law!

The Oasis of Truth and Freedom

Our freedom as a democratic nation depends on sincerity and truth. In chapter 1, we discussed the oasis as a symbol of hope, order, peace, and prosperity which depends on doing the right thing always, creating an environment of inclusion and not exclusion. We referenced Psalm 107 in our discussion and would refer to it again: "He turned rivers into a wilderness, and the water springs into dry ground. A fruitful land into barrenness, for the wickedness of them that dwell therein" (Ps. 107:33–34). Spiritual wilderness sets in when we reject the truth and promote lies through misinformation, disinformation, and propagation of false conspiracy theories. Remember that manipulation of truth to cover up crimes and corruption is equally as offensive as the crimes committed. "So, for one who knows the right thing to do and does not do it, for him it is sin" (James 4:17 NLT). Similarly, if you know that you must uphold the laws of the land and choose to break them, you have committed crimes against the people. True freedom comes by upholding the rules, and upholding the rules depends on upholding the truth surrounding the rules. All factors and evidence of the truth is summarized in the golden rule, "Do unto others what you wish that they do unto you," and the statement "that all men were created equal." This requires me to see you as me and for you to see me as you.

In America and across the world, divisiveness is caused by the wilderness of miscommunication fully imbedded in falsehood. It is like cancer that spreads one cell after another and moves at rates that could make it impossible to be stopped. If you lie to your neighbors, fellow employees, employers, your constituency, your family, acquaintances, and friends many times as could be counted, you have raised a trust barrier between them and you. You cannot be trusted, and your words cannot be relied upon because you've shown no evidence of truth and have enslaved yourself in their minds. You are not free! They are not free! The environment around you becomes toxic and exclusive as people literally avoids your presence. The same goes for spreading misinformation, disinformation, and propaganda through social media which enslaves the minds of the people. For example, the disinformation of people about the COVID-19 vaccine massively carried out by conspiracy theorists led to massive loss of live during this once in a hundred-year pandemic: lies told that the vaccines contain chips to monitor the citizens, the vaccines exert damages to the brain and turn people into zombies, and that whoever takes the vaccines would become impotent. Thousands and tens of thousands whose lives should have been saved died, even with the remedy at their fingertips.

The chief of lies, the adversary, the devil, and his agents of lies continue to seek your destruction in many ways that we cannot begin to imagine. According to the legendary singer, Bob Marley, "Emancipate yourselves from mental slavery, none but ourselves will free our own minds." You can be mentally enslaved by what you believe when you decide not to test the validity and reliability of such beliefs. The truth is that it is impossible to develop a microchip small enough to pass through a pinhole. Millions of people who have taken the vaccines are not walking the streets like zombies, and no one has complained of impotency after being administered the medication. Let the oasis of life repel the wilderness of falsehood from our minds, then we can be free and free indeed.

The oasis of life is basically the spirit of truth which is poured out by God unto us by his divine mercies. It is not restricted to a few but given to all people. "And it shall come to pass afterward, that I will pour out my spirit upon all flesh; and your sons and your daughters shall prophesy, your old men shall dream dreams, your young men shall see visions" (Joel 2:28). This promise is as good today as it was then. The United States of America and majority of other nations are embodiment of its validity and reliability. God has given everyone the spirit to decent between truth and falsehood and choose to do the right thing always. Our lives here and hereafter depend on how we apply this truth. "Your sons and your daughters shall prophesy" means that when we know the truth, we must tell the truth, carry out our duties truthfully, live the life of truth, and propagate the truth in opposition to falsehood. "Your old men shall dream dreams" meaning that the senior citizens must envision a better society for the next generations. We must make changes to our past mistakes for the benefit of our children and our children's children. I would have loved to present the whole speech by Dr. Martin Luther King Jr., explaining what it is to dream dreams, but a part of it will suffice.

> *Let us not wallow in the valley of despair. I say to you, my friends, we have the difficulties of today and tomorrow. I still have a dream. It is a dream deeply rooted in the American dream. I have a dream that one day this nation will rise and live out the true meaning of its creed. We hold these truths to be self-evident that all men are created equal.*
>
> *I have a dream that one day out in the red hills of Georgia the sons of former slaves and the sons of former slaveowners will be able to sit down together at the table of brotherhood.*
>
> *I have a dream that one day even the state of Mississippi, a state sweltering with the heat of oppression, will be transformed into an oasis of freedom and justice. I have a dream that my four little children will one day live in a nation where they will not be judged by the color of their skin but by their character. I have a dream today.*
>
> *I have a dream that one day down in Alabama, with its vicious racists, with its governor having his lips dripping with the words of interposition and nullification; that one day right down in Alabama*

little black boys and black girls will be able to join hands with little white boys and white girls as sisters and brothers. I have a dream today.

I have a dream that one day every valley shall be engulfed, every hill shall be exalted, and every mountain shall be made low, the rough places will be made plains, and the crooked places will be made straight, and the glory of the Lord shall be revealed, and all flesh shall see it together.

This is our hope. This is the faith that I will go back to the South with. With this faith we will be able to hew out of the mountain of despair a stone of hope. With this faith we will be able to transform the jangling discords of our nation into a beautiful symphony of brotherhood. With this faith we will be able to work together, to pray together, to struggle together, to go to jail together, to climb up for freedom together, knowing that we will be free one day.

This will be the day when all of God's children will be able to sing with new meaning "My country 'tis of thee, sweet land of liberty, of thee I sing. Land where my father's died, land of the Pilgrim's pride, from every mountainside, let freedom ring!"

And if America is to be a great nation, this must become true. So let freedom ring from the hilltops of New Hampshire. Let freedom ring from the mighty mountains of New York. Let freedom ring from the heightening Alleghenies of Pennsylvania. Let freedom ring from the snow-capped Rockies of Colorado. Let freedom ring from the curvaceous slopes of California. But not only that, let freedom, ring from Stone Mountain of Georgia. Let freedom ring from every hill and molehill of Mississippi and every mountainside.

When we let freedom ring, when we let it ring from every tenement and every hamlet, from every

> *state and every city, we will be able to speed up that day when all of God's children, black men and white men, Jews and Gentiles, Protestants and Catholics, will be able to join hands and sing in the words of the old spiritual, "Free at last, free at last. Thank God Almighty, we are free at last. (https://kr.usembassy.gov/martin-luther-king-jr-dream-speech-1963/)*

This truth we believe to set us free, cuts across cultures, traditions, and values of all people. The truth is that for you to be free, I must be free too. For freedom to reign, the truth must be confirmed through equality and fairness in justice because justice is the confirmation of the evidence of truth. Only when we allow God to pour his spirit of truth on us would we be able to dream of a better society. To create a better society, we must correct the mistakes and injustices of the past. Discriminating against anyone is a nightmare and not a pleasant dream of truth. Going back in history to retrieve racial plays from racial playbooks and reproduce them in the present society is being stuck in a nightmare loop. If you continue to think that United States is owned by the White race only, then you are still in a nightmare of racial injustice. America is a multicultural democracy owned by all the people, a republic with the promise of freedom, liberty, and equal justice under the law. The same dream that Dr. King had is the same dream we must all dream today for our country. According to Gloria Steinem, "Without leaps of imagination, or dreaming, we lose the excitement of possibilities. Dreaming, after all, is a form of planning." America may have realized the dream of scientific and technological advancement but is still cropping in its attempts toward a more perfect union because of hate, greed, cultural fights, exclusive policies, oppression of minority groups, and economic suppression of the less-fortunate ones.

Another phase of the truth is that the founders of our country structured the government to reflect the dominant culture of the period. For several generations after, the diversity of the country expanded and demanded the restructuring of the system to accommodate the demographic changes. For obvious reasons, such as fear of losing control of the existed status quo and the desire of the White population to slow the progressive development of new ways of doing things and maintain their privileges, have created political and cultural turmoil such that we are lost in a loop. Over and over and over again, the tendency of violence based on cultural grievances and assumptions has slowed, if not derailed, our growth toward a more perfect union. Deceptive politicians who traffic in strategic fearmongering to gain votes have created very dangerous wilderness of chaos among us: "They are coming for your guns, they say," "Your women and children are not save if you allow the other side to win, they taunt," "The Mexicans have initiated inversion of our country, and we have to stop them," and so on.

Each election season is ladened with this vicious propaganda to enslave the people's minds with fear, suspicion, and hatred for assumed enemies. Then the cycle of disinformation and propaganda continues, forming a loop of the same issues. At this point, the blame must be put on those who are victims of these atrocities because you have chosen to believe the lies than explore the truth. "One who deceives will always find those who allow themselves to be deceived" (Niccolo Machiavelli). The deceiver sees you as a lucrative target, understands your major weakness of accepting any idea without checking, and concludes that his deceptive strategies will always work on you. At the end of each election, you don't see people coming to harm your wife and children, the Mexicans have not invaded our country, and the government have not taken your guns away as presumed. You have been deceived. First-time deception may be an eye-opener to you, second time means you are having problems in analyzing reality, and the third time we may conclude that you are a fool.

The unfortunate thing about those who are deceived is their unintended consequences of deceiving other deceivable persons or passing the bug to the next person, and to the next person, until the wilderness becomes a full-blown desert of disinformation and propaganda. According to Saint Bernard who was a Burgundian Abbot and a cofounder of the Knights Templars, "In truth, opinion may be taken for understanding; understanding cannot be taken for opinion.

How so? Surely because opinion may be deceived; understanding cannot be. If it could, it would not be understanding but opinion. For true understanding has not only certain truth, but the knowledge of truth." Someone who lies about you creates his opinion of you and not understanding the truth of who you are. A conspiracy theorist generates his own opinion of things, situations, events, histories, and realities then presents them to you, wholesale. If you buy them, he giggles with satisfaction; if you don't, he reinvents the same opinion for the next phase of his deception. The cycle continues! Therefore, it is a divine assignment to all flesh to search for the truth, uphold it, preserve it, spread it, and make it ours.

Falsehood can only be debunked by the truth. Lies cannot debunk lies; they are birds of the same feathers that flock together. The scriptures stated, "Submit yourselves, then, to God. Resist the devil and he will flee from you" (James 4:7). We can only resist evil with God's word for his word is the truth. Also Saint Bernard pressed the issue of understanding further by saying, "We seek for truth in ourselves, in our neighbors, and in its essential nature. We find it first in ourselves by severe self-scrutiny, then in our neighbors by compassionate indulgence, and, finally, in its essential nature by that direct vision which belongs to the pure in heart." In agreement with Bernard's assertion, we can only attain understanding by intuitively searching for it, observing our immediate environment for evidence of truth, and believing with acceptance the evidence of truth coming from other seekers as well. The truth is that the world does not revolve around us, but we are part of it, we move within it, live in it, rise or fall within it, and survive or thrive within it together.

Therefore, our knowledge of the truth that all men were created equal, that "All have sinned and have come short of the glory of God", and that "Whatsoever we wish others to do for us, we should do the same for them!" should create the sincerity within each of us that will free us from the chains of darkness, mental enslavement, nets of suspicion or fear of our fellow men, and the self-centeredness that motivates people to deprive others of the resources meant for all. If you and I achieve this understanding, then we will wish for a good life for all and insist that all must have equal opportunity to achieve it. We will vote, despite the differences in opinion or culture, to silence the racism of racists, put a stop to the propaganda of deceivers, and repel autocracy from our democracy. The savior declared, "If ye love me, keep my commandments. And I will pray the Father, and he shall give you another Comforter, that he may abide with you forever; Even the Spirit of truth; whom the world cannot receive, because it sees him not, neither knows him: but ye know him; for he dwelleth with you and shall be in you." – John 14: 15 – 17. What is his commandment? "Love the Lord your God with all your heart and with all your soul and with all your mind.' This is the first and greatest commandment. And the second is like it: 'Love your neighbor as yourself." – Matthew 5:37 – 40. If you love him, you will not hate your neighbors, their skin color notwithstanding. If you love your God, you will not pick up your AR-15, a deadly killing machine and go into a church, a temple, a synagogue, or a mosque to kill innocent worshippers because of your hatred for them. If you love your creator, you will not deprive well-qualified students from low-income families the opportunity to attend any Ivy league school by selling their slots to less-qualified students from wealthy homes. If you understand that our freedom of choice was given by the creator, and confirmed by the constitution, you will not attack and kill fellow citizens who are LGBTQ believers, for we all have the freedom to do religion or not to do religion under the constitution. God gave that freedom to choose to obey or not to obey him, freedom to love him or not to love him. But obedience to him is a sign of our love for him, disobedience is apathy toward him that surely leads to death. The verdict is his to declare, not ours.

Therefore, to uphold a free society, we must uphold the truth, apply the truth, and make decisions based on the truth always. In John 8:31–32, the Savior declared again, "Then Jesus said to those Jews who believed Him, 'If you abide in My word, you are My disciples indeed. And you shall know the truth, and the truth shall make you free.'" This truth sets us free from the bondage of lawlessness or the penalty of sin. If more people, if not all, uphold the truth, our growth toward a more perfect union will be faster and smoother than our present journey. The truth does not give us the permission to break the law but the power to uphold it. First, we must know the truth then abide in it (internalize it), and live by its evidence in all things. The truth that our love for our neighbors should reflect our love for self should free us from the habitual lawlessness of stealing from our neighbors, killing our neighbors, bearing false witness against our neighbors, deceiving the people by lying to them, and covering up crimes committed against them. With the truth, our diversity will be celebrated and not despised! With the truth, suspicion among the citizenry will fiddle away! With the truth, irregular mountain ranges and valleys of privileges will be reduced to a flat land for equal opportunity for all! With the truth, freedom will ring, and liberty will reign in this nation!

CHAPTER 6

The Peoples' Oasis: Freedom, Liberty, and Equal Justice

Here, let's begin with the question of freedom, liberty, and equality: How do they relate to each other? Maybe we never considered this important relationship question before. Here is an idea, a person who is serving a prison term in a maximum-security facility wakes up every morning and yells out to fellow inmates, "I am free! I am free! I am free!" Many will think that he is crazier than the rest. How could you be free while in shackles? Others may ask, what are you free from and how were you set free? Answers to these questions are imbedded in the mind of the declarant of freedom. All other alternatives are assumed answers from the hearers of his declaration. In another scenario, a wealthy man's son committed a vicious crime and was sentenced to ten years in jail. Similarly, a poor person's son committed a vicious crime and was sentenced to the same number of years in jail. Each day the wealthy man's son complains of the quality of food served, while the other ate his food with gratitude. In frustration, the warden decided to confront the situation in front of the inmates. So he pointed at him.

"I am aware that you don't appreciate the food set before you! Well, you must get comfortable with it for you have a long time to consider your situation and you must be alive to accomplish that." The warden continued, "Here, we are all equal, and your superiority exist only in your mind!"

This, of cause, is the open truth: we have all sinned and have come short of the glory of God because all "men" were created equal, and none is perfect or superior in any way. The warden's rebuke is because if we deserve any privileges, they must be shared equally, and any punitive measures applied equally too. There are no personal truths, there are no group truths, and there are no cultural truths. Truth is universal; it is evidence of occurrence of events, existence of phenomena, and the confirmation of actions and behavior.

Relatively, knowing the truth and acting on the truth must be the foundation of our freedom. We the people must seek the truth, understand the truth, and apply the truth for real freedom to reign among us. A former president of the United States of America who knew the truth that he loses the 2020 presidential elections yet persist in falsely carrying out massive propaganda of fraud is an enemy to democracy. His lies shackled the minds of his supporters and infused in them the madness that led to the attack on America's temple of democracy, the Capitol building. Although many of the perpetrators are being sentenced to prison for the crime of "seditious conspiracy" without the indictment of the former president, the truth would have been perverted, and that will display injustice against the victims of his crime. The truth is that this injustice is against you and I because "no one is above the law" in America. What is going to be for you? The truth that will set us free or falsehood that will enslave us and our generations to come. Do not be deceived, the new generation are more sensitive to injustice than you may give them credit for. They will question your lukewarmness and will blame you for the dent in our history; you can be rest assured of it. Therefore, if we deserve to be free, we must seek the truth, understand the truth, imbibe the truth, and appreciate the truth no matter how bitter it may be to us.

"I Wish You Are Either Hot or Cold…"

It is important to be aware that our actions or inactions in any situation create equal and opposite impacts on our destinies and our national progression toward a more perfect union. The impact may lead to neutrality or excesses on either side of the fulcrum. In the words of Victor Webster, a well-known Canadian actor, "Everything we do, even the slightest thing we do, can have a ripple effect and repercussions that emanate. If you throw a pebble into the water on one side of the ocean, it can create a tidal wave on the other side." Our actions or inactions can create ripple effects in our lives, families, communities, or country. Wanting to remain neutral in most things may sometimes not be advisable. It may create an illusion of taking sides but not ready to commit to your real opinion or belief. Being neutral in a moral confrontation is as bad as taking side with immorality.

The divine rebuke meted out to the Laodiceans for lukewarmness is equally applicable to us today as individuals, groups, and a nation. Christ sternly declared, "I know your works, that you are neither cold nor hot. I wish you were cold or hot. So then, because you are lukewarm, and neither cold nor hot, I will vomit you out of My mouth. Because you say, 'I am rich, have become wealthy, and have need of nothing'—and do not know that you are wretched, miserable, poor, blind, and naked—I counsel you to buy from Me gold refined in the fire, that you may be rich; and white garments, that you may be clothed, that the shame of your nakedness may not be revealed; and anoint your eyes with eye salve, that you may see" (Rev. 3:15–18). In most cases, lukewarmness creates a sense of self-satisfaction, false feelings of independence, and a haughty sense of self-centeredness. We could try to illustrate its devastating effects using the laws of thermodynamics.

First, the zeroth law: "The zeroth law of thermodynamics states that if two systems are in thermodynamic equilibrium with a third system, the two original systems are in thermal equilibrium with each other." This means that when systems are in a state of thermal equilibrium, they cancel each other into neutrality (lukewarm).

Second, the first law: "The first law of thermodynamics states that energy can be converted from one form to another with the interaction of heat, work and internal energy, but it cannot be created nor destroyed, under any circumstances." It means to a layperson, energy is there, it's always there, and can only be transformed from one form to another.

Third, the second law of thermodynamics states that "the state of entropy of the entire universe, as an isolated system, will always increase over time. The second law also states that the changes in the entropy in the universe can never be negative." The question you may be asking is "What is entropy?" To a layperson, it means disorder in any system of things, degradation of matter or material existence of the universe, or deterioration of trends of things. "The degradation of the matter and energy in the universe to an ultimate state of inert uniformity." If we allow chaos and disorder to exist, the trend will continue without averting until we reorder the state.

Fourth, "the third law of thermodynamics will essentially allow us to quantify the absolute amplitude of entropies. It says that when we are considering a totally perfect (100 percent pure) crystalline structure, at absolute zero (0 Kelvin), it will have no entropy (S). Note that if the structure in question were not totally crystalline, then although it would only have an extremely small disorder (entropy) in space, we could not precisely say it had no entropy." What this means to us who are imperfect beings is that we cannot reach a state of perfection that will eliminate entropy entirely, but we can make the effort of growing closer and closer to reduce the chaos to barest minimum.

At this point, you may be wondering why we are talking about thermodynamics. Perhaps reminding us that the universe is a ball of energy that we tap into everyday to create things, do things, and transform things; we will better understand why we have chaos in our system of things and how we can arrest the entropy by bringing order into our thinking, our feelings about each other, and our dealings with our fellow human beings.

I hereby invite you to see things from the divine perspective, God's own view, which is perfect and eternally attached to his universal laws of existence.

Heat energy and the sun

Almost all the sources of energy on earth comes from the sun: potential energy (stored energy), solar energy (energy from sun rays), kinetic energy (energy from movement), chemical energy (energy from material things), mechanical energy, electromagnetic energy, gravitational energy, thermal energy (energy from heat), sonic energy (energy from sound waves), nuclear energy, and ionization energy. In most cases, if not all, heat is involved in the process of energy transformation. Consider a pot of water at room temperature set on a stove with a regulated heat applied. At a certain temperature, the water begins to simmer, we can observe tiny movement of bubbles that indicates that water molecules are starting to break away from their bonds. Then at 100 degrees Celsius, the water begins to boil with a more aggressive breakaway of the molecules, forming steam and moving further away from the source into the atmosphere. Even in its simplest form, heat energy makes things move; the early steam engines portrayed the concept more vividly. Other examples include steamboats, steam mills, steam-driven cars, electricity generation from steam turbines, and steam-cleaning devices. Although today we have discovered how to convert other solvents and liquids into mechanical and kinetic energy of movement, steam is still the purest form energy among the rest.

In the spiritual and moral sense, to be hot is to always do the right thing. A heart that is hot is one that is bent toward righteousness and not evil. A person whose heart is hot or warm is one who shows compassion to his fellow men, neighbors, and even those he does not know. Someone whose heart is hot or warm is one whose purpose or intentions are pure, whose love for self is same as his love for others, and one whose wish for himself is the same as what he wishes for his fellow men. As heat makes things move, so is a warm heart which is prone to action for the right reasons and for righteousness.

We can do no good with frozen hearts

In contrast, let us consider water at room temperature in a plastic container, putting the container in a freezer for some hours and then observing the gradual transformation of the water into ice. What the freezer does is suck the heat from the water as it changes from liquid to aqueous form, then to icy chips at zero degree Celsius before turning into solid ice below zero degree Celsius. Ice does not make things move; it dampens every molecule of substance into inseparable bonds that restrict movement. Under extreme cold, living tissues die because live activities cease: bacteria stops acting, viruses cease their movements and activities, parasites stop sapping their hosts, and animals or man buried under ice soon die. Extreme cold does not generate life or can it maintain it for an extended period. The only useful application of cold is to lower the temperature of things. Icy temperature preserves dead tissues and not living ones. We refrigerate things, such as raw meat, raw fish, perishable food materials, even medications, to stop microorganisms from acting on them. Also cold water or even ice is used in cooling down nuclear reactors, water for cooling down carburetors, etc. The bottom line is that extreme cold temperatures keep the movement of molecules of materials in check, creating inseparable bonds that stop any mechanical or kinetic energy. So illustrating human behavior based on the effect of extreme cold on material things and biological life-forms on earth is to present us with the best analogy of being cold in moral and spiritual sense.

According to Wim Hof, a Dutch motivational speaker and extreme weather athlete, "Cold is merciless. It shows you where you are. What you are." Coming from someone who has experienced its devastative effect on the body and mind, we should be rest assured of the truism of being cold. A coldhearted person shows no regard for the welfare and well-being of other people; his focus is always on himself, and his sight does not extend beyond his nose. He is selfish to a fault. Maya Angelou, the legendary American poet, expressed this more profoundly by stating that "if you find it in your heart to care for somebody else, you will have succeeded." A coldhearted person does not care about other people; the "spiritual molecules" in his heart lumps together and become so hardened that the possibility of breaking out and reaching out to others is zero to none.

On a daily occurrence, coldhearted individuals have cold-bloodedly kill innocent people using guns, with no feelings of compassion or restraint. Only coldhearted people will embezzle taxpayers' money behind the cotton of darkness without any feeling of guilt. A great example is Bred Favre, yes, Bred Favre! Here's the story, "Former Green Bay Packers Quarterback and Hall of Famer Brett Favre has been accused of using his 'special access' to former Mississippi governor Phil Bryant and other officials in his home state in order to influence roughly $8 million in welfare payments for himself, pharmaceutical company Prevacus, and a volleyball court for the University of Southern Mississippi, according to an expose published last week Mississippi Today—though Favre has not been charged criminally or accused of a crime" (https://www.forbes.com/). They committed a coldhearted crime of corruption against the less-fortunate members of the society by stealing their welfare benefits for their private use. The most depressing part of this crime is that people like Bred Favre are worth more than one hundred million dollars in assets but still decided to pilfer eight million dollars from those who needed the resource more. "Be ye not deceived, God cannot be mocked. For whatever a man soweth, he shall also reap!"

It is important not to confuse coldheartedness with indifference. Coldheartedness is an act of committing evil or doing the wrong things without any feeling of remorse or restrain. A cold-blooded killer is one who carries out vicious killings with no regard for the victims of his crimes. A coldhearted politician who lies to his or her supporters does not have any love or respect for them. The funniest thing about liars is that they tend to be very upset when others lie to them. We can observe this indecent behavior in politicians and other public officials as they heap blames on the opposition for similar misbehaviors they perpetrate behind the curtain. Like vinegar, they spread their sour taste to everyone around them while maintaining self-pretense as honey; that is what liars do.

A coldhearted person is insensitive to how other people feel about his or her actions. They hope for nothing because they care for nothing. Jeremiah 18:12 declares, "But they will say, 'It's hopeless! For we are going to follow our own plans, and each of us will act according to the stubbornness of his evil heart." When we lose hope in ourselves, in others, and in the general purpose of our existence, our hearts grow weary and hardened like ice. We then become prone to doing evil or watch it happening and do nothing about it.

A cold heart may be insensitive, but a hardened heart is a total blackout. "Render the hearts of this people insensitive, their ears dull, and their eyes dim, otherwise they might see with their eyes, hear with their ears, understand with their hearts, and return and be healed" (Isa. 6:10). People become hardened after taking several steps away from the warmth of love for others that should reflect on the love we have for ourselves. Like freezing water, a cold heart transforms from aqueous state to icy chips then to hardened blocks. A hardened criminal starts with unnoticeable small offenses to fully planned white-collar or blue-collar crimes. Also a full-blown racist begins with dismissible childish envy to small group apathy or discrimination then graduates to intense hate for people who don't look like him, worship like he does, or share the same beliefs with him. Be aware that racism is a state of mind that invades all racial groups, ethnicities, and tribes. Whether you are White, Black, Brown, Orange, or Oriental, individuals in every group have people who racially discriminate against other groups or individuals. However, it becomes institutionalized if deeply imbedded in the people's traditions, attitudes, and cultures. Basically, racism is part of sins of omission that in extreme cases do lead to the sins of commission. When we decide to omit or ignore the fact that "all men were created equal" and that "all have sinned and have come short of the glory of God," we tend to instigate superiority complex within ourselves which may lead to doing harm to others to prove our beliefs.

Seating on the fence is hypocrisy

We may wonder why God's anger is rekindled against lukewarmness every time his people are engaged in it! The understanding is simple, lukewarmness is indifference or being neutral. It is such an unacceptable human behavior that induces vomiting in spiritual sense. Let's refer to the stern rebuke again. "I know your works, that you are neither cold nor hot. I wish you were cold or hot. So then, because you are lukewarm, and neither cold nor hot, I will vomit you out of My mouth. Because you say, 'I am rich, have become wealthy, and have need of nothing'—and do not know that you are wretched, miserable, poor, blind, and naked—I counsel you to buy from Me gold refined in the fire, that you may be rich; and white garments, that you may be clothed, that the shame of your nakedness may not be revealed; and anoint your eyes with eye salve, that you may see" (Rev. 3:15–18).

The worst crime is to stand and watch while the evildoer perpetrates his or her crimes against our fellow citizens. Haile Selassie, the late Ethiopian leader, illustrated this very specifically by stating that "throughout history, it has been the inaction of those who could have acted; the indifference of those who should have known better; the silence of the voice of justice when it mattered most; that has made it possible for evil to triumph." Time and time again, we have experienced how the silence of those who were supposed to speak out or act to prevent heinous crimes stand by and do nothing, say nothing, while our humanity is ravaged by coldhearted criminals. If you are near the scene of crime by knowledge of what goes on and do nothing or say nothing, your lukewarmness hurts the most. He will spew you out!

Lukewarmness is a crime of indifference, a look-away attitude that permits evil, and grants a getaway pass for lovers of iniquity. A story of conviction by Jon Bloom, a staff writer of desiringGod.org, specifically identifies the look-away attitude when he wrote, "Lukewarmness is the dying of conviction. And conviction often dies the slow death of a thousand compromises. When I was 22 years old, I worked at a company where my supervisor was defrauding customers and asking me to comply by fudging inventory reports. I refused and raised serious concerns about his conduct. This got back to the company owner, who one day asked me into his office and sagely said, 'When I was your age, I also saw things in black and white. But I've come to learn that things are mainly shades of gray.' That was baloney. Fraud isn't gray. If the customer became aware of the fraud, the colors would have sharpened very quickly." Here, Jon refused to look away but stared sternly at the crime and called it by its real name, fraud. He stood his ground and maintained his conviction no matter how he was viewed or if the heavens came crashing down on him. It is abhorring to learn about the harm caused by indifference, but it is even more devastating to look away.

From Roger Waters's description of what scares him more than torture—"Not the torturer that will scare me, nor the body's final fall, nor the barrels of death's rifles, nor the shadows on the wall, nor the night when to the ground the last dim star of pain, is hurled but the blind indifference of a merciless, unfeeling world"—it is the indifference of people to the suffering of their fellow men. It is the indifference to the plight of Black, Brown, Oriental, as well as the neglected White people in America. It is the look-away attitude that allows crimes to be committed against all people, whether in America or any way else in the world. Ignoring the plight of less-fortunate people is more grievous than the actions of the perpetrators; God will spew you out because of your lukewarmness.

Although many may not fully understand the divine rebuke for lukewarmness, the consequences are for here and hereafter. If you are invested with the privileges of wealth, fame, position of power, or talent and you are at the right spot and at the right time to intervene in stopping or exposing the crimes against humanity but chooses to remain neutral and do nothing, the rebuke is for you. People who feel safe and indifferent within their confinement of wealth and comfort with the attitude of "It's their problem, not mine!" God has this for you, "Because you say, 'I am rich, have become wealthy, and have need of nothing'—and do not know that you are wretched, miserable, poor, blind, and naked." He is talking about spiritual poverty that will prevent you from reaching the pearly gates of heaven. In many cases of occurrence of disasters, it is the lukewarmness, indifference, or "I don't care attitude" of those who were expected to prevent them that led the way to the avoidable situations. Great examples of "boomerang" effects of indifference had aligned our historic timeline over and over and over again. In the *Spider-Man* movie, Peter Parker's indifference in not stopping the criminal assailant led to his uncle Ben Parker's murder by the same assailant. A police informant who feared the repercussion from a gang and avoided reporting to the cops their intended raid of another group led to his two children and wife being cut down through a drive-by shooting. Also a lawmaker who allows an unjust law to be passed may in the future become a victim of his own making if the situations are reversed. The effects of lukewarmness or indifference can be observed in every tenet of our lives, known or unknown; the impacts are far reaching as their chain reactions.

Lukewarmness Is Unacceptable!

We must understand that being lukewarm is as much a crime as being actively involved in perpetrating a crime. As astutely stated by Tim Holden, "The Holocaust illustrates the consequences of prejudice, racism, and stereotyping on a society. It forces us to examine the responsibilities of citizenship and confront the powerful ramifications of indifference and inaction." The crime of indifference is unacceptable by any ramification and must be fought against with similar courage and bravery as physical warfare. An indifferent person is a soldier whose courage has failed him, a warrior for justice that should have been but never was because of fear. If those in Hitler's inner circle had the courage to confront him on the atrocities he committed or was then about to commit, six million Jews would have been spared the ugly face of the Holocaust. Millions of other world citizens would not have perished in the Second World War.

Perhaps a similar situation closer home in America would paint a better picture of cruelty resulting from being lukewarm or indifferent. The courageous woman of the civil right movement, Rosa Parks, once said, "Time begins the healing process of wounds cut deeply by oppression. We soothe ourselves with the salve of attempted indifference, accepting the false pattern set up by the horrible restriction of Jim Crow laws." Time may begin the healing process, but time does not heal. A wound that does not heal from deep down is one that continues to surface whenever the same condition presents itself. One of those conditions is lukewarmness or indifference by those who were supposed to rise and declare that "enough is enough!" The wound had transformed from Jim Crow laws to segregation, from voting restrictions to economic isolation and from denial of slavery to police brutality. These conditions continue to raise their ugly heads, metamorphose from one form to another because so many on the right-hand side or the left-hand side of the equation remain on the fence, lukewarm, indifferent, unconcern, and display of total apathy toward the plights of their fellow citizens.

Dante Alighieri stressed the disheartening part of neutrality or lukewarmness by saying that "the darkest places in hell are reserved for those who maintain their neutrality in times of moral crisis." Dante Alighieri (AD 1265–1321) was an Italian poet and politician whose most famous book *Divine Comedy* gave insights into how our life here determines our life hereafter. Dante revealed that "you shall find out how salt is the taste of another man's bread, and how hard is the way up and down another man's stairs." People who show indifference to other people's plights do so because they have never tried walking in the same shoes.

Imagine walking in the shoe of an impoverished fellow citizen who is homeless, hungry, and hopeless of what the next day brings, knowing that it is your lukewarmness in raising rent, inflating prices of things, and cutting his job to make more profit that led to his condition. Imagine, imagine that your resistant to raising the minimum wage of all Americans due to your corruption in taking money from special interests to vote down every attempt to change the situation has dragged the economic and social progress of hardworking Americans. You were sitting on the fence then, and you are still sitting on the fence now. You looked away while the crimes were committed, and you are still looking away while the victims of your indifference are suffering. When would you get off the fence, the middle ground, the circle of coldheartedness, or remove your head from the sand and choose side?

Our heavenly Father would want you and I to be warmhearted for righteousness and justice, so he put his crown of glory on us, but

Finding Oasis Within the Wilderness of our Sociopolitical Ideologies

if you choose to be coldhearted, then you walk the walk of shame; it is your choice. However, curses are heaped upon the "lukewarmers," the fence sitters, and those who look away without any feeling or emotion. Know that like the boomerang, what goes around comes around; the crises your indifference is creating today may be your downfall tomorrow. If you want to be truly free, indifference is the wrong route to go about it for when you claim safety danger surfaces and when you think that crises will not come your way, that is when it comes flooding in.

Although I may not agree with Bill Maher on every topic regarding social and cultural issues, but in this case, we may have something in common from his quote, "Freedom isn't free. It shouldn't be a bragging point that 'Oh, I don't get involved in politics,' as if that makes someone cleaner. No, that makes you derelict of duty in a republic. Liars and panderers in government would have a much harder time of it, if many people didn't insist on their right to remain ignorant and blindly agreeable." From the rural voter who tends to vote for a party instead of the right person to the one whose only vote is for people who look like him or her, your continuous ignorance may be the worst indifference that our political system have suffered from through several generations.

Lukewarm means you are person who has decided to do nothing with the physical, mental, financial, and statutory capacity that natural talents and privileges have accorded you. It means that you are a wasted resource that no one can benefit from. In simple terms, you are selfish or self-centered. Remember, "To whom much is given, much is expected." You don't expect a low-income earner to spearhead the fight against corrupt legislators because he has less capacity to carry out that function. However, if he or she digs deep enough to jump-start a movement with the help of other individuals, we can say that such is extraordinary and must be applauded. The focus is not on the hero's heroics but on you to whom much is given. If you are a talented speaker, then speak against corruption, racism, and oppression of the less-fortunate members of the society. Let your talent be sharpened to tear through the veil of the lying politician with passion that fears no one, favors no one, and gives no one a pass. Yes, you have been given much, and much is expected of you.

According to John Stuart Mill, "The person who has nothing for which he is willing to fight, nothing which is more important than his own personal safety, is a miserable creature and has no chance of being free unless made and kept so by the exertions of better men than himself." I could not say that better. John had done that for us, a straight verbal shooter, an English philosopher, a political economist, and a member of the parliament (MP), born on May 20, 1806, in London, England, and died on May 8, 1873, in Avignon, France. The fight for the soul of America is deeper than the cultural fights that people are constantly initiating to cause commotion among the people of the United States of America; it is more extensive than the unfortunate situation where some states are trying to mono-culturize their regions with religious beliefs that only the dominant races in those states practice. We must, at least, remind ourselves that America is a multicultural democracy and does not require a constant discharge of cultural bullets at each other. For there to be peace, we must aim at inclusive union and not exclusive islands of cultural values. It is not insurrection that will destroy democracy but the indifference of those who are supposed to defend it, you and I. In the words of Carrie P. Meek, "Until we all start to take responsibility, until we do all we can to improve the character of our communities, we'll never break the cycle of violence and indifference." For us to be truly free, all of us must be free.

For Anyone to Be Free, All Must Be Free!

In many instances people tend to see freedom from myopic self-aggrandizement. They believe that freedom is to run away from whatever that holds them captive, the tendency to put a great distance between the location of danger and the spot of liberation. A young man once determined to search for jobs that would liberate him from the chains of financial difficulties. His journey took him to several workplaces as he spent his entire young life working for other people, with the hope that he would save enough money to start his own business. Despite his every effort to accomplish this purpose, success tends to elude him, that deep desire to escape his unfortunate situation drove him deeper and deeper into the hand of his situational captor, poverty! When he finally realized that his situation was a product of his own mental slavery, he refocused himself on self-emancipation. He decided to avail himself of education, information, and skills acquisition that expanded his horizon of options and pathways toward freedom. He finally eluded his captor, took full control of his life by breaking the chains of enslavement that were partly his and partly the product of society.

There is nothing worse than the mental prisons we created for ourselves then willingly shove ourselves into them and remain there, even with the door wide open. Marcus Garvey held up a mirror for us to truly see our predicament when he stated, "Emancipate yourselves from mental slavery, none but ourselves can free our minds!" We can only be free if all of us are free! We can only enjoy freedom if we share meals of freedom with other people. To many people, freedom means not to be restricted, deprived, controlled, or dominated. However, freedom may be viewed deeper than that if it is freedom for all people.

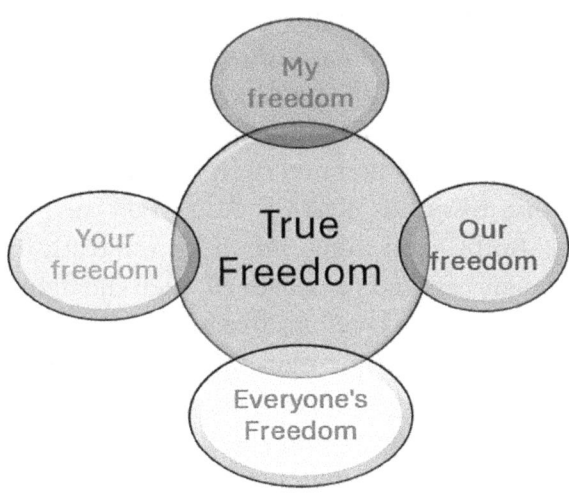

The etymology of the word could be the key to unlocking its true meaning. From two words, free and domain, we can come to the terms that freedom may mean "free domain" or "free from domination." According to *Merriam-Webster Dictionary*, freedom means "the quality or state of being free: such as the absence of necessity, coercion, or constraint in choice or action: liberation from slavery or restraint from the power of another: independence: the quality or state of being exempt or released usually from something onerous freedom from care: unrestricted use of privileges..." Those are quite extended definitions of the same word, but they mean the same thing. To be free, we must have an object of freedom since we are the subject of freedom. What are we supposed to be free from? How are we supposed to fight for freedom from the object of our enslavement? When we can sincerely find the answers to these questions, then we can come to full understanding of freedom and how our individual freedoms are tied together. For me to be truly free, you must be free too, and for you to be truly free, I must be free as well. So many people have the sentiment that freedom is being free to do whatever we like or being free to display indifference. That is far from the truth. Such misconceptions could lead to individual or group bondage beyond our desire to be free. While we are trying to be free, we end up entangling ourselves with nets of personal slavery that may become a chain reaction that pulls others in as well.

To some people, freedom is the power to exercise one's will, desire, purpose, goals, and the tendency to accomplish our individual missions in life. When a spanner is thrown into this spinning wheel of life, our freedom becomes compromised, and our trajectory to achieving our mission is diverted. Also when the purpose of our freedom is to do the right thing, search for the truth in all that we do, and express fairness and justice for all, then the fight for freedom is worth all the efforts. Therefore, freedom is not being free to do the wrong thing but to do the right thing. If you desire to exercise your freedom of expression or free speech, it must be for the truth, to build and not to destroy, to heal and not to hurt, to bless and not curse, to lift up and not to suppress others, and to "let your light so shine before men, that they may see your good works, and glorify your father which is in heaven" (Matt. 5:16). This is the true freedom of expression or freedom of speech, letting our light to shine out for all to see and say thank God for him or her. To tell the truth is to shine our light; to show compassion to others, even our enemies, is to shine as the day. To show fairness, even behind the curtain or beyond the prying eyes of the world, is to shine the light of freedom for oneself and for those you have shown fairness.

To be truly free is to be free indeed because freedom is active and not passive. We are free to do something right and not free to do nothing or nothing right. Soren Kierkegaard faulted our continued demand for freedom of speech but doing nothing with it when he said, "People demand freedom of speech as a compensation for the freedom of thought which they seldom use." Our speech is the projection of our thinking, and our thought process is a mirror of our souls.

As it is written, "A good man out of the good treasure of his heart bringeth forth that which is good; and an evil man out of the evil treasure of his heart bringeth forth that which is evil; for of the abundance of his heart his mouth speaks" (Luke 6:45). This passage explains it all, our freedom begins from within us and not from without. A person who chooses to defame another person does not begin from the truth of who his object of hate is but from his assumption that the character of the person must be assassinated. The defamer is not free and the defamed is enslaved by allegations and assumed crime he did not commit. Therefore, for any one of them to be free, both must be free. The character assassin must be free from his hate for his victim to be free. The dog whistler must discard his whistle for those he insults to be free from his disrespect. The liar must emancipate himself from his lying spirit for those who he had deceived to be free from his deceptions.

The late former first lady of the United States, Eleanor Roosevelt, pressed the issue further when she declared, "Freedom makes a huge requirement of every human being. With freedom comes responsibility. For the person who is unwilling to grow up, the person who does not want to carry his own weight, this is a frightening prospect." This means that I must be responsible for my freedom not to let it become a chain of imprisonment for others. To know the boundaries so not to encroach into someone's free domain is the requirement needed to maintain true freedom. "Freedom consists not in doing what we like, but in having the right to do what we ought," added Pope John Paul II. Similarly, Bob Dylan, the American iconic singer/songwriter and poet, wrote, "A hero is someone who understands the responsibility that comes with his freedom." Therefore, true freedom is making sure that our free domain does not in any way incite dominance over any other person or groups of persons.

Leave No Citizen Behind, Liberate All!

Our understanding of this section of the book demands a careful study of the word "citizen" and the word "liberation." As part of the ironclad motto of the United States Marine Corp, and all the other sections of the United States Military, "Leave no man behind!" has developed into a high sense of brotherhood, responsibility for each other's safety on the battlefield, and the mandate to complete any mission, get everyone home safely, as well as retrieving the remains of a fallen brother or a sister. While training for their missions, the warriors have come to know each other well, feel their joint presence in the training camps, go through rigorous training sessions that incites respect among themselves, and appreciate the sacrifices their individual families have made because of them going away to fight for their country. The motto works well with the military because it is a closely knit fighting force with clear goals, specific visions, articulated procedures, and well-ordered mandates. Therefore, "Leave no man behind!" is a command they passionately carry out, not because they are forced to, but because they love to. Family is supposed to protect and care for members in all respect, and each member is expected to care for the family as well.

However, the expression "Leave no man behind!" feels completely different when it comes to civilians, governments, and political domains. It becomes more difficult to express due to the multicultural, multiethnic, and multiracial nature of our society. The cultural values, goals, aims and objectives, rules and laws, processes and procedures are more verge and subject to multiple interpretations in a civil society than in a military or a team setup. Political institutions may have some clear-cut goals, but the implementation of the goals is marred by people whose personal objectives tend to corrupt the general good of society. Perhaps our understanding of who a citizen is and what roles he or she is expected to play in the efficient function of society may help in tapping down most, if not all, resistance resulting from our differences. When we finally appreciate our differences as our strength, then the motto "Leave no one behind!" becomes meaningful and applicable to all the citizenries.

First, let's begin with the definition of the word citizen. According to the Free Dictionary Online, a citizen is "a person owing loyalty to and entitled by birth or naturalization to the protection of a state or nation. A resident of a city or town, especially one who is entitled to vote and enjoy other privileges there. A civilian. A native, inhabitant, or denizen of a particular place:" A citizen owes loyalty to the cite of his or her citizenship: contributes through paying taxes, participates through voting for representative government of the cite, keep and uphold the laws of the land, and contributes in many ways to maintain order, development, and progress of the domain for which he or she is a citizen.

Also we can view a citizen as a person whose country owes certain rights and benefits that must be relinquished to the beneficiary, even when not demanded, especially when demanded. *Encyclopedia Britannica* explains, "Citizenship is the most privileged form of nationality. This broader term denotes various relations between an individual and a state that do not necessarily confer political rights but do imply other privileges, particularly protection abroad. It is the term used in international law to denote all persons whom a state is entitled to protect. Nationality also serves to denote the relationship to a state of entities other than individuals; corporations, ships, and aircraft, for example, possess a nationality." As citizens of the United States of America, we are also American nationals that our country owes protection, opportunity to access good welfare, better health care, right to work for and enjoy the fruits of our labor, and prosperity. President John F. Kennedy expressed one side of this contract by stating, "My fellow Americans, ask not what your country can do for you, ask what you can do for your country." Every day, citizens of this great country continue to ask what they can do for their country, do them to the best of their abilities, and achieve the greatest honors for self and country. However, the other side of the contract is where our country is having difficulty in fulfilling—asking what it can do for her citizens and not what it can milk out of them.

The etymology or the roots of the word "citizen" can give us a better understanding of the fundamental responsibility of a citizen. It originated from the Anglo-Normans' language or culture between AD 1066 and AD 1154, *citesein* or *citezein* meaning "city-dweller, town-dweller citizen." From the Anglo-French words *cite* and *sein*, *cite* refers to a site or a settlement for people and *sein* which means protector or benefactor. Therefore, we can conclude that the word "citizen" means a city benefactor, one who provides for the upkeep of a dwelling place, place of settlement, or a site where people live. A benefactor pays taxes to the city, state, or a country for its upkeep; he or she works for the entity by providing skills, competencies, and efficiency to maintain standards or improve on them. The online encyclopedia, www.investopedia.com, explains it better, "A benefactor is an individual that provides money or other resources to an individual, group, or organization. Being a benefactor does not require an individual to be wealthy, though the term is most frequently associated with significant financial gifts to charities and university endowments." It means a believer-supporter of something, other individuals, groups of persons, organizations, or government. Relatively, we can visualize John F. Kennedy's idea of who is a citizen and why we should ask what we can do for our country, not what our country should do for us.

Although the late president's idea is a great one, it is only one side of the whole equation and must be balanced to be regarded as a complete idea. A citizen is also a beneficiary of the government for which he is a national whose loyalty is completely attached. According to *Merriam-Webster Dictionary*, a beneficiary is "a person or thing that receives help or an advantage from something: one that benefits from something. The main beneficiaries of these economic reforms law: the person designated to receive the income of an estate that is subject to a trust: the person named (as in an insurance policy) to receive proceeds or benefits." These definitions may seem limited to financial and insurance benefits only; it is more than that and must be explained for better understanding by each and every one: a worker who worked and retires at the age of sixty-two had paid his dues and is entitled to the benefits from his retirement and Social Security contributions; a disabled worker or veteran who was injured or became sick while in the job is entitled to government financial and health protection; and a deceased worker's dependent children, spouse, dependent parents are entitled to his or her benefits after his or her passing. These are entitlements because the citizen had paid his or her dues, and the government must make sure that he or she reaps the fruit of their labor.

As we build our understanding of who a citizen is, the responsibilities associated with being one, and the benefits the status demands for being loyal to the government, we may as well think deeply of the word liberation and how it is related to "Leave no one behind" so we can truly replace it with "Leave no citizen behind." We can truly understand liberation from how it feels to those who have experienced it throughout history. To the European nations who were invaded by Nazi, Germany, it meant breaking the claws of Adolf Hitler from the necks of his victims, the nations he raided with brutality. To the Africans who were invaded then enslaved by the cruel Europeans and brought to the shores of the continental America in AD 1619, it meant emancipation by one of the greatest American presidents, Abraham Lincoln. To the American women who fought for their right to vote and enjoy the same rights that the men fraudulently deprived them of, it meant the ratification of the Nineteenth Amendment of the United States Constitution on August 18, 1920, allowing them to express their right to vote (end of women suffrage campaigns). Also to the Black people who were deprived of quality education through the false narrative "Equal but separate!" it meant breaking the barriers that created racial separation in our schools. To all those whose rights to vote were trampled upon by autocrats within our democracy, liberation means enactment of the Voting Rights Act in 1965 that reminded all the people that their rights to vote under the Fifteenth Amendment of the Constitution of the United States remains intact as stated, "The right of citizens of the United States to vote shall not be denied or abridged by the United States or by any State on account of race, color, or previous condition of servitude." Unfortunately, the same voter-deniers in the South illegally prevented the Black people from voting are at work again. This time, they are passing unjust state laws to throw numerous obstacles in the pathways of African American voters, as well as other minorities, to discourage them from going to the polls.

Liberation is not always a one-time thing but a continuous pushback on the unfavorable conditions until they are pushed off the hill and down the cliff. Norman Finkelstein, a famous American political scientist, activist, and author, described this situation when he made the statement, "People must liberate themselves, because liberation is not a single act. It's a question of eternal vigilance. Otherwise, you'll just become enslaved by someone else." People should not take an act of liberation for granted. They must remain vigilant to avoid the conditions of their enslavement from sneaking up on them again. It is true that the price for freedom is steep, but we must pay it for everyone if we truly desire to be free. The Black people and other minorities have suffered a lot of injustices in America due to the culture and history of the European tribes that dueled along the southern coast of the United States of America. This culture of violence, cruelty, enslavement of people, and forcefully dominating those who are unsuspecting did not begin in America, they were imported by the Vikings, Nazis, Germania tribes, Hungarian Vandals, the Portuguese raiders, the Dutch pirates, and the invading Anglo-Saxons. True believers in the freedom of our people may have fought back the colonial monarchs but did not vanquish the principles they symbolized. Those principles continue to rear their ugly heads in form of racism, discrimination, Jim Crow laws, Ku Klux Klan, Fascism, and White supremacy activities. For true liberation for freedom to be attained, we the people must fight the elements that are against freedom with the seriousness and certainty that our desire to be alive and thrive demands. Hence, the saying "All for one, and one for all!" This ethos confirms that liberation is for all, and all people are destined for liberation.

To be free, truly free, we must be both liberated and emancipated. We must make every effort to liberate and emancipate other people. Despite the general view that the words liberation and emancipation may be referring to the same concept, there are unique differences that we need to pinpoint for clarity and understanding of the terms. They differ as nouns. "As nouns, the difference between liberation and emancipation is that liberation is the act of liberating or the state of being liberated while emancipation is the act of setting free from the power of another, from slavery, subjection, dependence, or controlling influence." Indeed, liberation implies going after the source and site of imprisonment to set the victims free. It requires an external force that may be more powerful than the perpetrator to liberate the victims. On the other hand, emancipation is a force from within the circular existence of the crime that forces the hands of the perpetrator to let go of the victims. To some people, this analogy may seem a little difficult to understand, but, no, it can be appreciated from the point of who is doing what. To liberate, we must be the ones ready to exert the force needed to stop the enslavement of other people in all respects. Every act of liberation begins from within us, from our sense of good and evil, and from our desire to eliminate the source of evil and expand the contentment of righteousness. So we go after the source with the persistency, consistency, and courageousness required to pull down the high places of evil. As we mentioned, the fight for liberation may not be a one-act but a life journey; we must be ready for it always.

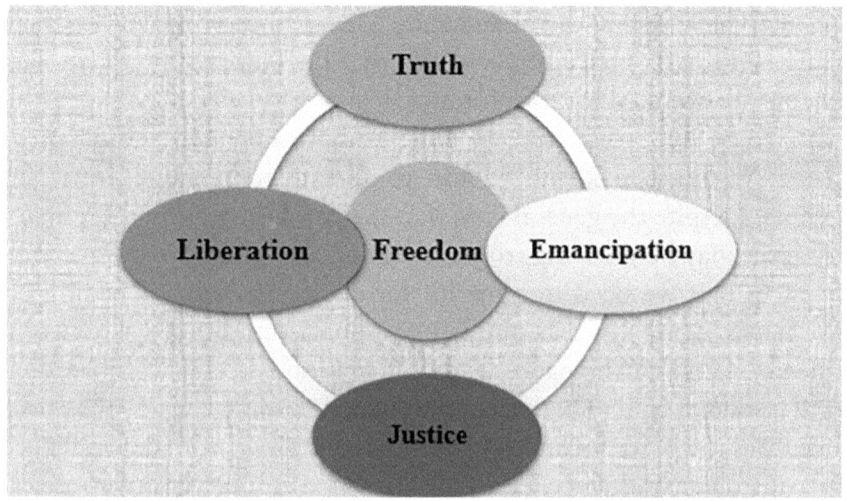

To be truly free, liberation must be the song in the hearts of all people, emancipation must be the sun that shines upon all, and justice must be the foundation by which we must build our citizenship. And in all, let the truth be the scepter of our freedom.

The truth about liberation is that it is a concept that we can observe visually. We behold those who come to set us free, we can observe laws created to relieve us from our sufferings, and we may even observe physical battles being fought to snatch us from the claws of the enemy. However, we may have some reservations when it comes to emancipation. Since emancipation is attached to how we feel after liberation, it may take some time to get used to. A young cub was rescued from the South African safari after its mother was killed by poachers. For several years it lived in the game's reservation among the workers, known and loved by all, and free to roam the confinement of the camp. When it was time to return "Boba" to the wild, the camp director instructed the lion tamers to organize an emancipation or send-off party for Boba, then release it at the nearest jungle. After every release, Boba returns to the camp at the end of the day. Reluctantly, the camp director ordered that Boba be put in an international games exchange to be transported to the Serengeti National Park in Tanzania. Boba was free to go but was not ready to leave. He felt the camp was his home and the people were part of his family. He may not be far from the truth, but the truth is that the campers were his captors who treated him well because it was their job to do so. We are not too different from the young lion when it comes to emancipation; emancipated prisoners do get confused on what to do with their newfound freedom, and emancipated youths who demanded freedom from their parents or guardians are often left frightened at the idea of living alone. No matter our situations, it is far better for us to be free to pick our battles, make our decisions, and plan our lives without the interference of other people. How we use our freedom is as important as how we achieve it. Therefore, it is important for us to know that our freedom is connected to the freedom of all other citizens, in America and across the world.

We may easily recover many American values, but when freedom is lost, America is lost forever. For the United States of America was established under the tenets of freedom, liberty, equal justice, and truth, without these, our great nation will disintegrate into history like other fallen empires. Freedom is truly free when everyone can enjoy the fruit of it. Liberty is real if everyone can feel the power of liberation, and emancipation can only be accomplished if we are freed both from within and from without. Sandra Cisneros only confirmed this thus, "Revenge only engenders violence, not clarity and true peace. I think liberation must come from within." I think so too. When we really understand that revenge is retaliation for a past sin, then we will know that liberation is prevention to an ongoing one, and emancipation is protection against future occurrences. Therefore, we must usher in our inner strength and courage to liberate ourselves and to liberate others. Also in agreement, Gloria Steinem stated that "Liberation does not come from outside." Of course not, anything that is related to human feelings comes from within our very souls. And at such, it is both an issue for men, as well as for women.

"For all men were created equal" stands for both men and women. "Those truly committed to liberation must reject the banking concept in its entirety, adopting instead a concept of women and men as conscious beings and consciousness as consciousness intent upon the world" (Paulo Freire).

A close friend of mine once asked, "Why does the military say 'Leave no man behind?'" Well, I can understand where she was coming from. In the early beginnings of the United States Military, only men were sent to battle while women carried out other noncombatant duties. But in our modernized military setup, men and women fight side by side on the battlefield, hence the expression, "Leave no person behind." Consequently, many of such gender-imputed expressions have either been modified or put on the chopping block. Thus, liberation is for both men and women, no difference. We all have something to be liberated from even if it is still inside us and holding us captive without end. We must liberate ourselves, then others.

It is possible that we desire something so deeply that we become entangled with every thought of it. According to Archibald Macleish, "There are those who will say that the liberation of humanity, the freedom of man and mind is nothing but a dream. They are right. It is the American dream." No matter the obstacles we encounter along the way while pursuing our dreams, we must first liberate ourselves from the internal obstacles before we can truly overcome the external ones. One of the greatest African leaders, Nelson Mandela, once said, "I was called a terrorist yesterday, but when I came out of jail, many people embraced me, including my enemies, and that is what I normally tell other people who say those who are struggling for liberation in their country are terrorists." He was right; liberation is the battle against evil in all its ramifications, without kid gloves! We battle against evil within us and without us. To overcome from without, we must overcome from within.

To illustrate the situation of "Leave no citizen behind!" I would like to reveal one of the on-the-spot lessons I learned some time ago. As a law-abiding driver, I pay a lot of attention to my side-view mirrors while my rearview mirrors tend to synchronize with my front view. As I move forward, I can observe activities in front of me, ahead of me, as well as behind me simultaneously, then it occurred to me that to be safe moving forward, I must be alert to what I am leaving behind or what is approaching me from behind as well. The truth about life is that our history is a record of what we leave behind in

Finding Oasis Within the Wilderness of our Sociopolitical Ideologies

time, our present is where we are writing that history, and our future is the anticipation of what the next chapters will be. The next chapters are not written until their plain pages drop down to the present from above, and the historic past cannot be deleted or modified, no matter how we may try to subvert or alter them. The funny thing about time as fluid is that my present or my past would become someone's present or near future, and someone's past becomes my present or near future because we are moving forward on the highway of life at different points in time. Some people may say that "History repeats itself!"; maybe true or not, but it could be that reality is just living out myriads of possibilities of similar situations that can only be controlled, determined in the present by us or by fate. Therefore, to understand the idea of leaving someone behind, we begin with ourselves and build the illustration outward.

Many people, in many respects, have left themselves behind without knowing it, me included. The reason is that we may not even realize what we have done to ourselves, not to mention others. An African American middle-class family moved into a neighborhood that is predominantly of a White population. The community is built in a close-knit fashion that you can easily see what your neighbors are doing in their front yards. In their first year in the new community, they felt alienated or not appreciated, but all was just about to be changed. Their ten-year-old daughter had a birthday party, and only her friends and family members were invited by her parents. Children from the neighborhood were watching from their porch or from the side street walks with keen interest. Thirty minutes later, Betty the birthday girl did the unthinkable, she crossed the street to invite other children to her party, as many as she could talk to or try to persuade.

She waited for several minutes to see if anyone from the neighborhood would attend, and her father said to her, "They won't come!"

Betty responded, "They may not come because you did not believe enough as to invite them, Dad."

Surprisingly, the neighbors began trickling in to drop off their children for the party, and some even stayed for a moment to enjoy the party alongside their children. Why this story? The lesson here is that Betty's parents had left themselves behind mentally and psychologically by thinking that their present experiences are mapped to the historical past of their race. They are chained down by history, instead of controlling the presence. On the other hand, the neighbors had liberated themselves from the past and are living in the presence, breaking the chains of the past, modifying today for a better tomorrow. For us to be truly free, we must make the conscious effort to liberate ourselves and others from the chains of darkness that were used to bound us or ones we unfortunately used to intrinsically enslave ourselves. Hatred is a chain of darkness that swings from within us, jealousy is another dark chain that eats through our very souls, and bitterness is the dark chain that corrodes our hearts. Let us emancipate ourselves from them then help to emancipate others as well. We can only be free if all of us are free.

In a similar fashion, with the table turned, a Caucasian man was suffering from a heart disease. He needed a heart transplant for a new heart, well, another heart, not necessarily new, to replace his damaged heart. For several months he and his family waited patiently for the availability of this precious organ. Finally, heaven's blessings fell at their doorstep, a healthy heart from a Black man who died from a car accident. Known to his family, the Black man had donated his heart and some other organs in case of his death, but unknown to the White man, his heart was immediately assigned to him. The crop of the matter is that the White man had a deep hatred against African Americans in general, and his wife was afraid that if he knew the source of the heart, he will not even consider it implanted into him. She said to the surgeon, "Let's keep it a secret then for the sake of saving a life from the loss of another."

Several months after his surgery and recovery, he requested to personally meet the family of his heart donor, with the intent to reward them financially. His wife knew who was coming to dinner but kept everything under wrap. On the scheduled date and time, while he was seating patiently in his living room, anxious to see whose DNA has become part of his, a nineteen-year-old African American young man walked toward him with his hand stretched out for a handshake. He quickly retorted, "I am sorry, I did not ask for you to be employed in my house. Why are you here?"

The young man responded gracefully, "No, sir, I am not your employee, rather I am the son to the man whose heart is beating in your chest. Do you want to give it back? I rather you keep it because it was a good heart!" The young man's composure and mannerism made a very positive impression on the White man, and they interacted for several minutes, discussing the life of his heart donor, who he was, why he donated his heart to save another's life. At the end of the meeting, he presented a check to the young man who declined by saying, "No, it was a gift. You don't pay for gifts that give life, you accept them and cherish them as much as you can. You may not see me again, but I am always in you!"

The worst "left behind" is when we leave ourselves behind. Like the rearview mirror, we must view the past as a lesson to change the present and create a better tomorrow. If you hold a public office or a position in the civil service and make the decision to give a less-qualified job seeker a job, to the disadvantage of a more qualified one, because of your personal bias toward their skin color, race, age, disability, religious beliefs, sexuality, or gender, you are still enslaved by your past and you need to emancipate yourself from those chains of darkness to be free. Unfortunately, your past has put a chain of restrictions around the presence of someone else without their knowledge of what you've done. Their opportunity to work for their dreams are taken away because of you. The chain reaction is enormous and could be very difficult for the victims of your crime to bear.

Another instance of leaving someone behind can be seen in people who are corrupt and fraudulent in getting ahead of everyone else. Speeding ahead of everyone to get ahead may lead to devastating implications in the highway of life. A member of an Ivy School Board who accepts bribe to deprive an economically less-fortunate student the opportunity to achieve their dreams and grant the same opportunity to a less-qualified student from a wealthy home has done injustice to the unsuspecting student and the nation that would have benefited from his or her natural talents after development. Maybe, just maybe, the student whose opportunity you have blocked could have been the scientist to discover the cure for cancer or any other terminal disease, a technologist who would have come up with a new method of generating electricity without fossil fuels, or an architectural designer who would have designed the new energy-efficient homes for low-income households. But your spirit of discrimination from the past stands in the way, and events that could have been are either pushed further into the future or completely lost in existence. By keeping your chained heart in the presence, you have enslaved the lives of many people, causing a spiritual chain reaction of a massive proportion in chaotic conditions.

Today we need more than a heart transplant; we need a soul transplant. The heart is a muscle and does what muscles do, move, and react, but the soul is our human connection to our heavenly Father, Creator, and Redeemer. Unlike the heart, the soul requires a total transformation to be changed. In describing this phenomenon, Dr. Martin Luther King Jr. stated, "Darkness cannot drive out darkness; only light can do that. Hate cannot drive out hate; only love can do that." To generate light, we require just a spark, and to nurture love, we need to let the stream of living waters flow through our souls. Relatively, Soren Kierkegaard reminds us again that "life can only be understood backwards; but it must be lived forwards." We learn from our history and from the history of others. We change what we need to change, cut off what we need to cut off, file out the rough edges, and polish our gemstones until they shimmer in the sun. This is how we leave no one behind! By empathizing with our fellow citizens, we can learn to love them as we love ourselves. George Washington Carver explains this vividly saying, "How far you go in life depends on your being tender with the young, compassionate with the aged, sympathetic with the striving and tolerant of the weak and strong. Because someday in your life you will have been all of these." We are going through the same stages of attainment as our parents and fore-parents, but we must do better with the knowledge we have now by converting them to wisdom in more efficient ways than they did because "To whom much is given, much is expected!"

In truth, the expression "Leave no one behind!" can be misconstrued in many ways. A great educational program was established by

President George W. Bush entitled "No Child Left Behind" but its implementation was a disaster. Good intentions don't always result in good outcomes as this failure has shown. Politicians have good intentions, but their strategies in achieving them always hit the snag unfortunately. A real educator would have perceived the moniker to mean not leaving the child behind mentally, in conceptual understanding of lessons, in knowledge acquisition, in learning progression, in educational standards and achievement, and in application of knowledge. A good teacher would have understood it from the perspective of using multiple strategies in instruction, differentiating lessons to meet the needs of the variety of students in the classroom, and building conceptual understanding of students from simple to complex ideas. A good administrator would have understood that after all said and done, students who meet the requirements must be promoted to the next level, and those who did not must repeat the level. By promoting everyone to the next level, those who did not meet the requirements are left behind mentally. They begin reading and doing mathematics at below level, struggle with creativity and self-confidence, and may drop out of school if the chain reaction continues for longer than necessary.

The parents may argue about the psychological part of the chain reaction on the students if they are required to repeat a grade level to make up for the shortfalls. They may insist on protecting their kids from the social stigma of falling behind in class and demand that they be promoted anyway. However, the parents may not understand that the little time they did not spend in monitoring their student's homework, assignment, and extra practice at home could have contributed to the situation than they know it.

The Department of Education, the Board of Education, the Congress, and all other shareholders in our children's education have contributed directly to the situation by complaining about the financial effects that holdovers may have on their budget: building more schools, recruiting more teachers, and spending more to accommodate the students' needs. They set the teachers up for failure by creating large classes with teacher-student ratios that are ridiculous and impracticable. To the politician, the teachers and parents are to blame for all the failures while they control the cover-up narratives.

The victim here is the child whose only guilt is trusting the adults to initiate him or her effectively, to becoming an informed, educated, and well-prepared contributing new member of society. Unfortunate situation indeed, our most important building block, our children, are in jeopardy of not competently carrying the baton when we are gone. Surely, our carelessness, incompetency, and lack of vision may come back to haunt us.

As a teacher, I have many instances of how not to leave a child behind. I was shopping in a Walmart Superstore some time ago, and a young man approached me with a stretched-out hand for a handshake. As I shake his hand, he stared at me, and I stared back at him, "Sir, I believe you don't remember me," he said. "I was one of your students." To cut a long story short, this student struggled in my mathematics class; his behavioral antics then was a call for help, I noticed. So I scheduled a student-teacher conference with him where we decided to work on his deficiencies by setting specific goals for him and I. He worked very hard to modify his academic, as well as his social behavior because he felt that somebody finally paid attention to him. We were both motivated to accomplish one thing, "educational justice," through liberation and emancipation. My mission was to liberate him, and his purpose was to emancipate himself from the factors that entangled him.

"I thank you for believing in me, even when I did not believe in myself!" he continued. "Today, I am a qualified medical doctor, specializing in sports medicine, and I owe a great deal of that to you!"

"Thank you", I responded. "But I was only a catalyst in your self-discovery. You emancipated yourself and worked hard to shine out the real you!"

This is one of many successful liberations we can accomplish in our communities, the little lights that we can shine in our small little corners to attain true freedom for all.

Therefore, we can finally understand that "Leave no one behind!" is a concept that permeates all aspects of our lives. It means that we should offer our shoulders for whoever needs our help, treat each other as you wish to be treated, and show no favoritism for anyone based on race, tongue and language, social status, or relationship. It is written, "Carry one another's burdens; in this way you will fulfill the law of Christ" (Gal. 6:2). To carry one another's burdens means to leave no one behind. To leave no one behind, we must reach out to other people, no matter their race, status, education, and position or rank.

I believe that Aaron D' Anthony Brown spelled it out clearly when he wrote, "When supporting others, sometimes we may want to pick and choose who we give attention to. We may give preference to fellow believers, members of our family, only people outside of our family, or just our friends. Are we allowed to exclude others?" No, not at all! For the benefit of freedom is not for a close few but for all, and they include all those in your neighborhood, people you never met, as well as people you pass by every day.

CHAPTER 7

True Justice Must Be Equal or No Justice!

Almost everybody has a different understanding of what justice is all about. We may have observed children complain about adult decisions, particularly when they, the children, are directly involved, and expressions such as "It is not fair!" "I think that is not right!" or "Why should I be punished, and he is not?" vehemently rants through the air. Don't be taunted by those expressions because when you were of the same age, you viewed justice and fairness from your perspective only. As a child, you felt that others do not deserve equal justice and must not be granted similar privileges, so you thought. The Apostle Paul mentioned this in 1 Corinthians 13:11, "When I was a child, I talked like a child, I thought like a child, I reasoned like a child. When I became a man, I put the ways of childhood behind me." Therefore, to fight for justice we must transform our understanding from the childish version of justice to the level known as "fairness" which is a more balanced reasoning to equal justice for all.

Considering the different definitions of justice portrayed by most dictionaries, online or in book form, the version that is more down-to-earth is that from Freebase Dictionary: "Justice is a concept of moral rightness based on ethics, rationality, law, natural law, religion, equity or fairness, as well as the administration of the law, taking into account the inalienable and inborn rights of all human beings and citizens, the right of all people and individuals to equal protection before the law, and their civil rights, without discrimination on the basis of race, gender, sexual orientation, gender identity, national origin, color, ethnicity, religion, disability, age, or other characteristics, and is further regarded as being inclusive of social justice." This definition surely portrays the true meaning of the word "justice," which encompasses all the phases of human existence and include all members of the human family, man.

Since this book is focused on reaching a layman on the street than serving academic debates, it is important to always look at the etymology of very important words, terms, and concepts for the purpose of activating individual reasoning and understanding of the concepts being discussed. The actual coining of the English word "justice" may be more than eight hundred years old, but the origin is as old as the dawn of time and beyond. From an ancient French Latin word *justitia*, which means "righteousness" and "equity," the word justice was derived (www.thewordcounter.com/meaning-of-justice/). Also *justitia* could be traced back to an old French word *justus* or *justius*, which means uprightness, equity, vindication, or right judgment. Many see justice as punishment or reward, instead of right or wrong; they may perceive it from the point of building or destroying something instead of factual truism or distorted falsehood, and they may even promote the idea of winning or losing, instead of meritorious or unmeritorious rights. Whatever point of understanding you choose to follow, justice is always doing the right thing and rejecting the wrong things, even if the heavens fall. You must promote justice and fight against injustice anyway and every way for it is the very essence of human existence.

The day God created man, he breathed into his nostrils the breath of life, and man became a living soul. He imputed into the DNA of man the element of justice, which is always doing the right thing. The manifestation of his justice is in our conscience or consciousness. "And God saw everything that he had made, and behold, it was very good. And the evening and the morning were the sixth day" (Gen. 1:31). "Thus the heavens and the earth were completed in all their vast array" (Gen. 2:2). God saw that everything that he had made was "just right" or "justified." Mahatma Gandhi confirms this spiritual existence by stating thus, "There is a higher court than courts of justice and that is the court of conscience. It supersedes all other courts." This court is the most aggressive court that prosecutes every human thought, finds us guilty or not guilty, and demands that the guilty must change their ways and the innocent must become warriors for justice and truth. Each one of us, at one time or the other, had gone through the struggle with our conscience as a prosecutor.

Three young men, between the ages of fourteen and seventeen years, decided to meet in some wood for an age-group initiation or welcoming ceremony. They selected this location to avoid the prying eyes of the adults and to activate their yet-to-be-earned age-related rights to partake in the use of alcoholic drinks. The party started when a group of invited friends arrived and continued through the night under the radiating heat of burn fires made from piles of wood. As the night grew, everything else seemed to be quiet, except the blaring noise from this group of drunken teenagers. The noise in the woods attracted the attention of Mr. Palmer as well as his dog Freddy. With his hunting rifle, he set out to investigate the commotion. Unaware of the approach of the old man, the teenagers continued their secret but loud activity. One of the young men, Kurt, who went for a bathroom break came face-to-face with Palmer, who asked him "What are you doing in my woods?"

Kurt replied, "Nothing, sir!"

Not getting the right answer, Palmer retorted, "That looks far more than nothing to me. I want you all to get the hell out of my property!"

Freddy attacked Kurt in defense of his friend, and Kurt fought back by striking the dog with a piece of wood he picked up from nearby, killing the dog instantly. In reaction, Mr. Palmer cocked his gun ready to shoot at Kurt, who jumped quickly and grabbed the gun as both were locked in a fight to take possession of the rifle. Unfortunately, to dispossess the old man of the gun, Kurt struck him with the same tree branch that killed his dog.

However, the party was still going on when a single shot rang out, bringing all the noise to a stop. They all ran toward the direction of the shot, and there was poor, old Mr. Palmer on the ground in

Finding Oasis Within the Wilderness of our Sociopolitical Ideologies

the pool of his own blood. Kurt—unfortunately frozen with fear, in his hand was a small tree branch sterned with blood, not his blood but Mr. Palmer's—could not give any account of what happened. Teenagers doing what teenagers do when faced with a difficult situation they are not equipped to handle choose to run away with the secret of, "Don't tell, don't volunteer info!" They all ran home with their various consciences prosecuting them for the cover-up! But unknown to any of the teenagers, Mr. Palmer was still alive, barely able to move or yell out for help.

Throughout the night, Kyle, who was part of the group, was being gruelled by the court of his conscience. He struggled between being faithful to his peers or telling the truth of what happened. Maybe if you had gone through such an ordeal before, you will understand what Kyle went through. At last, he succumbed to the rational and moral interrogation of this God-imputed prosecutor and decided to tell the truth. Consequently, the cops got to the scene in time to save Mr. Palmer. Let me be clear here, Kyle is not a hero in this story. He is a repentant coconspirator who was forced by the spirit of God to turn around from evil to doing the right thing. A defender of the truth would stand up against his friends without second thought, no hesitation or respecter of persons, and would not mind the consequences of his actions.

We all go through similar ordeals in our daily life, but God does not expect us imperfect beings to become perfect suddenly, rather to humble ourselves and seek his help in doing the right thing. According to 2 Chronicles 7:14, "If my people, which are called by my name, shall humble themselves, and pray, and seek my face, and turn from their wicked ways; then will I hear from heaven, and will forgive their sin, and will heal their land."

To let fairness and equal justice be done for all people, we must allow justice to be done within us with an open mind that leads to fairness. Justice can only be appreciated if viewed from all perspectives.

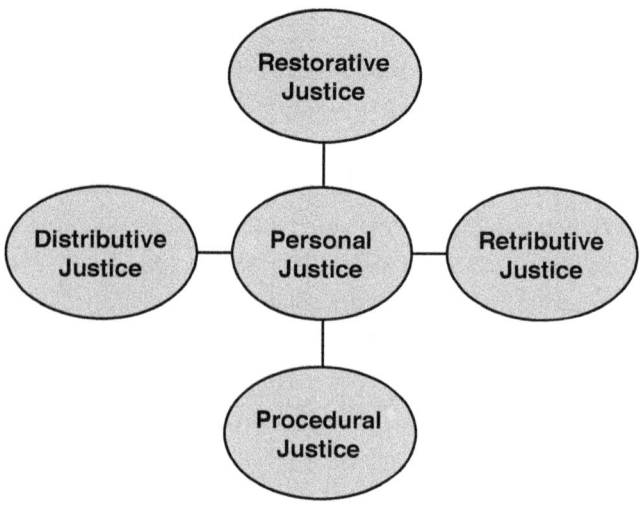

Figure 1. The Four Perspectives of Justice

The four perspectives of justice are really tied to personal justice. It is from the justification of our behavior and actions or inactions that all the other forms of justice can come alive.

Retributive Justice: Vindictive or Justification?

A judge or a prosecutor who pursues retributive justice must be honest, truthful, sincere, open to all possible factors, be fair in evaluating evidence and facts, and applying the law accordingly. He or she must understand and follow the critical race theory in refusing the sentiments of race from interfering with their judgments. In the constitution, an offender has rights that must be protected, as well as the rights of the offended. An accused is innocent until proven guilty, and the process of proving someone guilty or not guilty must be done following due process with careful consideration of facts and evidence.

The Fifth Amendment of the United States Constitution is where the rights of every individual not to perjure or testify against oneself, the right to be presumed innocent until found otherwise, and the right not to be held accountable for the same offense more than once. The question is, "How can we presume someone innocent without personal biases?" With human error and imperfections swelling around us and within us, it becomes an unsurmountable psychological, emotional, spiritual, and moral obstacle to scale over. Equity and justice begin from within you and not from without you. The fact is that we are always gruelled by the God-imputed prosecutor, our conscience, when we are making the decision to go against the truth. Therefore, it is far better to work with the prosecutor of conscience than to work against it. If your decision-making will determine somebody's guilt or innocence, then your morality and spirituality must be at the highest level.

We have seen or heard time and time again how innocent people have been sentenced to prison terms, even death, for crimes they did not commit. We can recall with nostalgia the famous "Central Park Five," a group of five Blacks and Hispanic teenagers who were accused of beating, raping, and leaving for dead a White twenty-eight-year-old investment banker. Trisha Meili was jogging in the Central Park on April 19, 1989, when she came face-to-face with her attacker who beat and raped her brutally. She survived without recollection of what really happened, who did that injustice to her. But innocent young men from Harlem, New York, took the fall despite not being near the crime scene when the moment of the crime was unfolding in real time. The corrupt police detectives pinned the crime on them without any physical evidence tying them to the crime. They applied all the methods at their disposal to coerce the unsuspecting teenagers to admit to the crime they did not commit.

This unfortunate incident took place because those who were the custodians of the process of proving guilt or innocence did not attain personal justice. Within the court of conscience, their individual prosecutors did not come alive. From the lead detective to the CSI who collected evidence, and from the police officers who made the random arrests to the attorneys who prosecuted the case against the teenagers, they lacked one thing, personal conviction or personal justice. The five men, then teenagers, Raymond Santana, Yusef Salaam, Kevin Richardson, Korey Wise, and Antron McCray suffered cruel injustice inflicted upon them by the corruption of these officers. Although the victims of this cruelty were finally released from prison, the effect of it will forever remain a scar on each man's history, both the perpetrators and the victims. Madison Feller wrote the concluding account thus, "Then thirteen years after the crime occurred, Matias Reyes, a convicted murderer and rapist who met Wise in prison, came forward to admit that he was the one who had attacked Meili, saying he did so alone. DNA evidence linked Reyes to the crime, and his confession reopened the case. (It should also be noted that Reyes had committed another rape near the park, days before he assaulted Meili.) Ultimately, in 2002, the Central Park Five's convictions were vacated, and in 2014, New York City paid the men $41 million to settle a civil suit they filed." It sounded like a fairy tale story. Not at all, it was a full-blown retributive injustice inflicted on them based on their age (ages fourteen through nineteen), color (Black and Brown), economic status (low income, lives in Harlem), and presumed guilty until proven innocence (stereotyped, labeled, or prejudged).

There were so many people in the New York Police Department that knew about the injustice committed against these young people but turned a blind eye: the DNA experts knew that the DNA of the boys did not match the sample found at the crime scene; the investigators knew that the interrogators coerced the teenagers to admitting to the crime they did not commit, yet they used the conflicting false confessions to prosecute the case, making the defendants to perjure themselves; and using false information to convict them. All these anomalies wouldn't have taken place if the personal justice of the city prosecutors were intact and at the highest levels needed to allow retributive justice based on truth and fairness to be achieved.

According to Equal Justice Initiative (EJI), "There are more innocent people in our jails and prisons today than ever before. The rate of exoneration continues to rise, revealing an unreliable system of criminal justice. A lack of accountability for police and prosecutors, reliance on junk science and mistaken eyewitnesses, and the indigent defense crisis are major contributors to wrongful convictions that have undermined the credibility of our system and ruined the lives of innocent men and women." Despite these factors being ascertained as the major causes of wrongful convictions, it is the personal injustice of the custodians of the judicial process that are the real perpetrators of wrongful convictions. Why are so many wrongfully convicted? If their cases were carefully considered without personal bias, without stereotyping, without prejudgment, without social stigma, and with careful investigational procedures appropriately applied, maybe so many wouldn't be sent to jail unfairly.

From EJI's work and data collection, over 3,175 exonerations were achieved since 1989, according to the National Registry of Exonerations. Out of the bunch, about 375 cases were exonerated through DNA evidence and with a combined total of 27,200 years of prison terms for crimes they did not commit. Also we can note that out of ninety-five convictions integrity units in the United States, only forty-two (45 percent) have recorded exonerations. By implication, there are still thousands of innocent people in jail hoping to be liberated. Basically, we must focus on changing the system to avoid wrongful convictions and not trying to exonerate them after convictions. It is far more difficult to undo a bad process than to stop it from happening in the first place.

The worst feeling about this is that many are sent to jail because of their racial, physical, cultural, social, and economic differences and not for the actual crime committed. We can recall the examples of people who were sentenced to long jail sentences or death for reason far from the truth of their guilty verdicts: Diane Jones and Walter McMillian were wrongfully convicted in Alabama; Anthony Ray Hinton who spent thirty years in an Alabama prison; Beniah Dandridge who spent twenty years in prison after being wrongfully convicted based on an erroneous fingerprint match; and Diane Tucker, a woman with intellectual disability who was wrongfully convicted of murdering an infant by obtaining medical evidence that proved the baby never existed. Many more had gone through this ordeal several years earlier: Rubin "Hurricane" Carter convicted in 1966 without evidence but only the description of an eye witness; Joe Arridy wrongfully put to death in 1939 for the crime he did not commit, rape and killing of a fifteen-year-old girl in Colorado;

also Darryl Beamish was sent to prison for the crime of killing a twenty-two-year-old chocolate heiress Jillian Brewer in 1959, a crime he couldn't have committed being an eighteen-year-old deaf and mute man who was far from the scene of the crime. If your sense of justice is alive, by now you will be feeling the desire to find justice for these people. You will be feeling the euphoria of bringing the liars, cover-up perpetrators, and corrupt lawmen and women who convicted these people without sincere, honest, and truthful procedures in the legal process. This is surely where you and I are expected to rise to the highest levels of our personal justice, our personal convictions that all men are created equal and deserve equal justice and fairness. We can read more at https://www.insider.com/innocent-people-convicted-of-murder-2018-3.

Distributive Justice: Fairness or Pretense?

All around the world, and in the history of every nation, people have fought one way or the other for distributive justice. Many emigrate to locations with more resources, for better opportunities, as well as peaceful environmental conditions to live in. We may think that distributive justice is focused only on material distribution, but Legal Dictionary Online defines the term distributive justice as "Fairness in the way things is distributed, caring more about how it is decided who gets what, rather than what is distributed. In modern society, this is an important principle, as it is generally expected that all goods will be distributed throughout society in some manner. In a society with a limited number of resources and wealth, the question of fair allocation is often a source of debate and contention. This is called distributive justice." In the United States of America, the debate and contention are far more gruesome due to the concentration of the massive wealth of this nation in the hands of few people. Today, we have about one thousand billionaires, an increase of six hundred from the 2016 record of four hundred billionaires.

The issue is not getting wealthy but getting wealthy while systematically pushing the rest of the country down the ladder of poverty. So many people today are in the business of stealing from unsuspecting citizens. Dreams monthly subscriptions in such basic accounts as Netflix to the unavoidable ones, such as rent or mortgage payments, people who are expected to achieve the American dream are being sucked dry by these companies or businesses. Since subscribers make automatic monthly payment to these accounts, as demanded by Netflix and other similar companies, the payments are never late and are regular income to Netflix but regular giveaway by the customers. Today, statistics shows that Netflix has over two hundred million subscribers in the United States and closing in on company's market cap of three hundred billion dollars as at the end of 2022. The idea that people may not watch great movies and TV programs without subscribing to online streaming is where injustice tends to reign. Monopoly of the market by these companies, hands over economic and social control of our society to the powerful hands of few. According to Albert Einstein, "In matters of truth and justice, there is no difference between large and small problems, for issues concerning the treatment of people are all the same." This may not be your cup of tea, but it is a problem for many in our community. Distributive justice is not exactly about how wealth is distributed but how citizens can have equal access to resources that will help them to realize their dreams.

Consider the basic things like housing, personal injustice by fellow citizens who think that speeding ahead of everyone else on the highway of time is what is needed for them to make it in life. Every living thing has a habitat, and they don't have to pay to live in them, but human habitats are the only ones we must pay to live in. As far as habitat is concern, there is a great distributive injustice done to all Americans and American citizens. Here is a simple account of a family that fits the case of a distributive injustice: this family moved into a two-bedroom apartment at a monthly rate of $1,150.00 in 2011. The city of Paramount, California, saw no reason to protect renters from greedy landlords by voting down on establishing rent control in the city's ordinances, allowing the landlords to increase rent at their own discretion. By 2023, the same apartment is being rented at the rate of $2,040.00 a month. Today, the same family that had lived there for about twelve years are out in the cold because they cannot afford the rent. Almost 100 percent rent increase, $890.00 to be specific (77 percent). The head of the family became unemployed due to the pandemic, and the lady of the house became disabled and could not go back to work. If they spend about 60 percent of their combined income on housing, how much would they spend on food, clothing, miscellaneous, medications, transportation, utilities, etc.? Put yourself in their shoes and you may understand. Thousands of residents of various big cities are homeless, and hundreds are being added to the list daily. The best reason is that those, like the greedy landlords, who are helping to put the people into housings are the same people who are throwing them out in the cold.

Without doubt, the system has shown no compassion to the generality of the citizenry. You can connect the banks to the situation as they prefer to provide loans to those who purchase homes for the purpose of making big money from them. Individuals who want loans to purchase single-family homes are denied resources on flimsy excuses, such as credit score and credit history. The irony of the whole situation is that the banks use the combination of the people's payroll deposits, bill payments, servings, money transfers, and other transactions to make these loans available to the greedy landlords while depriving the real owners of the financial resources of any access. If this is not a distributive injustice, what is it?

In many ways, injustices are being committed against unsuspecting citizens of the United States of America through distributive fallacies: low credit scores allow credit card companies to suck you dry with high interest fees; monopoly of markets allows few corporate bodies to dominate distribution of services, thereby generating inflation at will; a fixated minimum wage allows employers to rip off their employees by not raising their wages, rather raising their burdens of work. If the employees complain about their condition, they are told to either decide to stay or leave, a dilemma that most employees are left to deal with, without governmental protections. I cannot blame you if you feel that people who are supposed to serve your interests have conspired against you because they have! Fredrick Douglass wrote with specificity, describing this feeling thus, "Where justice is denied, where poverty is enforced, where ignorance prevails, and where any one class is made to feel that society is an organized conspiracy to oppress, rob and degrade them, neither persons nor property will be safe." This statement was true then, it is true today, and it remains true as long as human activities continue. Without distributive justice, the mere idea of an American dream becomes a nightmare to many people, because dreaming of making it big or becoming successful, with avoidable obstacles being thrown in your pathway, frustration, and retreat become eminent. Instead of putting in work and effort in building assets, the people resort to fighting for survival. Therefore, fairness and equal justice is required to make changes to how opportunities and resource distributions are set up for the benefit of all Americans and not the rip-off by few.

Procedural Justice: Truthful or Subjective?

The definition of procedural justice may be the vehicle through which the other four aspects of justice are achieved. "Procedural justice is the idea of fairness in the processes that resolve disputes and allocate resources. One aspect of procedural justice is related to discussions of the administration of justice and legal proceedings. This sense of procedural justice is connected to due process (US), fundamental justice (Canada), procedural fairness (Australia), and natural justice (other common law jurisdictions), but the idea of procedural justice can also be applied to nonlegal contexts in which some process is employed to resolve conflict or divide benefits or burdens" (Wikipedia). I believe that the importance of this section of chapter 7 cannot be overemphasized. Procedural justice determines fairness in retributive, distributive, and restorative justices, without which the achievement of fairness and equal justice is but a dream. However, it is personal justice that produces the transparency that leads to the feeling of fairness in any due process. Personal justice must be based on personal convictions of truth, judgment based on facts and evidence, and total alienation from all forms of preferences or bias. Our individual prosecutor (conscience) must be alert and active in prosecuting our morality and sincerity within the conscience court, raising our sense of justice and fairness to the highest standards as God intended. Then we will be ready to create and follow due process with fairness, confidence, efficiency, and competency.

If a police officer lacks personal justice, he will allow personal bias to soil his decisions, cloud his mind with preferences, nepotism, racism, stereotyping, preconceived notions, labeling, profiling, and prejudgment that will lead to subvention of due process and wrongful convictions. The same goes with a judge who will disregard evidence, facts, and logical conclusions, thereby sentencing an innocent person to jail or death. It is important that "hearing all parties before a decision is made is one step which would be considered appropriate to be taken in order that a process may then be characterized as procedurally fair. Some theories of procedural justice hold that fair procedure leads to equitable outcomes, even if the requirements of distributive or restorative justice are not met" (Wikipedia). This may be true to an extent when the judge or decision-maker is personally convicted by the truth or justified by fairness and moral equity to pass the right judgment. However, a custodian of proceedings who is personally unjustified would follow the order of hearing from all parties but will be unconvinced by the truth, unprotected from bias, stereotypes, nepotism, and discrimination as to decide a case with preconceived notions.

For true procedural justice to be achieved, no matter the setting, courtroom, classroom, workplace, sports ground, Congress, or any other identified context, fairness must be envisioned by all the groups involved. Every component of procedural justice must be evaluated and determined to be fair. According to Gerald S. Leventhal, "The seven types of structural components are: selection of agents, setting ground rules, gathering information, decision structure, appeals, safeguards, and change mechanisms." For fairness, these components require preset ground rules for evaluation. Therefore, in his postulates, also known as "Leventhal's Rules," he stated that, "The six justice rules are: consistency, bias-suppression, accuracy, correctability, representativeness, and ethicality."

Finding Oasis Within the Wilderness of our Sociopolitical Ideologies

Although many custodians of due process do follow the components of the procedural justice system judiciously, their moral status is so low as to negatively impact the process of justice. A police officer who stops a driver for breaking a traffic rule may show fairness in the process by explaining to the driver the rules he or she broke and why the ticket is given, where to go, and what to do to resolve the issue. When the whole procedure is carried out respectfully without bias, stereotypes, and preconceived notions or negative attitude against the driver based on the color of his or her skin, then all who are involved will go home trusting that the process was fair. However, when the police officer's personal judgment is clouded by all the negative or unjust practices that tend to disrespect the driver, demands total submission to the position of the officer, without any explanation of the rules broken, no provision for information on how and where to go for resolution of the ticket and more subvention of the process, confrontations and fracas tend to result, in most cases the death of the driver or in some cases that of the officers.

In workplaces, the process of promotions, gender equality, sexual harassment resolutions, and the promotion of a welcoming atmosphere for all people must follow the concept of procedural justice without cutting corners. Maya Angelou's statement, "It is impossible to struggle for civil rights, equal rights for blacks, without including whites. Because equal rights, fair play, justice, are all like the air: we all have it, or none of us has it. That is the truth of it," should be our focal point of understanding of justice in general. No matter your race or ethnicity, your gender—male or female—your religious or cultural orientation, procedural justice is required to generate the spirit of fairness that will lead to highly productive workstations that respects women and men alike.

As sincerely impressed by Ban Ki-moon, "Sustainable development is the pathway to the future we want for all. It offers a framework to generate economic growth, achieve social justice, exercise environmental stewardship, and strengthen governance." Continuous development and growth are necessary for the survival of human civilization and must involve every member of humanity. Therefore, it is by upholding procedural justice that we can carve out the best possible strategies to make this happen. The late reverend Desmond Tutu of South Africa gave a clear picture of neutrality as injustice, particularly when it concerns procedural justice, "If you are neutral in situations of injustice, you have chosen the side of the oppressor. If an elephant has its foot on the tail of a mouse and you say that you are neutral, the mouse will not appreciate your neutrality." Relatively, it is our constitutional and humanitarian responsibility to hold the custodians of our procedural justice system accountable for their indifference and dereliction of duty.

Women in the workplaces are not satisfied to see sexual abusers get away with their heinous crimes. I don't believe that the people of United States of America are happy that very rich people avoid paying their fair share of taxes and no one does something about it. You don't believe it either! So why are you upset with the party or the people who are fighting to restore this balance? Young college-age students are not satisfied to behold the selection of students into Ivy League schools being shrouded in secrecy! It is unjust to allow rich former athletes like Bret Favre to collude with custodians of our procedural justice to defraud the less-fortunate citizens of their rights to survival! It is against the will of the Almighty for custodians of our judicial processes to cover-up crimes, twisting facts, and tampering with material evidence and sending innocent people to jail for crimes they did not commit or sending the wrong people to the gallows. "Be not deceived; God is not mocked: for whatsoever a man soweth, that shall he also reap" (Gal. 6:7).

Restorative Justice: Punitive or Reclamation?

At this point in our lives, many people have become frustrated that the wilderness of injustice continues to encroach on our oasis of life. The question becomes, how can we stop the devastating approach and restore the breaches? We can take solace from Cesar Chavez's advice, "It is possible to become discouraged about the injustice we see everywhere. But God did not promise us that the world would be humane and just. He gives us the gift of life and allows us to choose the way we will use our limited time on earth. It is an awesome opportunity." We can decide to use our limited time to complain about the injustices done to us, or we can guide our loins with the girdle of faith and trust in our God-given talents and proceed to vanquishing our oppressors.

Restorative justice is a call to return to him who created us. It means finding, again, the pathways that will restore our humanity through righteousness. It is a call for you, a call for me, and a call for everyone else. Late senator Robert Kennedy explains this precisely as follows, "Each time a man stands up for an ideal, or acts to improve the lot of others, or strikes out against injustice, he sends forth a tiny ripple of hope, and crossing each other from a million different centers of energy and daring, those ripples build a current that can sweep down the mightiest walls of oppression and resistance." Restorative justice is for all the poor, the comfortable, the above averagely comfortable, and the wealthy. Restorative justice is to restore the truth in us and provide us with the spiritual and moral power necessary to search for the truth, do the right thing, and let the truth set us free. When we love the truth, it means we love God because he is truth. A faithful Muslim, H. Rap Brown, stated, "I seek truth over a lie; I seek justice over injustice; I seek righteousness over the rewards of evildoers, and I love Allah more than I love the state." When you love God more than the state, it means your love for your country is second only to God. And your love for yourself must equal your love for your fellow men.

The Centre for Justice & Reconciliation at Prison Fellowship International (May 2005) gave this simple definition of restorative justice, "As an approach to justice that seeks to repair harm by providing an opportunity for those harmed and those who take responsibility for the harm to communicate about and address their needs in the aftermath of a crime." It means to restore their love for others after crime committed against them has devastated their lives and status in society. We cannot attain restorative justice without taking care of our personal justice. Like I said before, this book is not dwelling on religion or religious beliefs but what religion does in restoring our personal judgment. If you are a Christian, no matter your denomination, your belief must make you more honest, sincere, and fair. If you are a Muslim, your love for Allah must make you a more loving person who is always ready to assist other people, no matter who they are or when they need your help.

To attain restorative justice, we must attend personal justice. It requires Christians to come to workplaces already prepared to be honest in every dealing with other people, it requires openness and sincerity, it demands being respectful and protective of all people. Restorative justice wants Jews to do business with fairness and be considerate in their transactions. It means that White Evangelical Christians must not regard other Christians as baseless and must be ready to restore what their ancestors did to other groups within the same ecosystem. It means "showing up" for justice and not "covering up" crimes. Allah, or God, says in Quran, "O you who have believed, be persistently standing firm in justice, witnesses for Allah, even if it be against yourselves or parents and relatives. Whether one is rich or poor, Allah is more worthy of both…." (Quran 4:135). Our heavenly Father requires each one of us to be persistent in fighting for justice even if it is against those we love.

The same call for restoration that God made to Israel is the same call that he is making to us today: "Cry aloud, spare not, lift up thy voice like a trumpet, and show my people their transgression, and the house of Jacob their sins" (Isa. 58:1). This is a call to restorative justice for you and me. It means we must change our ways, attend to our personal justices without which our restorative justice may not be attained.

"Yet they seek me daily, and delight to know my ways, as a nation that did righteousness, and forsook not the ordinance of their God: they ask of me the ordinances of justice; they take delight in approaching to God" (Isa. 58:2). Unfortunately, as a nation, we ask for God's blessings and prosperity and receive a little to none because the effects of our personal injustices are every way, generating a wilderness of corruption, shading of innocent blood, and defrauding the poor.

"Wherefore have we fasted, say they, and thou see not? Wherefore have we afflicted our soul, and thou take no knowledge?

Behold, in the day of your fast ye find pleasure, and exact all your labors" (Isa. 58:3). An unjust person will never find justice for self. You pray and seek the face of God and find nothing because of your injustice toward the innocent.

"Behold, ye fast for strife and debate, and to smite with the fist of wickedness: ye shall not fast as ye do this day, to make your voice to be heard on high. Is it such a 'fast' that I have chosen? a day for a man to afflict his soul? Is it to bow down his head as a bulrush, and to spread sackcloth and ashes under him? Wilt thou call this a fast, and an acceptable day to the Lord? Is not this the fast that I have chosen? to loosen the bands of wickedness, to undo the heavy burdens, and to let the oppressed go free, and that ye break every yoke?" (Isa. 58:4–6). People will stop at nothing to protect their religious doctrines and their denominations, but the lifestyle that these teachings demand is far away from their thoughts. We have seen time and time again how people attend churches, mosques, temples, and synagogues to learn about their religion, and yet remain unchanged or take up a different image in public. God is saying in this, if your heart is right with me, set the captives free. Stop laying burdens on others too heavy to bear. Break every yoke you have placed on others. Do unto others, as you would have them do unto you. Love your neighbor as yourself. Above all, love God with your whole heart. This is the acceptable fast to God. It means don't allow your colleagues in the Congress to force you to vote for an unjust law or policy meant to punish others for their religious or cultural beliefs. Abrogate the laws that cut taxes for the wealthy, that puts undue burden upon the average man on the street to shoulder the responsibilities of the state. It means stopping the stereotypes of profiling the minority as criminals and giving presumed privileges to those who do not merit them.

In addition, restorative justice includes how we treat the less fortunate among us. You may continue to believe that taking care of the hungry, homeless, the jobless and those who are disabled is not your responsibility because you have not experienced any of these conditions, but remember that you may become one of those anytime. The Creator of all things is concerned with how you work for them, as well as how he makes you prosperous. "Is it not to deal thy bread to the hungry, and that thou bring the poor that are cast out to thy house? when thou see the naked, that thou cover him; and that thou hide not thyself from thine own flesh?" (Isa. 58:7). Some people who claim to be Conservatives in many ways have tried to do away with "food stamps" meant for the hungry families. They have in many ways placed undue burdens of eligibility on them or have these programs cut. The irony is in their stress that these people should look for jobs, yet jobs are not provided for them. Should they die of hunger because they are not as fortunate as you? Through your economic policies, you have created the wilderness of poverty and wretchedness for these people and still blame them for the crimes you committed against them. Beware, heaven is always watching, and when you really believe that you are safe and comfortable, the hammer of God descends on you.

The scriptures explain the connection between how we deal with the poor and our relationship with God: "For I was hungry, and you fed me. I was thirsty, and you gave me a drink. I was a stranger, and you invited me into your home. I was naked, and you gave me clothing. I was sick, and you cared for me. I was in prison, and you visited me. Then these righteous ones will reply, 'Lord, when did we ever see you hungry and feed you? Or thirsty and give you something to drink? Or a stranger and show you hospitality? Or naked and give you clothing? When did we ever see you sick or in prison and visit you? And the King will say, 'I tell you the truth, when you did it to one of the least of these my brothers and sisters, you were doing it to me!" (Matt. 25:35–40). Whatever riches you have accumulated is not meant for you to devour in greed. He has a purpose for letting you have it, and that purpose is to be a steward in his vineyard.

"Then shall thy light break forth as the morning, and thine health shall spring forth speedily: and thy righteousness shall go before thee; the glory of the Lord shall be thy reward" (Isa. 58:8). When we deal with the poor as we are dealing with God, with love, sincerity, respect, and concern for their welfare, then the oasis of life shall spring forth in all that we do, and the glory of God shall fill our land. "Then shalt thou call, and the Lord shall answer; thou shalt cry, and he shall say, Here I am. If thou take away from the midst of the yoke, the putting forth of the finger, and speaking vanity" (Isa. 58:9). God will not withhold any good thing from you when you have a generous heart to others. He repays you in every way. You will prosper and be in good health. You will not go hungry or thirsty because you have given to others.

Restorative justice involves everyone, the victims of crimes and the perpetrators, the custodians of procedural justice, those who are given the burden for fair distribution of resources, and the wrongfully accused and the false accusers of the innocent. The call for restoration is a trumpet that blares into our very souls. "And they that shall be of thee shall build the old waste places: Thou shall raise up the foundations of many generations; and thou shalt be called, the repairer of the breach, The restorer of paths to dwell in" (Isa. 58:12). It is not a literal interpretation of this verse which was meant for ancient Israel but the applicative interpretation that is meant for the United States of America and the rests of the world today. Corruption in the high places has created a massive wilderness or waste places within our nation. Now is the time to generate several oases of truth to counter the wilderness that has enveloped us.

From the secretary in the office to the director of every government department, state or federal, put away the old waste that makes our political and social establishments ineffective in administering to the people's needs. Stop the bureaucratic bottlenecks that frustrate the citizens to the point of quitting. Remove the unnecessary veils used in restricting people from accessing their constitutionally recognized rights to resources, privileges, opportunities, and freedom to pursue their own happiness. End the myth that certain races are supposed to be given the first and the best seats on the table, whether knowingly or unconsciously, "For all men were created equal!"

True restorative justice requires making amends to situations and conditions that lead to harm being done to the masses. If you are a legislator or an elected government official, your continuous resistant to reformation of how our police departments should operate makes you a traitor to the people, families, and individuals who in one way or the other have been negatively impacted by the brutality of men and women in uniform, adorned with badges, and armed with lethal weapons. Why must a police officer be given immunity to any consequence resulting from his or her job performance? No matter the reasoning in your mind at this moment, if the conclusion is that it is alright, then it is alright for the surgeon to recklessly take the life of a patient without consequences; it is alright for an attorney to circumvent a court order and not be disbarred; you are as well insinuating that a corrupt judge should not be impeached for doing his or her duty unfairly; and that a governor of a state can embezzle the state's money and not be prosecuted. If we let one department off, then we can as well let all of them off!

Without a doubt, restorative justice rests a lot more on the shoulders of the custodians of the process of justice to make amend to their unfortunate legal chaos that has created the untrustworthiness in the minds of the citizenry today than ever before. According to Justice Sonia Sotomayor, "We educated, privileged lawyers, have a professional and moral duty to represent the underrepresented in our society, to ensure that justice exists for all, both legal and economic justice." Her statement confirms that aspects of restorative justice require the legal minds of society to pull away from politics and focus on true justice. If your mission in life was to be a lawyer, be a damn good one. If your aim was to become a judge in the later years of your professional life, then become an incorruptible one and stick to the truth as a needle is to the pole. We have witnessed many who have fallen from grace to grass because of greed.

Why did you become a lawyer if your mission is not to represent the underrepresented, uphold, and defend the law no matter if heaven falls? Sometimes, even fallen angels do proclaim the truth. According to Fidel Castro, "The equal right of all citizens to health, education, work, food, security, culture, science, and wellbeing—that is, the same rights we proclaimed when we began our struggle, in addition to those which emerge from our dreams of justice and equality for all inhabitants of our world—is what I wish for all." If one of the worst dictators in world history could mutter such beautiful proposal for the people, before darkness took over his personality, then it is possible for all those in position of authority to make amends to their thought process that were based on corruption and injustice and become the real custodians of justice and fairness for the people. To become the bulwark of societal defense against injustice must be the true state of heart of all our elected officials. Also it is time for "we the people" to get off the fence of dependability and demand fairness and equal justice from those we elected to public offices by voting in the right people, voting out the corrupt ones, and setting moral and ethical standards for the politicians that are not written in books but imbedded in our sociopolitical unity as the owners of the government.

CHAPTER 8

Restoring the Oasis within Our Wilderness

The United States of America—a Country, a Nation, or Both?

In the minds of every citizen of the United States of America is the physical vision of the greatest nation the world has ever seen. We can easily visualize the aesthetic high-rising buildings of some of the greatest cities in the world: New York City with the towering Lady of Liberty Statue, well-lit skyscrapers that provide entertaining shows of light displays, architecturally well-designed avenues, and boulevards, a city that never go to sleep, and the environment that displays class and generates the euphoria of wealth. In the West Coast is Los Angeles, the city of angels, where the avenues are lined with tropical palm trees, inviting blue waters of Santa Monica Beach, Manhattan Beach, Long Beach, Laguna Beach, Santa Barbra Beach, Huntington Beach, Oceanside Beach, etc. The imposing Hollywood sign, a constant reminder of who is who in the entertainment industry. Also mansion-laden green woods of Beverly Hills, Palo Verdes, and the desert cities of Palm Springs, Coachella Valley, Yucca Valley, Twentynine Palms, to mention but a few, generates the feeling of American dream in everyone whose feet had treaded these places.

It would be regarded as unfair if the great city of Las Vegas was not mentioned at all. However, the purpose of these descriptions is to give you an idea of what our focus of discussion is about. Even if we want to move forward, the neon lights of Las Vegas would disagree. A desert city that sprang up from an oasis within a traveling route, the most popular vacation destinations of citizens and foreign visitors alike. A city whose coined moniker "What happened in Vegas, stays in Vegas!" has been the defining symbol of experiences garnered by all visitors and residents who cared enough as to touch Vegas with a finger known as Las. We can as well add Phoenix, Arizona, to the mix now or struggle to find a place for them later, but I prefer now. A great industrial and cultural center whose influences in technology, industries, and trade is comparable to other cities mentioned. Whether all the cities in the Western region that should have been mentioned and are not, the focus is to give us the idea of how great the United States of America is in our eyes as citizens and in the eyes of the world.

We can talk about the middle United States regions by looking closely at the regional belts that makes up this vast and extended, mineral-rich, agriculturally based economic areas that have contributed in no small ways to the greatness of the US. The Bible Belt for example is "an area of the US where evangelical Protestantism plays an especially strong role in society and politics. People in the Bible Belt tend to be socially conservative and have higher church attendance rates than people in other parts of the country. The Bible Belt is thought to include almost all of the Southeastern US and runs from Virginia down to northern Florida and west to parts of Texas, Oklahoma, and Missouri" (*The Business Insider*). Also, we have the Rust Belt which covers the Midwest and Northeast regions that have states, such as New York, Pennsylvania, Ohio, Michigan, Indiana, Illinois, and Wisconsin. The famous political swing states that impose great influences on how the United States president is elected. This country owes these regions to the once thriving iron and steel industries that built America. Today, the industries and factories are abandoned, leaving urban decay and ghosting of once prosperous cities since 1970s, thereby, justifying the name "Rust Belt."

Although the term "Belt" was used extensively to describe the economic, industrial, and cultural diversity of the country, the Black Belt was the description of the dark fertile soil that was rich for planting a variety of crops and plantations for valued crops like cotton and tobacco, covering a stretch of counties from Virginia down through the deep South and including parts of Texas and Arkansas. Unfortunately, today the same term is used to describe the massive number of African American citizens living in the region. Their dark skin has become synonymous with the color of the soil, still being incited by the same people who would prefer to keep the Black people enslaved forever.

The Corn Belt is a region of the Midwest that produces most of the nation's corn and wheat. It is a long stretch from Ohio to parts of Kansas, Nebraska, and the Dakotas and includes parts of Minnesota in the north and Missouri and Kentucky in the south. Also this range includes Iowa and Illinois that produce more than one-third of the nation's corn, making them the heart of the nation's corn production. Unlike the Corn Belt, the Cotton Belt is a region that focuses on producing cotton as a cash crop. Rooted in slavery, this region of Southeast United States had exploited the enslaved Africans from the late 1500s to the early twentieth century, even to the late 1950s. The labor of the Black people had contributed immensely to the building of this country, and they deserve the fruit of their labor without questions, but their labor was forced, and the benefits were taken away from them by the cruelty of evil men through enslavement. Although there are other existing Belts, such as the Frost Belt, Salt Belt, Jell-O Belt, Rice Belt, Snow Belt, Stroke Belt, Sun Belt, Unchurched Belt, and the Wheat Belt, our purpose here is to paint a picture of America's diversity that probably determines the soul of this country or nation. Is the United States of America a country or a nation? This is the million-dollar question that many may have difficulty answering. What we know is that it is the greatest empire of states in the history of this world.

However, for us to fully understand the topic at hand, we must be aware of the differences between a country and a nation. By definition, a country is a political entity with specified borders and domiciliate area of control. It may encompass people who may not necessarily be of the same nationality. For example, Israel and Palestine, Kosovo and Serbia, the Kurds and the Iraqis, and the former Soviet

Union which was made up of fifteen nationalities before its break up. In many instances, countries with multiple nationalities tend to be involved in continuous warfare and struggle against each other due to cultural, religious, and ethnic differences.

On the other hand, Wikipedia explains that "a nation is a community of people composed of one or more ethnicities and possessing a more or less defined territory and government, usually formed on the basis of a combination of shared features such as language, history, ethnicity, culture and/or society." From the early 1500s to the period when the United States of America became a political entity, the territory defined as colonial or continental America was more of a country than a nation. It was a country of European immigrants, enslaved Africans, and Native Americans (the original occupiers of all the Americas, northern, central, and southern areas of America). According to the National Geographic Society page on Education (2023), "European colonization of North America expanded through Spanish colonists establishing themselves in present-day Florida in the 1500s, and English colonists doing so farther up the East Coast in the 1600s. North America's Indigenous peoples preserved their cultures and dignity through this period, despite facing violent dispossession by the colonists; enslaved Africans did as well, amid the horrors of their forced transportation to North America and inhumane treatment by their enslavers." History has shown that people tend to conglomerate around other people with like kindreds, similar cultures and traditions, beliefs and religious affiliations, and the tendency to bend toward primordialism. Fortunately, or unfortunately, no country has remained fixed in terms of makeup for over a thousand years. They are as dynamic as the humans that duel within their borders. Population of the world is a dynamic phenomenon and not a fixed and immovable outcome.

Perhaps, we should now revert to the United States of America, an entity that we can describe as a nation, as well as a country. A unique phenomenon whose diversity is the secret of its greatness and success. It did not evolve from primordialism, neither did it borrow all aspects of Ethno-Symbolism, but enough to guarantee its identity, and it is not a descendant of mono-nationalism, but a modernization theory that favors multi-nationalities, multi-cultures, and multi-racially imagined community. Benedict Anderson (1983) explains that "a nation is an imagined community in the sense that the material conditions exist for imagining extended and shared connections and that it is objectively impersonal, even if everyone in the nation experiences themselves as subjectively part of an embodied unity with others. For the most part, members of a nation remain strangers to each other and will likely never meet." A definition that portrays the United States of America as a country of many nationals which we may describe as immigrants and indigenous people which we refer to as the Native Americans. Based on Anderson's description, the United States of America is a socially constructed community as imagined by the Founding Fathers and modified by generations that follow for over 245 years of existence. By its design as a democracy, it is a nation of multiple nationals who have come from far and wide, with talents and resources that have contributed to building America into the greatest nation on earth. By its ownership as a republic, it is a country that belongs to all the people, 100 percent of them. Therefore, the United States of America is both a nation as well as a country. As a country, it is an entity of political boundaries shared by all the people as a republic. As a nation, it is a domiciliate of multiple cultures, variety of traditions, numerous religious and political ideologies that defines it as a multicultural entity that is ruled not by persons but by the rule of law, and a nation where decisions are made by the people and not by a king or an emperor. In simple terms, a democratic nationality where power belongs to the people and not the government.

Restoring the Soul of the United States of America

It is impossible to restore something if you don't really know what it is. Almost hopeless to find a missing gem if you do not have a picture of such a gem in your memory. I can still insist that it is senseless trying to reverse-engineer a process if you have no idea of what steps led to the undesirable outcome in the first place. What is the soul of a nation? According to Boyed Matheson's written explanation on "The Soul of the Nation," "The soul of the nation is found in that inner self-respect, self-determination and selfless commitment to community and country. It is also grounded in respect for the dignity of others and tolerance, valuing the unique value in every life, at every stage and in every station." I could not agree more! It is imbedded in love for country and love for fellow citizens but true love for oneself as well. Believe me, it is deeper than the above definition and wider than what our thoughts could absorb or comprehend.

In many instances, people think that the best way to go is separate religion from politics; they are right, there is always conflict when the two interface. But we cannot separate a righteous person from policymaking and expect a true balance. For the soul of a man is the spirit of truth that connects man with the Divine God. As it is written, "And the Lord God formed man of the dust of the ground and breathed into his nostrils the breath of life; and man became a living soul. And the Lord God planted a garden eastward in Eden; and there he put the man whom he had formed" (Gen. 2:7–8). Without the spirit of God, the dirt from which man was formed remains dirt. It was and it's still the spirit of the Almighty that made man a living soul. The living soul is the state of overwhelming consciousness of God in us and around us as nature.

Perhaps when Adam became conscious of who he was, where he was, and whose face he was looking at, he did not require introductions; he knew because the "Spirit of the living God" was in him. I am sure he didn't call him God at first but "Father," which is more personal and closer identifiable relationship with the perfect being he was staring at. I am also sure that God did not respond to Adam by calling him "man" but "my son" because he created him in his own image. Therefore, no matter our understanding of what a soul is all about or our intuitive desire to define it based on our religious, cultural, and traditional affiliations, the trace will always bring us back to man's origin, the garden of Eden, where man became a living soul. Let us consider *Merriam-Webster Dictionary* definition of a soul which involves a little bit of every aspect of this phenomenon as stated, "It is the immaterial essence, animating principle, or actuating cause of an individual life." Also it is viewed as "a person's total self, an active or essential part of a moving spirit." Furthermore, the definition includes morality as well, "The moral and emotional nature of human beings, the quality that arouses emotion and sentiment, spiritual or moral force." Not only is morality involved, but the intensity of our feelings and sentiments binds all together, "a strong positive feeling (as of intense sensitivity and emotional fervor) conveyed by every human being."

We can only restore the soul of our nation if the soul of each individual citizen of this great country is empowered to shine. The soul is the light of God in us; we either trim the lamp for it to shine for all to see or put it under the bushel away from the view of others. To restore the soul of the nation, we must restore our connection with the one who created us. The spirit that moves upon us to love our God with all our heart, to love our nation only second to him, and to love our fellow men as we love ourselves is needed again to spark the flame of our souls into life. In his farewell speech, January 1989, Ronald Reagan gave a description of the United States of America as a city set on a hill. He gave a vivid assessment of what makes it the greatest nation on earth by saying, "In my mind it was a tall, proud city built on rocks stronger than oceans, windswept, God-blessed, and teeming with people of all kinds living in harmony and peace; a city with free ports that hummed with commerce and creativity. And if there had to be city walls, the walls had doors and the doors were open to anyone with the will and the heart to get here." This, of course, is what a true soul of a nation creates, individual lights that brightens a nation, individual talents and skills that built every facet of a vibrant life and living, and strong hands that extend in friendship to all who share the same principles of freedom, liberty, fairness, and equal justice under the law.

As it is written, "Ye are the light of the world. A city that is set on a hill cannot be hidden. Neither do men light a candle, and put it under a bushel, but on a candlestick; and it giveth light unto all that are in the house." The Lord sees us as light that shines and provides directions to the world as an example for all to follow, and he expects us as a nation to shine the brightest in a dark world. In addition, he expects us individually to shine within our little corners as bright as we can. Therefore, he gave the fervent command, "Let your light so shine before men, that they may see your good works, and glorify your Father which is in heaven" (Matt. 5:14–16). As the light of a city is a sum of the individual lights within its domiciliate, the soul of a nation is the combined power of the souls of her citizens.

Restoring the soul of our nation does not mean going back to the old ways of doing things, it means going forward to "*the new beginning*". In every individual is a moment of "*Stop and think again!*" or "*Stop and recalibrate again!*" This, of course, is the point of reset in our lives that is required to get rid of all the life junk that the system has dumped in our pathways. It is also the point of reset where we must learn from our mistakes and make corrections accordingly. The issue is that some people have been dealt so much systemic blow that self-recovering may be virtually impossible. Here is where the "government of the people, by the people, for the people" comes in to help in restoring the dignity of individuals who cannot help themselves.

To restore the dignity and self-respect of individual citizens requires providing housing for the homeless person that is living in the street, in homeless encampments, and temporary shelters. It means recognizing that these citizens are as important as those living in mansions and aesthetic buildings. In truth, they are not asking for donations, rather they are asking for their government to look out for them at the most pressing period of their needs. This does not require a democratic party solution or a republican party solution; it requires the American solution. It requires the constitutional provisions for every citizen of the United States of America as stated in the Bill of Rights. If you are living in a housing, an apartment building, a rented house or one own by you, an intimidating mansion, a country home, or a town house with all the warmth and comfort that you may not even realize you have, imagine that all goes away in a momentous sweep, and you are left in the street with no place to go. The feeling of self-doubt, fear of where your next meal is coming from, the emotion of disappointment and helplessness, all sending darting arrows of hurt through your heart may help our understanding of how the homeless feel as they are left in the cold.

I have over the years heard some very privileged people make jest of people who had lost everything: "It is their fault!" "They should have managed their businesses better!" "They should have gone back to school to get a better education!" and "Why should we waste the taxpayer's money in resettling the homeless?" Yet it is the insidious activities of these accusers that lead to the situations these people are going through. It is their resistance to raising minimum wage to a better living wage that may have contributed to many becoming homeless; their inflation of prices, thereby abusing the free market economy meant for general economic growth; their continuous increase in rent to the point that two-thirds of people's incomes are spent on housing; and the unemployment saga that are caused by billionaires who are eliminating jobs in order to make more money.

The soul of every individual is imbedded in the body for our body is the temple of the living God. Protecting the body from the elements of nature requires habitats or shelters, the first factor in restoring the soul of the nation. The body must be nourished with food to keep it strong and healthy for the habitation of the soul, which is the second factor in restoration. Indeed, without health care and protections against diseases or infections, the body dies naturally, the third factor. Education and free access to information is required to incite the mind to creative navigation of society's natural resources, which is the fourth factor of restoration. The fifth factor is immersed in acquiring and maintaining a job or a professional status that binds all the other factors into a consistent relationship. Therefore, to restore the soul of the United States of America means we must restore the dignity of all the citizens.

Although the government may not achieve all the above for every citizen of the United States in a sweep, but enacting laws that protects the individual from exploitation, extortion, economic abuse, and social degradation is one way of restoring the dignity of all the citizens. The USA may be the greatest economic and military power in the world, but when it comes to creating the social order that elevates the domestic status of the citizenry, the nation struggles. According

Finding Oasis Within the Wilderness of our Sociopolitical Ideologies

to the recent report released by the United Nations Organization (UNO) on the happiest nations in the world (2022), the greatest nation in the world, the United States of America, did not strike the first ten positions on the chart. For our nation to be rated sixteenth in the world should not arouse any indignation because we already know the reasons why. It is the inequitable distribution of resources, opportunities, and privileges that has created the dichotomy.

Happiest Countries (Top 20 by Rank)	Wealthiest Nations (Top 20 by GDP Rank)	Average Income Per Capita (Top 20 by Rank)
1. Finland	1. United States (18.57 T)	1. Monaco
2. Denmark	2. China (11.22 T)	2. Bermuda
3. Iceland	3. Japan (4.94 T)	3. Switzerland
4. Switzerland	4. Germany (3.47 T)	4. Luxembourg
5. Netherlands	5. United Kingdom (2.63 T)	5. Norway
6. Luxembourg*	6. France (2.46 T)	6. Ireland
7. Sweden	7. India (2.27 T)	7. United States
8. Norway	8. Italy (1.85 T)	8. Denmark
9. Israel	9. Brazil (1.8 T)	9. Singapore
10. New Zealand	10. Canada (1.53 T)	10. Iceland
11. Austria	11. South Korea (1.41 T)	11. Qatar
12. Australia	12. Russia (1.28 T)	12. Sweden
13. Ireland	13. Australia (1.25 T)	13. Australia
14. Germany	14. Spain (1.23 T)	14. Netherlands
15. Canada	15. Mexico (1.05 T)	15. Hong Kong
16. United States	16. Indonesia (0.93 T)	16. Finland
17. United Kingdom	17. Turkey (0.857 T)	17. Austria
18. Czechia (Czech Republic)	18. Netherlands (0.771 T)	18. Germany
19. Belgium	19. Switzerland 0.659 T)	19. Belgium
20. France	20. Saudi Arabia (0.639 T)	20. Israel

The United States is ranked seventh per capita income earning of her citizens in comparison with the rest of the world. But the US is the wealthiest nation in the world with a whooping GDP of $18.57 trillion. The disparity is that the wealth of the nation is in the hands of a small number of people, about one thousand billionaires to be exact. To restore the soul of our nation, there must be a calculated attempt to redistribute our wealth by making laws that will stop greedy capitalists from taking undue advantage of the rest of the citizenry. Finland is ranked no.1 on the "Happiest Countries Chart," ranked no.16 on the "Per Capita Income" earnings of her people but completely off the first twenty ranks of the wealthiest nations, indicating that the country's wealth is fairly and evenly distributed and the people are fairly satisfied with their lifestyle. In retrospect to their past rankings, Finland's life expectancy ranking of twenty-fourth in the world at an average age of 82.48 years is far higher than that of the United States ranked forty-sixth at an average age of 79.11 years. We can do better if we are ready and willing to dislodge special interests from our politics and economic endeavors.

Also restoring the dignity of our family units is a way of restoring the soul of our nation. We have more single-family units today than families with both parents living together. It is unfortunate that filing for a divorce is made easier and quicker today than four decades ago, with the stroke of the computer keyboard and the help of a legal aide, divorce can be settled in few months based on filed paperwork without physically appearing before the judge. Here, the children are the victims of these irreconcilable breakups; they suffer without end. Their anger and disappointment are transferred to other people, other things, including the school. We cannot begin to imagine the impact our self-centered divorce acts have on our children and their immediate environment! No one is asking anyone to stay in an abusive relationship, but if the situation is because of your inconsiderate behavior, then you really share the blame for what happened. When you took the oath to join with one and other for as long as death do you part, you agreed to work hard together to maintain and to uphold your relationship, to keep extended family influences out of your domain, and to turn a blind eye to other women and other men from putting asunder to your life of "one" and only "one." The most important part of the oath is your promise to rear your children as God would want you to, give them the love and nurture that they need to grow into responsible adults. However, due to your irreconcilable differences you have failed to uphold that oath, and the spirit of the oath will hold you responsible for breaking it. Therefore, to restore the soul of the United States of America, we must restore the function of the family unit that makes up the bigger family, our nation.

Also to restore the soul of the nation, we must restore the soul of each community and district within every county. In an earlier chapter of this book, we discussed the disparity in resources and facilities apportioned to communities based on unjust distribution processes that gives credence to some areas to the disadvantage of others. It is important that the people should be given proper orientations on how to participate in building their communities by restoring their confidence in the activities within their immediate communities. Representatives of the people are only seen when they are canvassing for votes during elections after which they disappear without any contact with the people, no town hall meetings to listen to their community complains, or give bimonthly reports of their achievements in the Congress.

Peter Drucker kind of hit the nail by the head when he opined that "management is doing things right; leadership is doing the right things." A leader is one whose aim is to do the right thing, and doing the right thing demands doing things the right way. Creating a management structure that will guide the people to achieving their goals and dreams. Relatively, we can only restore the soul of our community if we aim to restore the quality of leadership needed to pilot the community spirit to a greater height.

The famous Italian Dominican friar, theologian, and philosopher, St. Thomas Aquinas, stated with a conclusive alacrity that "if the highest aim of a captain were to preserve his ship, he would keep it in port forever." Leaders who tend to leave their communities the same way they found them are not worthy of the scepter of that community. To you, members of the community, comes the question, "Why do you continue to vote for leaderships that do not improve the way of life of your community?" "Why do you continue to give your support to a party platform that does not care about you as individuals or as a group?" By your nepotic behavior, party preferences based on racial makeup and the unfortunate belief that it is only your inner circle that must dominate or no one else, our communities have remained the same without progress. Therefore, to restore the soul of the United States of America, we must restore the original understanding that all men were created equal and have equal rights before the law. It is time to come to terms with the fact that God placed the best and most talented people within humanity, evenly distributed and not concentrated within specific ethnicities as some have continued to proclaim falsely.

In every community of human endeavor, it is the deep-rooted sincerity of members of the community that sparks the spirit of trust and cooperation. Without sincerity of understanding, acceptability, appreciation of each community member, and sincerity in being fair to all, the community trust cannot be fully expressed. If your yes cannot be truthfully your yes and your no cannot be truthfully your no, you have no right whatsoever, either morally or spiritually, to lead anyone. You have no right to even pretend to be a member of a vibrant community. We can only restore the soul of our nation when we can restore the sincerity of each member of our community. To be candid, sincerity and integrity is so important to the soul of our nation that Douglas Adams stressed that "to give real service you must add something which cannot be bought or measured with money, and that is sincerity and integrity." It is the spirit of sincerity that can break all the cultural, traditional, ethnic, political, and racial barriers that have prevented us from reaching a "more perfect union."

Using a simple, but a more understandable example of the effect of sincerity on our communities, Princess Stephanie of Monaco stated, "Circus is what real life should be like. It's sincerity, feeling, emotions. All real. There are no lies in circus. There are artists working together to give a smile. It's a world where people help one another. It's the only show where a family, everyone from children to their grandmothers, can sit together and all be entertained by the same thing."

In conclusion, we can only restore the soul of our nation by going forward to "the new beginning!" and not back to the old ways. Restoration of each individual soul is required to boost the national spirit of liberty, freedom, and equal justice with fairness. It takes the twinkling lights of each home or abord to light the city, and each

Finding Oasis Within the Wilderness of our Sociopolitical Ideologies

small light must increase in intensity to create a city of lights set on a hill as an example to all the world. These must include the restoration of the dignity of the homeless by giving them a second chance to functional habitat and protect the citizenry from self-centered landlords who are relentless in raising rents. Stopping the cruel capitalists from cutting jobs for the purpose of making more profits and challenging the politicians to their responsibilities toward their communities and not toward special interests would be the best method of making sure that the wealth of this nation is fairly distributed for all the people to experience the American dream.

CHAPTER 9

Making Our Oasis Better than Before

Our journeys of a thousand miles as described in this book began with the first step of reading the introduction. Then you decided to continue reading the book or to drop it. However, if your interests had been sustained till this moment, and at this chapter, it means you have absorbed a lot of the principles that this book is calling your attention to behold and uphold. So far, we have likened the United States of America to an "oasis of life" within a wilderness. Since an oasis and a wilderness are both natural and dynamic phenomena, it is important to note that with some favorable or desirable conditions, an oasis could expand its beautiful topography and usefulness or a wilderness could encroach speedily and turn an oasis uninhabitable before any attempt at stopping it is made. If you fail to water your lawn on a consistent basis, the wilt that you begin to observe is the result of that error.

Negligence in rearing your children, of course, will lead to a dysfunction in their upbringing. Years of not participating in your community's political activities will hand power over to your inferiors while you rue your lukewarmness. Ignoring corporations' small penny price increases will finally lead to inflation that you may not have the capacity to bring down. Let's be honest to ourselves, as well as to others, it is the very thing that we tend to ignore that hurts the most when it comes to full manifestation. The hurt is that we could have done something but failed to make any attempt at arresting the effects or finding solutions to the problem. This situation is not yours alone, it is mine too, and it is a general habit that most people have enbibed consciously or unconsciously. However, we can find out ways of overcoming it by learning from others who at one time were in the same predicament but reversed their steps and moved toward a more positive direction. Or we can take personal initiatives at recalibrating our life goals and reverse-engineering our faulty steps.

The American Dream: Reality or Just a Dream?

Millions have crossed the great oceans of the world to reach American shores, some had brazed the harsh deserts and tough traveling conditions in search of the American dream. What is the American dream? Why is it so important to every citizen and non-citizens alike? Wikipedia gives the following description that may provide us with a simple understanding of what it is all about: "The American dream is the national ethos of the United States, a set of ideals including representative democracy, rights, liberty, and equality, in which freedom is interpreted as the opportunity for individual prosperity and success, as well as upward social mobility for oneself and their children, achieved through hard work in a capitalist society with few barriers." This definition simply displays the ideals that in normal circumstances may provide all citizens with the opportunity to dream of any attainment, work on the dream under conducive factors, and achieve their dreams with euphoria of successes. Also included in this dream is the transfer of assets to one's children, children's children, and for generations to come. It means that the pioneering generation may not always jump-start success. But with the proper upbringing and specified clear goals, the next generation may bring the family to a successful status or the journey or dream continues.

Besides the idea that no work, no pay is the hidden factor known as capital. America is a nation that believes in investing capital to generate profits. The freedom of investment and the liberty to work at one's dream is the atmosphere that the United States of America offers to anyone who finds a way to reach her shores with good intentions. So many immigrants had graced this land with talents and skills that have built America, and you have equal opportunity to do likewise. The most important asset or capital that we have and can be invested in our American dream is our mind: your intellectual property is your capital, your professional skills and training is your asset, your physical prowess is your bait in this card game, and your educational and academic training can lead you to many open doors if you can search for the right door.

Yet many people tend to search for assets in places that may not be the right sources but ignore the closest source which is from within. If you have the skills in fixing cars and other mechanical objects, it will be futile for you to go for a college degree that is not related to your natural inclination. The best way to go about your American dream is to focus on establishing an auto shop, learn everything you need to learn about auto mechanics, and build your dream one step at a time, one year after another, and from one level of efficiency to another. Success creates more success! If you build on your success, you can expand your business into a franchise. You may not be the success phenomenon of Henry Ford or the spectacular rise of the Dodge brothers, but you could become an efficient and competent repairer and modifier of Oldsmobile that will incite customers' confidence in your work.

Indeed, a carpenter can become a successful furniture designer if his or her dream is deep and extensive. From one's backyard or garage, a business could rise to become one of the best in the country if the dreamer is not stuck in the garage. It is important to note that it is a dream until we make it a reality, and a dream is a virtual reality that we can bring to life, or we may as well let it remain a virtual picture of what is possible if we do not put in the hard work. This is where our freedom of decision holds sway, it is where our liberty to take control of our status comes into play, and it is where our equality and fairness manifest into reality. Despite our misunderstanding of this philosophy, sometimes, of course, it is in this moment of our thought process that we can find the purpose of the constitution that states that we can "secure the blessings of liberty to ourselves and our posterity." It may have taken me a little time to come to appreciate this philosophy and may take most people almost a lifetime to even envisage the tenets, but the reality is that each of us will at one time or another be stunned by this aspect of our souls.

The beautiful thing about virtual reality is that it can always be recalibrated, redesigned, repositioned, or repurposed. The American dream is a virtual reality of what our lives could become if we put in good planning and purposeful efforts required to make them come to life. A police officer who applies his or her years of experience in inventing or designing a better body armor for saving lives would have recalibrated his or her American dream. A firefighter who works on the possibilities of developing better ways of fighting aggressive fires and better protective gear that will save his life and that of the victims of fire may have reinvented his dream, as well as protecting that of others. In the words of Mario Andretti, "Desire is the key to motivation, but it's determination and commitment to an unrelenting pursuit of your goal - a commitment to excellence - that will enable you to attain the success you seek." It takes a deep desire and motivation to unlock the great realms of our mental possibilities. Coupled with relentless commitment and undeterred effort, our imagination will take flight beyond our wildest dreams.

A teacher who is not just satisfied with teaching in a classroom but desires to design and produce better teaching materials, software, or hardware is on the flight to achieving for self and others. An educator who applies technology in his professional experience is a better designer of educational materials than an engineer who applies engineering to developing teaching and learning materials. The educator has what the engineer does not have, knowledge of how students learn, the feel of students' progressive achievement, students' learning styles, and how to differentiate instructions to accommodate the variation of students in a classroom.

Besides the success of achieving an American dream are the difficulties, resistance, and share frustration that we experience on our way to reaching our goals. The most grueling factor is that of being stuck in the loop of living the same lifestyle over and over and over again. You work in the same workplace, in the same position, a little bit above minimum wage, and follow the same routine year after year, promising yourself that you will break the loop and move forward. My fellow citizen, it will take a high-level willpower to break such a loop. Some people will sail through smoothly while others may go through difficult situations, but the journey is still the same. The unfortunate thing about how we all view the philosophy of American dream is that people tend to equate it to economic achievement alone, but I can tell you that it is beyond that. It is inculcated in what we desire most and how to achieve that desire while living in a representative democracy, a land of freedom, a conglomerate of liberty and rights of the citizens, and professed equality under the law.

Although the American dream allows for competition, it is the injustice committed by those who took undue advantage of others by claiming the privileges that doesn't belong to them that have created dissatisfaction, alienation, suppression, poverty among the minorities, and disadvantage of those who were brutally treated with the injustice of slavery and genocide like the African Americans and the Native Americans or Indigenous Peoples. According to Wikipedia, "In 2020, a poll found only 54 percent of US adults thought the American Dream was attainable for them, 28 percent believed it was unattainable for them personally, while 9 percent rejected the idea of the American Dream entirely. Younger generations were also less likely to believe in the American Dream than their older counterparts."

Yak! These statistical analyses of people's opinions of what an American dream means to most people has shown that we tend to associate our dreams to that of others who became successful and famous citizens. Note with sincere attention, this scenario is you having a deep desire for something, a dream of what you so earnestly want to achieve, and the process of creating plans to reach your goals, with purposeful effort focusing on them until successful outcomes are achieved. You will be consistently frustrated and disappointed if you focus on attending to someone else's dream or replicate their success for your own. In truth, the American dream is not asking you to be the next John Wayne, the next Bill Gates, or the next Mohammed

Ali, but to be you. George Bernard Shaw puts this in perspective by saying that "imagination is the beginning of creation. You imagine what you desire, you will what you imagine and at last you create what you will." He meant that your creation is from your imagination, and your imagination is from your desire. Therefore, stop trying to be like someone else and be yourself. If 28 percent of people believe that the American dream is not attainable to them, 9 percent don't believe in it, and most people of younger generation don't care about it, then we can ascertain that there is a deep misunderstanding in how people perceive this philosophy.

Surprisingly, the confusion and apathy that people feel about the ethos American dream is from the poor perception of the early days of the birth of the United States of America. Then people thought it was meant for White property owners, people who hold positions in the society, the highly educated or well-informed members of the community who are male and Caucasian, and specifically those who were descendants of the early immigrants. These people unjustly suppressed the growth of others who were not part of their inner circle, commandeering privileges that were meant for all members of the community. They created a disparity that has endured through many generations and for more than two and half centuries of our existence as a nation. However, we must change things for ourselves and our posterity and mentally reverse the unjust acts that were committed against us. From Janet Jackson's perspective, "Dreams can become a reality when we possess a vision that is characterized by the willingness to work hard, a desire for excellence, and a belief in our right and our responsibility to be equal members of society." We can expressively give credence to our rights and responsibilities as members of a democratic society by truly pursuing our dreams and happiness, thereby putting a stop to the activities of privilege suckers. Under our direct or indirect tutelage of our children or young generation, we can reposition their thought process to view a dream as a dream, the projection of our inner desire to achieve excellence in anything that we focus our minds on. Also to inspire young people to aim for the stars despite the failures of the present or past generations.

Complete deception was perpetrated when the Founding Fathers of this nation expressed the ethos "the American dream" in the preamble of the constitution. They did not really mean that the dream was for all the citizens. Although the ethos was first coined in 1931 by James Truslow Adams, the reality is that it is the same dream that propelled us to come to USA, it is the same dream that moves you to become the best in your field of endeavor, and it is that inner desire that gave you the impetus to become the first in your family to go to college. It is the same dream but achievable in the American way: following "a set of ideals including representative democracy, rights, liberty, and equality, in which freedom is interpreted as the opportunity for individual prosperity and success, as well as upward social mobility for oneself and their children, achieved through hard work in a capitalist society with few barriers." It does not matter that you have failed in your first attempt at achieving your personal goals, what matters is that you have decided to recalibrate your focus, chosen to reinvent your dreams, and you are persisting in your effort to bring your desire to life no matter what it is. What matters is that you are believing in yourself again.

Not only should we focus on our individual American dreams but also focus on the soul of the nation imbedded in each of us. We may find it highly difficult to achieve our dreams if the national dream of a better society is not achieved. As clearly expressed by Bayard Rustin, "If we desire a society of peace, then we cannot achieve such a society through violence. If we desire a society without discrimination, then we must not discriminate against anyone in the process of building this society. If we desire a society that is democratic, then democracy must become a means as well as an end." Our American dream is intertwined with the soul of our nation, and it is our responsibility to rescue the nation from the forces that are threatening to destroy it from within and from without. It is time to stop people who have, through corrupt means, been occupying our public offices. It is our responsibility to prevent people with ulterior motives from making laws that are meant for taking away our individual constitutional rights from us while we become helpless and unable to intervene. If we choose not to control the narratives of our political and economic systems, then we should not complain when morons and incompetent people make bad decisions over our lives.

In conclusion, we can ascertain that our pursuit of happiness is not always smooth; sometimes we walk through thorns and thistles, sometimes we journey through smooth highways, and sometimes we climb hills or trek across deserts. It is your dream, your virtual reality, you and only you can edit it and no one else. In the words of E. B. White, "I arise in the morning torn between a desire to improve the world and a desire to enjoy the world. This makes it hard to plan the day." It may have been hard for E. B. White to decide on which to do, but I believe we can do both since one depends on the other.

Transferring Our American Dream to the Next Generation

As illustrated in the last section, one of the advantages of representative democracy is to "secure the blessings of liberty to ourselves and our posterity" and to transfer assets from the pioneering generation to the next generation. As stated earlier, the pioneering generation may not be the success story in every American family, and first attempts may not always result in our desirable outcomes. Despite many years of continuous learning and acquisition of professional and social experiences, parents of different backgrounds persist in making the same mistake of assuming that their children will turn out well without them being there to administer proper training and upbringing. As the scriptural proverb goes, "Train up a child in the way he should go, even when he is old, he will not depart from it." This statement was true then, it is true today, and it will be true forever. Many prominent people who have in one way or the other graced our community have expressed their gratitude to parents and relations to whom they owe the upbringing that had contributed to their success. Statements such as "I owe my gentleness to my father teaching me how to show courtesy to others!" "Without my mother's cooking lessons, I wouldn't be this good of a cook!" "I will forever be grateful to my elder brother. He made a man out of me!" "We learned many good things by watching our father's examples!" etc.

As these praises and credits put parents on the pedestal of honor, so does parental neglect bring kids down to the lowest possible human behaviors. We have in instances heard people vent their frustration on their erring parents and relationships by making utterances, such as "I wish he wasn't my father. He cared more about his work than his children!" "His excessive drinking brought my family to a complete disrepute!" "My mom abandoned us and showed no regard to us as her children!" "I became a gangbanger because he was one of them!" etc.

Be not deceived, God cannot be mocked. For whatsoever a man sowed, that shall he also reap! If you desire a functional family, you must sow the seeds required to train them into responsible adults. You cannot sow neglect and expect to reap responsible kids, neither should you display apathy to your children's education and expect them to be highly educated. The training of your kids begins the moment they are born into this world. The baby starts learning about his environment through sound, smell, and touch, and the mother's voice is the very first lesson for him. He differentiates the mother's voice from the rest of the voices around him by consistently relating the sound to a gentle touch of care and a familiar smell of food (breast milk or baby food). The baby perceives, without understanding, that all he must do when he is hungry, needs attention, feels wet, or needs company is to cry and all his needs are delivered to him, no questions asked. With time, he begins to associate with other voices, such as father's voice, siblings sounds, and even strange voices from visitors. Do not be surprised, the baby learns faster than we do when it comes to facial recognition. The mother's face is the most recognizable one, followed by the face of whoever assists the mother in taking care of his needs. He decides his favorite sibling based on whose face is always by the crib to play with him and which one takes too long to visit.

As the baby continues to create new memories, his capacity to learn about the environment increases, and his transition to the next stages of life becomes smoother and naturally more efficient. The parents' understanding and guidance through these early stages of life is very critical to the child's development, as well as the development of a functional family unit. It is the responsibility of the parent to learn how to wean the child away from the base instincts of early stage to the control stage, through gradual but consistent efforts at impressing on the mind of the child why certain satisfactions could be delayed or controlled. They may not get whatever they want by just crying for them anymore, but through a little understanding of timing and childlike negotiation, the child will come to understand how patience works, what meritorious privilege is, and how to take advantage of them while seeking to satisfy his needs.

Most parents go through the early stages with little or no major challenges. However, it is the teenage or adolescent period that proves more herculean to handle. At this stage of life, the child is about to become an adult, and logical reasoning is required to communicate with your children; practical principles are needed to master skills and procedures. Here, the mind has shifted from creating memories by recognition to retaining them through mastery. This period is one when your child learns by symbiotically comparing your life, examples, behavior, and attitude to the ideals you want him to acquire. You either become the hero he is trying to imitate or the bad example he will question or resist. Many parents react negatively to their children's challenge of their parental authority without understanding the hormonal changes they are going through. Well, you must remember that you once passed through this stage as a teenager, whether you had help or not; it is your responsibility to offer as much help as may be required for them to successfully negotiate this stage of their life.

Indeed, it is the small things that will build the character of your kids more efficiently than you care to realize. Begin from your child's self-care or organization: discuss with your child the importance and practicality of personal hygiene and organization, show examples by demonstrating the procedure of waking up with or without an alarm clock. Practically demonstrate how to use the toothbrush with toothpaste, the strokes of brushing one's teeth, rinsing the mouth thoroughly, at least twice a day, morning and nighttime, and how to dress up with shirts fully tucked in, shoes laced, and belt buckled up properly. The mother should guide the girls on how to dress properly.

Some fathers know how to help their girls dress up in their early adolescence and should if the situation demands assistance.

We should not only teach our children how to take care of their personal hygiene but also guide them on how to arrange their rooms orderly. Every parent would be proud to know that their teenage children's rooms are clean and orderly and, of course, by the courtesy of their learned responsibility. These do not happen in a vacuum but through your time investment and parental guidance. For example, you may say to your teenage son, "Johny, I believe you will like a more organized room than what you have now. We can work together to get it organized so we can observe the difference." Take pictures of before appearance and pictures of after-work appearance. Don't do the work yourself but assist by guiding him to accomplish most of the chores. Use the opportunity to have some discussions on lessons you want him to learn. Explain reasons for every expectation you want them to accomplish because teenagers respond more favorably when you treat them like would-be adults and not like children.

On the other hand, a mother must teach or guide her teenage daughter to learn many things, including cooking. Begin by having your daughter do little things, such as chopping onions, cutting carrots, or drying dishes while you do the washing. Next time, have her wash the dishes while you dry them. Here she will begin to learn that homekeeping is an unavoidable responsibility that must be carried out with care on a consistent basis. Without doubt, both parents and kids may interchange instructors, partnership, or instructions. The mother can teach the son how to cook in the kitchen, beginning with basic things, such as boiling eggs, microwaving noodles or soup, and sorting things for the kitchen. The father can teach his daughter how to organize her room, make up her bed, sort and arrange her clothing for various occasions, etc.

In addition to home training and domestic skills acquisition is the ability to relate to other people with a positive attitude and sincere courtesy. Specifically impress in the mind of your teenage children that "all men were created equal!" Discourage them from feeling superior to anyone based on their financial or social status or feeling inferior to other people because of their societal attainment. Let your children understand the principle that before God, we are the same, "For all have sinned and have come short of the glory of God!" And under the Constitution of the United States of America, and the statement from the declaration of independence, "We hold these truths to be self-evident, that all men are created equal, that they are endowed by their Creator with certain unalienable rights, that among these are life, liberty, and the pursuit of happiness." Not only should they understand our equality under the law but must also be productive members of the society by honing their God-given talents through hard work and persistency. They can become whatever they focus their mind to achieve, become the best in any endeavor and reach the stars, if they would.

However, it is our most ardent responsibility to transfer the best ideals to our children, not the worst parts of our history as a nation or the failures of our past generations. For there to be freedom, liberty, and equality for all citizens, we must fight against racism, discrimination, nepotism, sectionalism, bigotry, and corruption in all their ramifications. Please do not give our new generations injustice by transferring the feelings of unjust behavior to them. They should not bear the heavy burden of the past but put on the springing hope for the future. They should be the generation to jump-start the growth to a "more perfect union" by achieving a more inclusive union of loving their fellow men as themselves.

In conclusion of this section, we must reiterate the fact that it is our responsibility as parents to provide the informal education our children require to become useful citizens of society. Note that it is not the responsibility of the school or the teachers to teach your children how to wake up in the morning and prepare for school but to teach them the curriculum meant to initiate them into the culture and traditions of society. Be aware that your child's respect for teachers and other adults at school is a projection of the respect he or she has for you. For them to transfer the spirit of hard work to their formal training at school, they must be taught how to be organized, make decisions after thinking through the issues, develop the sense of routine, and the desire to achieve on a high level. If you as a parent make time and effort to inculcate these ideals in your children, then you may have provided them with the tools they need to excel in life.

Let Us Meet in the Town Hall to Make Our Oasis Better

It is unfortunate that we somehow believe that our participation in politics begins and ends with us casting our votes. If this is the case, then we have somehow deviated from the full meaning of our political system, representative democracy based on a presidential system of government. As earlier defined, it is "the government of the people, by the people, and for the people!" The government is the people's business. It is my business, it is your business, and it is our business. No big business with shareholders allows the board of directors to control everything without the contribution, evaluation, input, and decision-making of the shareholders. Precisely, that is what the structure of our political system tended to exhibit. Since the establishment of this system of government, elected representatives have in many ways defy the will of the shareholders, the people, without any atom of regard to those who elected them. Unlike regular businesses where managers can report back to the owners of the business, the representatives of the people's business believe that they don't have to report back to the owners of the business. So many representatives of the people have declined conducting a town hall meeting for fear that the people will question their representation activities. Year after year, they have carried out the "dodgeball" game of coming back to their districts to canvass for votes then disappear after being reelected. The barrier of communication is so thick that it is so difficult to have access to them. Well, here is the big problem: the missing link, no town hall buildings, or facilities!

Maybe, just maybe, this missing link of not having town hall facilities in each district was meant to cut off the community from having contact with their representatives. If that is the case, I believe the residents should rally around to build their community town halls and provide clear and direct contact with their representatives. A town hall with high standards communication equipment, not just a telephone system but a system with access to state and federal databases, with email and text messaging system to reach out to residents. With a meeting hall capable of holding more than five thousand residents in a seat, the representative or representatives would be able to have face-to-face communication with the people. It is the right of the people to insist that their representatives give reports on how they are representing their districts in the state or federal Congress. It is time to hold them accountable for any redundancy exhibited by them, any misplaced loyalty must be questioned and addressed, and any misdirected votes in the Congress that is not to the interests of the residents must be counted against their reelection.

In addition, the town halls must be equipped with a standard secretariat managed by people who are knowledgeable in statistical analysis, information technology, communication designs, public relations, and legal representation of the residents of the districts. As a modern society, we must modernize our political system, beginning with our facilities, then raising the standards of our policymaking processes. The residents must have the freedom to contribute to whatever proposals the representatives take to congress through messaging mediums that are regularly attended to by the secretariat. Above all, they must be able to put their complaints through to the legal representatives when their civil or constitutional rights are tampered with or violated.

Besides organizing consistent town hall meetings, the development and launching of a functional website will bring the activities of the districts to the residents with ease of access and the convenience of messaging, filing complaints, making suggestions, and availing oneself with most current information about the districts. A website showing profiles of would-be candidates for election cannot be overemphasized. On many occasions, voters had been deceived by candidates who lie about their profiles and get elected without much scrutiny. They must wait for another two years to correct their errors at the polls, which creates more distrust, anger, frustration, and feelings of betrayal. According to Charles W. Pickering, "A healthy democracy requires a decent society; it requires that we are honorable, generous, tolerant and respectful." Truly, we cannot argue against that, but the task of searching for decent people could be herculean to many in a society that is a high-speed chase. A touch of truth and verifiable profile is what people need to make the right decisions. An efficient, functional town hall secretariate will surely provide the boost needed in this regard.

Although a town hall is a secretariate, it is also a forum of bringing political parties or platforms together, providing the quorum for people of various ideas and philosophies to discuss the districts problems and propose solutions that are acceptable to all the people, almost I mean. One-sided decisions will always generate dissention and apathy. However, we cannot avoid one-sided decisions if most residents choose to stay away from participating in town hall meetings. We have quoted Plato more than twice in this book, we will hear him again. He stated that "one of the penalties for refusing to participate in politics is that you end up being governed by your inferiors." You become governed by people whose suggestions are below the required solutions. They are the loudest in the mix, insist on others accepting their suggestions without questions, and make suggestions that allow them to benefit more than everybody else. Unfortunately, you allow them to control all the narratives because you choose to stay home. "An empty vessel makes the loudest noise!" Since people tend to pay more attention to the loudest messages or messages that go viral, it is imperative that we make sure that one that goes viral is the one with the truth, the solution to a problem, the one that brings peace, freedom, inclusion, and acceptability to all the people.

Plato also stated, "A good decision is based on knowledge and not on numbers!" If you are a medical doctor, your community needs your input in making health decisions. If you are an educator, the district requires people with your knowledge and experience to make suggestions about your school curricula. A local engineer could be the defense against misuse of resources or spending too much for too little in any project. Your community may need your help as an attorney when it comes to legal matters; they may want your professional contributions if you are an architect, and volunteers are really needed by any community to help in any way possible.

Contrary to the popular belief that good representatives must be given the free hand to represent the people without interference, it must be fully noted that they are only representatives of the people and not community administrators. They are messengers or envoys or ambassadors of the people that must bear the general views of the community on cultural, economic, social, security, and national or local political opinions at the state or national assembly. They are to defend the rights of all the citizens at the congressional gatherings. Debate and vote against alternate views that are intended to deprive us of our right to life, freedom of speech, freedom of movement, liberty to pursue our own happiness, and to work for our success and prosperity, as well as our posterity. If our representatives are with us and for us, they will not be avoiding town hall meetings. They will refrain from taking any money from special interests. They will stop the idea of opposition and build collision in the bit to solving our community and national problems. They will turn away from party loyalty and follow the truth. Although we expect the best from our representatives, their loyalty is not always guaranteed because of their hidden intensions of running for any public office, the unknown influences behind their motivation, and their deep-rooted bias to treat some population better than others. Without doubt, these are human weaknesses that we loath profoundly, but we can prevent people with such weaknesses from climbing our political ladder, let alone making daily decisions about our welfare, security, economy, social and political well-being.

Passing the Baton to the New Generation

Every generation deserves the right to progressively grow toward a better society. When such growth is not experienced either incrementally or astronomically, a society tends to deteriorate either gradually or with a fast-paced downward trend that leads to its collapse. In truth, the responsibility of preparing the new generation to take over the job of nation building rests squarely on the shoulders of the older generation. In an athletic relay race, the importance of understanding the strengths of a team's participating athletes is not only the focus of the team's head coach but that of the whole team, including the assistant coaches, physical trainers, medical team, equipment management team, etc. They require even the most basic information, such as body type, eating habits, sleeping schedules, medical history, etcetera, to put together a winning program for the team. After weeks and weeks of training, the head coach would decide based on the performance of each athlete who runs the laps. In many instances the best runner is placed as the anchor but may be placed at other circuit points for strategic purposes. A well-prepared team still requires the emotional and psychological understanding between team members to generate the feel for smooth baton exchange. Many relay teams who were expected to win a race fumbled in baton exchange and then loose scandalously. They may have trained together, even for a long time, but the feeling of baton exchange is needed to give the team a smooth transition from one circuit to the next.

There is no difference between a relay team's baton exchange and how we transition our young generation into the responsibility of nation building. Like an athletic team, we must educate our children on the structure of our government, its functions, and responsibilities to the citizenry, and in turn, the citizens' responsibilities to the government. This is where civic education comes into play. Our children must be initiated efficiently with the quality of education needed to prepare them to receive the baton smoothly then run their own race in a more progressive manner. In the words of Benjamin Franklin, "An investment in knowledge pays the best interest." There is no knowledge worth investing in than one that will preserve our civilization, as well as improve every aspect of its existence. Unfortunately, our educational system tends to focus more on specialization and less on general knowledge that every citizen must attend for societal preservation. American history course is not necessarily civic education, and the study of American constitution as a coursework is not enough to teach civic responsibilities in our schools. Our children must be educated in civics beginning from elementary schools and all the way to college levels if we are to develop a pathway for them to take over our responsibilities when we are gone.

Abraham Lincoln stressed this basic but simple idea by stating that "the philosophy of the school room in one generation will be the philosophy of government in the next." Absolutely true for his generation, for the present generation, for the generations in between, and for generations to come. We should not expect a government of honorable people if we fail to teach our children how to be honorable, sincere, truthful, and fair to all people. It will be a misplacement of faith to hope that racism and discrimination will be vanquished without building the character of the new generation on the truth that "all men were created equal" and the heavenly command that we should "do unto others what we want them to do unto us."

Perhaps we can feel the importance of preparing our children for the tasks of inheriting our successes, our indecisions on matters that should have been straightforwardly decided but were not, and our messes, no matter how we made them. In the view of the former United States secretary of states, Mr. Colin Powell, "Children need to get a high-quality education, avoid violence and the criminal-justice system, and gain jobs. But they deserve more. We want them to learn not only reading and math but fairness, caring, self-respect, family commitment, and civic duty." We must train them to be good-thinking adults who exhibit balanced and knowledgeable perspectives of our social, economic, cultural, and political issues, with the deep desire to find solutions to them.

To emphasize the significance of well-prepared young people in continuing our civilization, Allissa Quart, an acclaimed author and poet, likens the situation to poetry by stating that "civic poetry is public poetry. It is political poetry. It is about the hard stuff of life: money, crime, gender, corporate excess, racial injustice. It gives expression not just to our rites but also to our problems and even our values; these poems are not about rustic vacations." Like poetry, our civic education must possess rhythm in expression, display rhyme in ideals, inculcate tonality of discuss, and provide consistent accent in movement. It must generate the patriotic spirit that will incite the euphoria of learning in our children. Rhythm in expression implies inculcating the language of respect for everyone's culture and background. Rhyme in ideals means that we all deserve freedom, liberty, and equal justice under the law. Tonality of discuss means to develop the tone that preserves all citizen's respect while we debate hard-core issues without violence.

To provide consistent accent in movement means that every citizen of the United States of America, born or naturalized, must know the basic tenets of our great country of multiple cultures: the constitution, basic laws, our civic duties, community responsibilities, our democratic values, and our shares in the Commonwealth of our republic. Therefore, smooth transition of our young people into nation building requires synchronizing civic education across the country. A young person in California must have the same exposure to the content of our civic education as a young person in Florida, Texas, New York, Iowa, Wisconsin, etc. Synchroneity of civic education generates that emotional, psychological, and mental understanding that will prepare the new generation to run the race of nation building better than the older generation.

It will be counterproductive to develop a civic curriculum that maintains the old ways of doing things instead of progressing to a better society. A civic education that continues to point at the mistakes or past errors without solutions to them is not worth teaching. If we are to get rid of hate, we must resist the urge to transfer White supremacy ideologies, hate groups agendas, racial rhetoric, and racial dog whistling to our children at home. It is important to have the young people visit museums of various cultural events and learn from every culture on how to understand each other, accept each other's traditional existence, and go beyond just tolerating to appreciating each other. Our civic education should include aspects of the various cultures in this nation: variety of foods, traditional clothing, cultural events, traditional occasions, cultural calendars, and traditional celebrations or ceremonies. The irony is that by being interested in one or more aspects of any culture may trigger appreciation for those cultures. If I love to put on the Japanese kimono dress, then learning the history behind it may not be a burden and showing respect to the people that created it should not be a taboo. The same goes when it comes to Black culture. It is unjust for you to love rap music then hate the culture that created it. Although rap music arose from the intense injustice committed against African Americans by the same people that enslaved their ancestors, your appreciation of this unique art should make you more empathetic to their course and collaborate with them in ameliorating their suffering. They are not the perpetrators of this injustice; they are the victims.

David Binder, a Tony Award-winning Broadway, off-Broadway, and West End theater producer and artistic director of the Brooklyn Academy of Music, gave a suggestion on how to build relationships between cultures using festivals. He stated, "Festivals promote diversity, they bring neighbors into dialogue, they increase creativity, they offer opportunities for civic pride, they improve our general psychological well-being. In short, they make cities better places to live." When people of different cultures meet on a regular basis to discuss issues or do joint events or enjoy sporting events, there is the tendency that familiarity is born and respect is established. Apart from large events, such as festivals, political workshops organized for our students will develop the spirit of collaboration among various ethnic groups which later are transferred to their professional life.

Let's not forget that the older generations may still have a lot of influence on the younger generation. Therefore, it is imperative to organize civic responsibility information workshops for them as well. To be candid, many adults do not have the knowledge of how our political system operates, and unfortunately, deceptive politicians take undue advantage of their ignorance. Over many years, they are persuaded into monolithic voting blocks that are rigid and homogenous, not open to new ideas, and unable to break away from religious or ethnic influences. They tend to vote for the same platform despite the platform's redundancy, favor certain race without the consideration that America is a multicultural democracy, and tend to be very suspicious of people whose political views or philosophy are different from theirs. We have observed instances where conservative politicians have used videos of caravans of people from Latin America heading toward the United States to incite fear among the voters. They proclaim that America was being invaded by the Latin American countries: "They are coming to take over your jobs, sexually abuse your women and children, and nobody is safe! Pitch in at least $20 to help in this fight, then vote me in for Congress or for president to put an end to these brutal assaults coming to you." This situation continues to surface in every election circle with no promise kept and no solutions offered.

If these older generations and other voting blocks were familiar with our democratic system of government, they would have known that for immigration and other laws to be enacted or amended, two-third of the Senate, which is sixty-seven out of one hundred members, must vote for the bill to pass. An outright majority votes in the House of Representative are required for the bill to be passed in the lower chamber as well. Civic education could have given them the information that the president cannot single-handedly enact any law without the congress. Ignorance among voters is one of the root causes of impasse in our legislatures across the country. Many voters continue to vote on ideas that are not in tune with current events or current views of the generality of the citizenry. Many bills that would have solved some if not most of our community problems are abandoned because of resistance from a few members of legislatures who would rather see the demise of such bills than the general good of society. The Congress is divided because some people are not open to new ideas, progressive enough to propel the nation to a new height. They are afraid of change, change that will provide equal opportunity to all the citizens, change that will eliminate the hoarding of resources by special interest groups, change that will place power in the hands of majority and the true implication of democracy and not the autocratic moves of the minority. They want to hold onto power for as long as possible if their political philosophies are not accepted or entertained by the new generation.

Contrary to the old saying that "with age comes wisdom," the older generation lacks wisdom because they seem to lack the knowledge associated with our fast-paced modern society. Wisdom as we know is the application of knowledge for the greater good of society. If our economic, technological, and scientific knowledge is growing at the rate that far outpaces our political system, then the process of making policies to sustain, standardize, and prevent abuse becomes slow and ineffective. Our society will suffer from incompetency, chaos in function, and decline in the capacity to compete with the rest of the world. In many of our state legislatures across the country, including the United States Congress, the average age of legislators tends to revolve around fifty-eight years. Based on the statistical analysis of the 117th Congress of the United States, the median age of the senators is 63.9 and that of the house members is 58.3, showing that older people are either being seated in Congress much more than the younger people. It could also mean that too many older generations are holding on to power by refusing to retire despite not having much to contribute to modern Congress. Whatever direction the focus is on, our Congress is getting older instead of younger. The older generations are resisting exchanging the baton of nation building with the younger generation so much so that the impasse in ideology is making the whole system nonfunctional and ineffective.

Apart from the median age of the US Congress becoming older, the median age of governors across the nation is also a bit concerning. Research and statistics show that by February 2023, four governors are in their seventies, sixteen governors are in their sixties, twenty-four are in their fifties, and six are in their forties. It means forty-four out of fifty governors are fifty years or older and only six are below fifty years of age. If the average age to become a governor of any state is thirty years as specified in most state constitutions, then more candidates below the age of fifty should be elected to office. This could mean that either the younger generation is not prepared enough to take over the responsibilities or that the older generations are still trying to impose themselves in the whole leadership setup without any consideration for the future of their children and grandchildren. At this stage of their lives, they should be serving as advisers to the younger generations and not as competition to them.

The oldest state legislature in the United States is New Hampshire with a median age of sixty-six years. As at the time of report, the youngest member of that body is Rep. Travis Bennett, twenty-three, a senior at Plymouth State University; he's one of the few millennials among New Hampshire's legislators. Setups like this presents opportunities to the older generation to make laws based on the old ways of doing things, muddled with their archaic feelings of discrimination, sectionalism, racial domination, and the unbelievable feeling that they are born to rule and others are meant to follow. You tell me, what kind of generational age-related suggestion can Travis Bennett ever propose to this body and would be accepted without prejudice? None! No matter how much effort he puts into his arguments, the decisions or voting outcomes will always be based on the majority ideologies. Any suggestion for progressive changes would incite resistance, anger, suspicion, and possibly the desire to expel whoever is suggesting.

According to Rebecca Beitsch in her Stateline article, December 23, 2015, "State lawmakers across the US are older than their constituents, an imbalance that might be tilting policymaking toward the interests of seniors and away from the country's largest living generation: millennials." This situation is warranted by the intentional lack of civic education to prepare the younger generation to pick up the baton, even when the older generations are reluctant to transfer power to them. We need new ideas, and the younger generations are the people who are going to provide them. We need more efficient ways of making policies, and our college-aged children are the ones we must bank on to take up the mantle. We need to have lawmaking institutions that make decisions based on facts, real data, and provable evidence, and our information technologically sound younger representatives must be our best bait. Therefore, it is time for the older generation to give it up and stop being generational obstacles to the younger generation. We must have confidence that our new generation will do the work, even better than their parents and grandparents; they are smart enough to handle the tasks, they are good with technological skills required to make faster progress, and they are more open to new ideas, better understanding, and culturally more inclusive than the older generation.

Without doubt, I believe that the philosophical ideologies of the new generation are more accommodating to the idea of a democratic nation than the split beliefs of the older generation. Since the older generations, traditionalists, baby boomers, and Generation X are mostly splits into Conservatives or Liberals, the younger generations, Generation Y and Generation Z, are more Progressive in their ideological beliefs. They tend to imbibe the philosophy that combines ideals from all the beliefs, extend their understanding across cultures, and provide psycho-social tents that attracts all races, allow interracial relationships, and encourages collaboration across the spectrum of America's societal structure. Therefore, the faster and smoother we can allow this beautiful oasis of human existence to geminate, grow, and expand, the quicker we can expel the wilderness of hate, bitterness, racism, discrimination, and sectionalism that has eviscerated our society beyond measures.

CHAPTER 10

Power in the Oasis Is the People's Power

As we come to the tenth chapter in this book, we should keep an open mind to understand and appreciate the idea of "power," what it is all about, and who is qualified to wield it and for what purpose. As a natural inclination, every human being desires and lusts after a position of power—power to tower over other people, power to control affairs in any setting, or power for security purposes. To some people, that desire remains just a desire, but to some others, it produces the drive to achieve power with any means necessary. When they finally achieve power, their desire becomes that of totally controlling everything, holding sway over everybody, and exacting superiority overall. At this point, autocracy sets in, cruelty begins to show its ugly face, vindictiveness pops up at any slightest provocation, and reign of terror begins to creep in gradually. These are the factors that berets individual's power grab.

The history of our world is clearly ladened with biographies of individuals who obtained power by dubious means and then abuse such powers in ruling their people with cruelty. From Adolf Hitler of Nazi's Germany to Idi Amin Dada of Uganda who systematically eliminated their people for the sake of dominance. We will never forget more than six million Jews that were incinerated in gas chambers and over seventeen million people who were killed during the Second World War that was started by him, Hitler. The cruelty of

Josef Stalin whose "Great Purge" tactics led to the death of over ten million Soviet citizens; intellectuals who opposed his harsh rule is indelible from the history of cruel dictators who unfortunately have been a part of our world history. Also history will never forget the evil that were committed by Vladimir Lenin of Russia, Kim Jong Il of North Korea, Emperor Hirohito of the Imperial Japan, Ho Chi Minh of North Vietnam, Kim Il Sung of North Korea, Saddam Hussein of Iraq, Pol Pot of Cambodia, Tsar Nicholas II of Russia, King Leopold II of Belgium, and Mao Zedong of Communist China.

In contrast to autocratic power of individuals is democracy, specifically American democracy where the power to rule belongs to the people and not the leaders. It is the people that choose their leaders and not the leaders who choose themselves. Unlike autocracy where the focus of power is on an individual or a group of individuals, democracy requires a structure, but it is not a structure. According to Michel Foucault, "Power is not an institution, and not a structure; neither is it a certain strength we are endowed with; it is the name that one attributes to a complex strategical situation in a particular society." Power of democracy is the power of the people symbolized in the "will of the people" and the ideals we hold dear as a nation, freedom, liberty, equality, and equal justice under the law. People's power is not an institution but requires institutions to channel its effects throughout the system of governance; it is not a structure but requires a well-defined structure to be effective; and it does not depend on individual strength but require individuals' sincerity, honesty, truthfulness, sense of justice, ability in fairness, and competency to operate in full capacity. It is a sense of collectiveness that pushes the will of the people to have a society of fairness, atmosphere of justice and truth that maintains the foundation that "all people were created equal and have the same inalienable rights." To exist and thrive, these rights must be implemented and protected with any means necessary.

The power that belongs to the people is not that of fear but that of love for our fellow men as we love ourselves. Mahatma Gandhi expressed this idea more profoundly by saying that "power is of two kinds. One is obtained by the fear of punishment and the other by acts of love. Power based on love is a thousand times more effective and permanent than the one derived from fear of punishment." Individuals tend to search for power for personal reasons, such as economic attainment, personality aggrandizement, shear desire to dominate other people, or fear of being personally harmed. They fear the assumed punishment of poverty or being poor, they fear being seen as insignificant among their fellow men, and they fear being held accountable for their crimes against society. Therefore, the only way of expelling these fears is to climb the hierarchy of power by any means necessary, dominate with impunity, and eliminate any threat from any source.

In contrast to the power wielded in autocracy is that expressed in democracy. The power of the people is an act of love among the citizenries. It is not wielded by any individual but rather an expression of our belief in one another's right to exist, be free to thrive, be liberated from any obstacle to our pursuit of happiness, and be given equal opportunities to resources, as well as and to be held to the same standard of justice no matter our cultural, religious, and political orientations. It is not an emotional feeling or sentimental state of mind; it is rather imbedded in the golden rule, "Do unto others what you want them to do unto you!" It is this power that propels us to go out and cast our votes, make changes to ineffective leadership, protest unjust acts perpetrated against our fellow citizens, and fight to keep corruption and corrupt politicians off our government. It is this power of the people that motivates us to defend the rights of our fellow men in our workplaces, community streets, local schools, and in our court system.

Although it is a quiet understanding that we share, its expression is often external and collaborative. According to Ann Landers, this power from love is "friendship that has caught fire. It is quiet understanding, mutual confidence, sharing and forgiving. It is loyalty through good and bad times. It settles for less than perfection and makes allowances for human weaknesses." Despite the humanistic nature of the power of the people that Ann Landers refers to as "friendship that has caught fire," authoritarians among us are still working extremely hard to erode the confidence that we the people have invested in it. They want to make sure that only a selected few wield this power, and since they have not stopped the barrage of continuous attacks on our democracy, why should we stop fighting against them?

In this chapter, we will critically look at the ways these enemies of democracy are working against the interests of every one of us, the citizens of United States of America, become alert to their nocturnal strategies, and develop methods of combining forces needed to destroy the stronghold of the enemy.

Overcoming the Wilderness of Ideological Differences

From the inception of the birth of this great nation, ideological and philosophical differences have remained the bane of its growth and development. As immigrants come from different parts of the world into America, they brought their religious beliefs, political views, cultural efficacies, traditional education, ceremonies, and celebrated holidays. Over four centuries of the existence of the colonial America and the United States of America, many ideologies and philosophies have graced this continental country. Some have contributed to the greatness of this sociopolitical entity, some have provided nothing but divisiveness, while the rests have only served as identifying factors. Today, as a political domiciliate, the United States of America is majorly populated as Conservatives, Liberals, or Progressives. Although another school of thought which encompasses most, if not all these orientations are gradually evolving.

In not long a time, this school of thought which is mostly expressed within the younger generation will blossom into the most powerful voting bloc in the country. All evidence shows that the younger generation is truly departing or turning away from the rigid political beliefs held by their parents and grandparents. They believe in freedom that is not worn down by ideologies, liberty that is not restricted by unjust laws, and justice that is not determined by anyone's racial, cultural, religious, or hierarchical status. To fully understand their thinking, it is important for us to know why they are putting aside some part of conservatism and focusing on some, why they are perceiving Liberalism from a different perspective, and why they are viewing progressiveness only from factual and evidential periscope.

Conservatism and its effects on American people's power

The sociopolitical philosophy known as Conservatism is one where people believe in limited government or small government, value individualism or ability of an individual to express an inert moral value without interference, believe in traditionalism or maintaining and passing traditional beliefs from one generation to the next. They believe in Republicanism without nobility status and believe in limiting the power of the federal or national government to the barest minimum. The foundation here is the support for Judeo-Christian values, moral absolutism, free market economy, unrestricted free trade, anti-communism, support for traditional family values, capitalism, and belief in American exceptionalism. Conservatives generally are antiabortion. They believe, based on religious and moral principles, that the human zygote, embryo, or fetus is a living person that must be allowed the right to be alive. Their stance on the matter of abortion tends to vary as the school of thought varies considerably. From Wikipedia Encyclopedia explanation, "There are diverse arguments and rationales for the anti-abortion stance. Some anti-abortion activists allow for some permissible abortions, including therapeutic abortions, in exceptional circumstances such as incest, rape, severe fetal defects, or when the woman's health is at risk." To some people, believing in total ban on abortion procedures of any form is their stance; their fight is for their religious beliefs and nothing else matters.

Also Conservatives are generally pro-business based on unrestricted capitalism and oppose labor unions which they believe is a threat to this individualized economic enclave. "They often advocate for a strong national defense, gun rights, capital punishment, and a defense of Western culture from perceived threats posed by both communism and moral relativism." United States' budgetary expenditures over many decades on national defense is basically the influence of Conservative politics on our democracy. They advocate for the freedom to possess, conceal, and carry guns without license as a means of protecting the Second Amendment rights of every American, by every American; we mean all those whose prefer to protect the guns and not human life. Conservatives tend to question disease epidemiology, climatic science, and evolution of species far deeper than other philosophies. In addition, they want low taxes or no taxes in certain cases, advocate for free markets, deregulation, and privatization of businesses. Furthermore, their preference for smaller governments, reduced government spending, and elimination of government debts tends to be turned with their preference for state controls, not federal control, or controls from a central-national government.

Although Conservatism had taken deeper roots in our sociopolitical set up from the early years of American democracy, its influence and efficacy has waned or is still waning today due to the rapid demographic changes across the spectrum of our society. There will always be a struggle among the various political philosophies until we can find a way of making them rhyme with the basic tenets of our beliefs. Conservatism was introduced by the early immigrants from Europe and the Middle Eastern Ancient empires based squarely on religious beliefs, cultural preservations, and the idea of power by conquest and dominance. The struggle to exist has become a power struggle within the wilderness of American political chaos, and the wilderness is widening at a lightning speed that may be out of control if not intercepted as soon as humanly possible. We must find the oasis that will restore peace, freedom, liberty, equality, and justice if we look inward within ourselves and have trust in others' ability to do the same.

Liberalism and why America needs some of it, and to forgo some of it!

In the year of our Lord 1690, the English philosopher John Locke published a foundational text of liberal ideology labeled *Two Treaties*. This book pigeon became the launching pad for modern

Liberalism, a philosophical ideology that led to a new idea of government all over the world. From this launchpad, the modern idea of liberal democracy came to life. Although prior to Locke's thesis, an English pamphlet writer Richard Overton had already prepared the ground for this with the belief expressed in his statement, "To every Individual in nature, is given an individual property by nature, not to be invaded or usurped by any…no man hath power over my rights and liberties, and I over no man's." The truth here is that all men were created free and equal. Also John Locke's philosophy was partly influenced by John Milton's belief in freedom in all its forms, which is also an undisputable truth from the beginning of man in the garden.

Despite some of the conflicted ideas like Communism, socialism, and Fascism, Liberalism as expressed in Locke's thesis insisted that government is not endowed by God as claimed by people who advocates monarchies, instead requires the permission of the governed to exist. He added that there must be a separation of church and state or the removal of religious sentiments from government for it to serve the people effectively. From his philosophical writings and ideological promotion of Liberalism, many nations of Europe and other countries of the world were able to break the monopoly of monarchies from their governments thanks to the social contract principles of Thomas Hobbes. In fact, this social contract that rose from the Enlightenment Age completely revolutionized the idea of government in Europe, insisting that all human beings have the right to life, liberty, and property or pursuit of happiness and no government, individuals, or groups should interfere with these God-given rights. In his book, *Leviathan* published in 1651, Thomas Hobbes advocated a monarchical commonwealth that should aim in protecting the people without interference. But John Locke insisted that government must be authorized by the people, and they have the right to retrieve such authorization if the government becomes tyrannical.

From the British Glorious Revolution of 1688 to the American Revolution of 1776 and from the French radical Revolution of 1789 to the nineteenth and twentieth centuries rise of Constitutional-

Nationalism in the Middle East, Liberalism have been the transformational catalyst that propelled the rise of democracy in many countries across the world. The Founding Fathers of the United States of America embraced most if not all the ideas of Liberalism that led to the establishment of this constitutional democracy that has become the greatest economic and military power the world has ever seen. It led to the establishment of the American constitution, promotion of individual freedoms—such as, freedom of speech or expression, freedom of association, freedom of movement, and freedom of religion—the right to trial by jury, and promotion of gender and racial equality. Liberalism also led to the establishment of independent judiciary in our democratic structure that in a way limits the interference of government, groups, or individuals in the process of executing equal justice to all the citizens, no matter their economic, social, racial, or hierarchical status in the society. In simple terms, the United States of America owes more to Liberalism than any other political philosophy. Although Liberalism had been headbutted by many philosophical ideologies over many centuries, its staying power is hunched on the principles that are mostly appreciated by most populations in countries where it is the foundation of the government.

In contrast to classical Liberalism, which was also a forerunner of American Conservatism, modern Liberalism is the basis of the modern American Liberalism. "It is a political theory that places the individual and individual rights as the highest priority and relies on the consent of the citizenry for the legitimacy of government power and political leadership. The ideas of natural rights, liberty, and property are the bedrock of the theory, and the state is used to ensure these rights from being infringed upon by foreign states or fellow citizens. Because of this, Liberalism views the state as a 'necessary evil.'"

Liberal ideals led to the declaration of independence written by Thomas Jefferson with the belief that "all men were created equal… with certain unalienable rights." And such rights are not to be infringed upon by the government. The fundamental liberal ideals as instituted in the American constitution includes freedom of speech, freedom of the press, freedom of religion, the separation of state and church, the right to due process, and equality under the law. In addition is the promotion of "welfare state" where one of the major duties of the government is to establish social institutions required to promote and protect the economic and social well-being of the citizens based on the principles of equal opportunities and equitable distribution of resources and wealth. Also liberal democracy promotes privatization but with certain basic regulations that prevent abuse of the system in any form. It promotes partnership with the state in giving the less fortunate or disadvantaged members of society the opportunity to make up the loss grounds. I believe that this should not be confused with "Socialist economy" or "Communism" where the state controls every facet of society with limits of achievement and red lines that must not be crossed.

Equally important to modern Liberalism is the ideal of creating a social network for society preservation and order. Since the focus is on how to make the government work for the people and not for special interests alone, as proposed by opposing political philosophies, American modern Liberalism inspired the advocation of measures that combines civil liberties, equality, social justice, and a well-regulated mixed economy to create a social safety network required for society to thrive. Modern Liberalism opposes corporations or businesses that tend to monopolize the marketplace using antitrust laws to prevent abuse in any form. Monopoly, if not checked, hands power and control to few individuals with capitalist resources who then control the social-political atmosphere without restrictions. Therefore, the role of the state in reducing inequality, increasing diversity, providing access to education and health care, regulating economic activity, and protecting the natural environment is increasingly more important today as the population and demographic status continues to expand.

Without doubt, modern Liberalism had brought about many innovations in civil rights implementation, such as expanding Voting Rights for the minorities, affirmative actions to integrate the underrepresented groups, women's reproductive rights, immigration reforms, and LGBTQ rights. Also despite the gruel and persistent obstructions from opposing political philosophies, American Liberalism had instituted such massive social and economic programs

Finding Oasis Within the Wilderness of our Sociopolitical Ideologies

like Woodrow Wilson's "New Freedom," Franklin D. Roosevelt's "Great New Deal," Harry S. Truman's "Fair Deal," John F. Kennedy's "New Frontier," Lyndon B. Johnson's "Great Society," and Barack H. Obama's "Affordable Care Act." Some of these programs have in several ways stood the test of time while some have fizzled away over time or as soon as their proposers depart from the office.

To be candid, modern Liberalism has pioneered so many great innovations in American democracy, as well as misfired in some. However, in comparable to others, it is the major philosophy that had laid the foundation to the United States becoming the greatest military and economic power the world has ever seen.

Progressivism: A growing movement or a splash in the pond?

My first contact with the word "Progressive" as an identifying description of a sociopolitical philosophy incited within me the notion of growth or continuous improvement in standards toward a better society. However, after studying numerous views from various analysts, my sense of direction in this case becomes slightly complicated if not distorted. Probably, many people feel differently about Progressivism or any other sociopolitical philosophy in America due to numerous reasons that could have emanated from cultural, religious, or traditional moral principles. In a simplified definition or description, we can appreciate that it is a political and social reform movement that focuses on making government more effective by improving its efficiency and accountability. Unlike other major sociopolitical philosophies that originated from individual philosophical ideologies, Progressivism is a political doctrine that advocates the reform of an existing system or institution instead of its abolition or replacement. Many analysts resort to describing the tenets or major beliefs of Progressives as a replacement to actual definition of what it is all about. Due to this academic misrepresentation, many tend to view Progressives as outsiders with completely new doctrines that are meant to replace their beliefs. While in contrast, it is a movement meant to reduce or eliminate redundancy in government, reassess and implement new methods of fighting corruption within our constitutional democracy, develop new ways of making government accessible to all citizens, eliminate monopolies and allow free market economy to thrive, and protect the constitutional rights of all citizens no matter their status in the society.

In retrospect, Progressivism defends aspects of Conservatism, advocates many Liberal ideologies as the Liberals themselves, and give credence to the foundational beliefs, such as freedom, liberty, equality, equal justice under the law, and environmental conservation or environmental justice. Although many have attempted to define American Progressivism based on individual perspectives, it is simply just making things better and more inclusive to all than the exclusiveness of other major sociopolitical philosophies. Unfortunately, due to political bias or sentimental aloofness against the movement, many have labeled or considered them to be left-wing, left-wing populist, democratic socialist, libertarian socialist, social democratic, and environmentalist. In truth, there is nothing wrong with Progressives advocating for a universal health-care system, wage equity and labor rights, economic justice, social justice, opposition to the military industrial complex, an increase in corporate regulation, the abolition of capital punishment, and action on climate change. After all said and done, government is expected to work for all the people and vice versa. That it is the duty of every citizen to defend our country against all enemies, foreign or domestic! However, to defend a government that is corrupt, ineffective, inefficient, and completely alienated from the needs of the people is nothing more than political injustice. Here, I believe, the Progressives are proposing more effective solutions, making it possible for the United States to progress toward a more perfect union by being more inclusive and not exclusive.

One very important focus of Progressivism is the effect of modernization on our society. Contrarily to the general belief that the Progressives' only mission is to eradicate or change institutions, Progressivism believes in solving problems that are results of natural and man-made progressions. They focus on how to make sure that population increase and quality of life of the people go hand in hand, how to apply science and technology in improving society, better strategies of establishing and operating industries without polluting the environment, and proper regulation of businesses and government institutions to improve social justice. From the Online Encyclopedia Britannica's description of the goals of Progressivism in American political atmosphere, it says, "The Progressive movement accommodated a diverse array of reformers—insurgent Republican officeholders, disaffected Democrats, journalists, academics, social workers, and other activists—who formed new organizations and institutions with the common objective of strengthening the national government and making it more responsive to popular economic, social, and political demands." From this description, we could have been cajoled to believe that the movement should be accepted by all, but the suspicious ways Americans view change is still the bane of this movement as well as others. From this perspective, citizens needed better education for the idea of a better society to be attained.

Educating the masses, although a very difficult prerogative to initiate, may probably be the best medium of transforming society faster than anticipated. Therefore, the Progressives' belief that education is more of a human and civil right than just a privilege is one of the foundational beliefs of this movement. In the Progressives' circumstances, the idea of providing every child with a basic free education, whether the parents approve of it or not, is tilted toward creating a more informed society than the mere issue of privilege. In addition, an efficient and competent government requires highly educated, highly skilled individuals in science, technology, business administration, economy, legal matters, medicine, sociology, and so on to be functional and effective. An organized society with a government that is functional and effective is bound to grow toward a more perfect union even with multiracial tendencies.

The cost of educating society has always been a matter of great importance among the Progressives. They advocate for lower educational costs for students who attend colleges and universities to acquire higher education. It is believed that attending higher education means contributing at a higher level to the benefit of society than most people can appreciate. The irony is that young people invest so much in time, efforts, financial pig banking, and natural talents to acquire knowledge and skills that corporations and government institutions take undue advantage of, without any investment, refund, or payback, or renumeration of any form. Hence, advocating for lower costs in higher education, part forgiveness of student loans, or total forgiveness in certain cases should be the prerogative of all and not just for the Progressives.

As much as other major sociopolitical ideologies have contributed to the foundation of this great nation, Progressivism has provided the catalysts to its rapid rise to the greatest military and economic power status. From the promotion of diversity in government to the fight for equality and equal access to resources and opportunities, Progressives have proved that God did not concentrate talents in certain ethnicities, or tribes, or race but has given to all people equally. Then access and privileges must be equally distributed for America to benefit from all the talents that have graced our land, no matter the race, financial, social, or political status.

Since Progressivism is not completely a new ideology or movement, its origin could be traced back to the "Age of Enlightenment" as are other major sociopolitical ideologies, and the main features of its movement are based on the idea that individual's life could be improved through the advancement in technology, effective social organization, and efficiently organized economic development activities. Hence, the idea of scientific and technological advancement as a means of improving the life of an individual, as well as the smooth progression of society, tend to be the major difference between Progressivism and other sociopolitical ideologies. It means that advancement in information technology is required to develop a better-informed society that can make decisions based on facts, evidence, and truth and not on sentiments and assumptions. It means that the citizens will have enough information on their leaders to vote them into or vote them out of office. It implies that citizens will be educated on means of accessing resources and privileges within their immediate communities without barriers.

Despite the good intentions and progressive proposals, like the pitfalls experienced by other major sociopolitical philosophies, the persistent influence of human error cannot be truly averted due to the persistency of negative human behaviors. Information technology may be an effective tool to improve citizens' knowledge acquisition and informed-based decision-making, but the negative impact of misinformation and disinformation due to corrupt human behaviors have generated obstacles so enormous that the capability of scaling over them is almost impossible. To be sincere, it is not the computer that is corrupt but the programmer who programmed it to behave that way. It is not the accounting program or cash machine that steals or diverts money to personal accounts; it is either the corrupt accountant or whoever has access to the system that is the culprit. Certainly, a budget allocator system is not the one that discriminates against low-income communities, rather it is the person who is at the pole end of the decision-making apparatus. The bulldozing earth-moving equipment doesn't determine the standards of construction or inspect their execution but the project managers whose major purpose is making money for themselves and the corporations they work for.

We cannot underestimate the impact that this negative human behavior, corruption, could exert on the growth and development of our society. If we ignore its impact, it will spread like wildfire and would bring down the nation, but if we choose to fight it without consistency, it will continue to change its loopholes such that pinpointing them becomes highly frustrating. Therefore, it will require more than just progressive ideologies in making improvement and exacting change in our sociopolitical systems. A workable philosophy may be one that borrows from Conservatism, Liberalism, even some aspects of democratic-socialism, collectivism, and humanism.

Finding the Oasis within Our Sociopolitical Wilderness!

There is nothing more divisive to a nation than divisiveness itself. There is nothing that creates divisiveness like held beliefs, ideologies, and philosophies. There is nothing that generates hate, chaos, and general societal anarchy than irreconcilable differences. Whether we care to believe it or not, within every problem lies the solutions or antidotes to such problems, but we must search for them, dig through the dirt if we may, and put in every necessary effort required to resolve the problem. In many cases, we just needed to trim the hedge and let the flowers bloom, cut the bushes to reveal the pathways, clear the boulders to allow the stream to flow, cuddle the baby to stop her crying, and cut down the shrubs to let the vine grow. In some other cases, we must exact change to make the difference; a bad idea is a bad idea no matter which direction you look at it. Also an applicable good idea remains an idea until you decide to apply it.

According to the great American self-help author and motivational speaker Wayne Dyer, "If you change the way you look at things, the things you look at change." This is the whole idea of perception; it changes our view of things when we change them. However, we should understand the simple fact that change must be initiated only when it is needed. Changing things for the mere desire to make changes is not only counterproductive but disruptive in many instances. On the other hand, if a change is necessary, it must be one aimed at improvement, development, and progressive growth. The truth is that "all change is not growth, as all movement is not forward" as Ellen Glasgow indicated.

Without any doubt, America and all-American citizens need a dosage of mental, psychological, emotional, and spiritual individual and societal changes that is required to emancipate us from the sociopolitical enslavement that our irreconcilable ideological differences have imprisoned us as a nation. There is no better author whose written books on change have positively impacted us than George Bernard Shaw. He wrote, "Progress is impossible without change, and those who cannot change their minds cannot change anything." This great author and society changer, who won a 1925 Nobel Prize in Literature, believed that everyone has the capability to step out of our self-enclosed cocoon for precise moments needed to see what is out there. Also Pres. Barack Obama in confirmation to Bernard Shaw's belief stated that "change will not come if we wait for some other person or some other time. We are the ones we've been waiting for. We are the change that we seek." Although Obama's assertion was to the younger generation, the older generations are equally invited to walk the same road if we as a nation must kiss ideological impasse goodbye.

Despite our distrustful feelings to change, the irony is that without it, we must be ready for extinction. According to Pres. John F. Kennedy, "Change is the law of life. And those who look only to the past or present are certain to miss the future." We must move away from the past into the present so that we can view the future with the telescope of the present. It is what we do today that determines how we will live tomorrow. Therefore, the call for the younger generation to stand up and assume the responsibility of leadership is more urgent now than ever. Also the appeal to the older generations to restrain from influencing our current political scenery with ideological sentiments that create divisiveness is ever more persistent today than yesterday. The question is "What would benefit a seventy-five-year-old person who decides to contest for a public office when he or she should be retired and enjoying the fruit of their labor?" The answer is best known to the individual!

In retrospect, people don't have much to contribute mentally or physically once they are past retirement age, and the resort is to impose outdated political views that are contrary to current problems and issues on society. In terms of knowledge and skills needed, can they keep up with modern technology and systems? Based on manpower management, do they have the pedigree to work with the younger generation whose sociopolitical views are more Progressive than Conservative? Can they cope with the stress and physical demands of the job? Maybe not! Why then do we encourage this age group by voting for them into office instead of electing younger people? Why do we primary them into representing our various political platforms, thereby blocking the opportunity of younger candidates from assuming the party representative candidacy? We may answer these questions if we can free ourselves from our sociopolitical mental stagnation and ideological enslavement. It is only by digging deep into what our true belief should be that we can find the oasis that would ward off our ideological wilderness, divisiveness generated by our philosophical differences, intolerance instigated by our persistency to hold on to the past instead of understanding the presence and looking ahead to the future, and our self-centered desperation to blame others for being different instead of changing our outdated ideologies. Anyone who resists change will end up in the museum of history not in the dynamism of the present and certainly not in the excitement of the future. Change must begin from within us, then to our neighbors, followed by our community, and our nation will be washed with a new feeling and given a new name.

In God We Trust! In the Constitution We Unite!

As we travel through this wilderness of sociopolitical ideologies, it is important that we search for the oasis of living water that will quench our taste, smoothen our pathways, strengthen our union, sharpen the general beliefs of our republic, and generate within us the peace that passes understanding. We trusted God who had brought us this far; we can trust him again. He is the Lord of the oasis who gives not sparingly but according to our needs. The beautiful thing about this whole phenomenon is that the oasis is within us, and we can find it if we search for it with sincerity of heart and efficacy of purpose.

Since we are a nation that trust in God, and our constitution confirms the trust, stating in the First Amendment, "Congress shall make no law respecting an establishment of religion or prohibiting the free exercise thereof; or abridging the freedom of speech, or of the press; or the right of the people peaceably to assemble, and to petition the Government for a redress of grievances." In this simple statement, every citizen of the United States of America has the right to do religion or the right not to practice it. It means that the government cannot enforce a national religion or deprive anyone of religious freedom. It also implies that no single individual or group can force anyone to follow any religion or barrier anyone from practicing any religion. Just as Christians have the right to worship God in their churches, chapels, and cathedrals, the Muslims have the moral and constitutional right to worship God following the Islamic principles in their mosques and prayer grounds. The same rights are invested on the Jews who choose to follow Judaism and worship God in their synagogues or tabernacles. Those who believe in the principles of Buddhism have equal rights to pray to God in their temples as temple monks or as Buddhists. Also Native American tribes reserve the right to worship God according to the principles of their ancestral religion with nature as their church. The same goes with all other religions not mentioned.

The practice of religion is a human right, as well as a constitutional right of all Americans and non-Americans alike. Let's be clear with this assertion, every one of us is free to practice our doctrines and tenets within the confinement of our homes or our worship centers or resolve not to follow any philosophical pathway. Even within our homes or families, family members do have the constitutional and religious rights to choose to do religion or not to do religion. No matter your religious belief, you should be truly aware that God who is the Lord of all religion never force any one to worship him. It is written, "'Come now, and let us reason together,' says the Lord: 'Though your sins are like scarlet, they shall be as white as snow. Though they are red like crimson, they shall be like wool'" (Isa. 1:18). The Jews were the custodians of the first or old testimony of God's dealings with man, his plan to redeem us from our sins, and the sacrifice of his dear Son to save the whole world. Subsequently, the custodians of the new or second testimony of God's dealings with man were the disciples first then to the whole world through "whosoever will." His proclamation then becomes, "For whosoever shall call upon the name of the Lord shall be saved" (Rom. 10:13) and "Come unto me, all ye that labor and are heavy laden, and I will give you rest. Take my yoke upon you and learn of me; for I am meek and lowly in heart: and ye shall find rest unto your souls" (Matt. 11:28–29). Through it all, the Lord of the universe always presents himself as the loving father to all humanity. He gave Adam and Eve freedom of choice in the garden of Eden; though they made bad choices, it was their decision to choose to worship or not to worship God. That is, they choose to obey or not to obey him.

As he commanded the early disciples to take the good news to all the world, he also sent great men and women from other nations to preach the good news of salvation. He met Saul on the way to Damascus in a shiny pure white light and transformed him from being an obstructionist to becoming the greatest pioneering apostle for Christianity. The same Lord through his angel Gabriel (or Jibreel) met Mohammed in a cave called Hira, located on the mountain Jabal an-Nour near Mecca. He gave him the same message of redemption and hope as a package known as Quran in the year AD 610. A message for all those who dueled in the mountains of Arabia, descendants of Esau and Ishmael. Wikipedia gave a little account of his encounter as written in Islamic tradition, thus, "When I was midway on the mountain, I heard a voice from heaven saying, 'O Muhammad! you are the apostle of Allah, and I am Gabriel.' I raised my head toward heaven to see who was speaking, and Gabriel in the form of a man with feet astride the horizon, saying, 'O Muhammad! you are the apostle of Allah, and I am Gabriel.' I stood gazing at him moving neither forward nor backward, then I began to turn my face away from him, but toward whatever region of the sky I looked, I saw him as before." It was God's will to send the message of the fulfillment of his promises to Abraham and his descendants and to the world symbolized as the stars of heaven.

No one religion is better than the other "For all have sinned and have come short of the glory of God." No one race or ethnicity is superior to another for we were all made a little lower than the angels. "But one in a certain place testified, saying, what is man, that thou art mindful of him? or the son of man, that thou visit him? Thou made him a little lower than the angels; thou crowned him with glory and honor, and didst set him over the works of thy hands: Thou hast put all things in subjection under his feet. For in that he put all in subjection under him, he left nothing that is not put under him. But now we see not yet all things put under him" (Heb. 2:6–8). Therefore, any one race or ethnicity that claims supremacy over another is claiming equality with the angels of the Lord, and unfortunately no man is an angel. If you claim superiority to others, you become spiritually inferior to humanity. Hence, the Declaration of Independence confirmed the truth, and we must confirm the truth within us as well. This is the oasis that will dispel the wilderness of hate, bigotry, envy, jealousy, discrimination, and racism. It is this deep-rooted awareness of who we are that we must search for, find it within every one of us, and release its flow in our communities for us and our posterity.

The United States of America has been in the forefront of racial injustice and yet is a nation with the greatest potential to attending racial harmony. It has been a sanctuary for religious freedom, yet the chaos of religious bigotry seems to know no bound. In June 2015, the citizens of this great nation were shocked when the most heinous racial killings in American history took place. Dylann Roof, a self-proclaimed White supremacist, murdered nine worshippers at the historic Emanuel African Methodist Episcopal Church in Charleston, South Carolina. Like a serpent, he crept into the church, pretending to worship alongside the innocent Black worshippers who welcomed him with open arms. As his nocturnal motive of killing those he claimed supremacy over, found the opportunity he was waiting for, he blasted them away with his gun. He took their right to life away. He accused them of crimes they did not commit, unknown crimes that they had no chance to defend themselves, one of which is the color of their skin and their religious beliefs and their right to assembly stepped upon and soiled with impunity. In his twisted mind, he believed that he was superior to those he killed, but in the eyes of justice, he is lower and inferior to the victims and their families. "Be not deceived, God cannot be mocked. For whatsoever a man soweth that shall he also reap." Dylann Roof sowed seeds of hate, and he will reap death and eternal damnation.

The real irony is that all religions believe in religious liberty for all people. According to the Islamic scripture, "The truth is from you Lord': Let him who will, believe, and let him who will, reject [it]" (Al-Kahf 18:29) which means that the Muslims believe in freedom of religion for all people. They believe in "whosoever will' as do the Christians, Jews, Hindus, Buddhists, Native Americans, etc. However, the unfortunate side of this religious principle of "whosoever will" is that some tend to fall beyond the tenets of these beliefs by going extreme. They tend to become the decider of what people should believe, who should believe them, and how they should believe them. The result is forcing people to go against their will by being violent and intolerant. Jesus Christ, the Lord of Christianity and the Son of God, vehemently declared in the presence of his disciples and the people, "For God did not send his Son into the world to condemn the world, but to save the world through him." The world was already condemned by sin, prepared for destruction, and set up for eternal damnation. So if you are a follower of this Lord and you believe that it is your responsibility to condemn your fellow men of sin, bring them to trial in your personal inferior court of judgment, find them guilty based on your religious sentiments, and execute them with your sword of unrighteousness, in this case your AR-15 military-styled weapon, then you have condemned Jesus again in your life and in the lives of your coconspirators. He told his first disciple, Simon Peter, "Sheath your sword, Peter. For he that draws the sword dies by it!" By this statement, he condemned violence in all its forms, even in the face of provocation. He did not say that his followers should not defend themselves when attacked but that they should not be the perpetrators or the ones to draw any weapon against their fellow men.

This commandment goes beyond his instructions to his disciples; it is an instruction to all whose belief in religious and social liberty is paramount in their lives. When you finally discover this oasis of peace, you will understand that your religious liberty depends on my freedom of existence, and my ability to pursue my happiness depends on me respecting your rights to equal justice and fairness. Many have tried to force others to their will instead of coexisting or co-sharing. They have instituted unfair laws to control others who happened to be the minority or even the minority who forcefully, through gerrymandering, take over the mantle of leadership to subdue the majority because of their sense of superiority over them. In all cases, these human atrocities never work out well; they bring chaos, crises, and wars. The ensuing wilderness is man's inhumanity against man, and we all pay deadly prices for them. If you may, go to hell to find out from Adolf Hitler if it was worth it at all, find out from Idi Amin Dada if he would have restrained himself from the numerous massacres he carried out against his people in Uganda based on the final outcome of his behavior, or go back in time to question the Papacy if the execution of the so-called heretics they burned at stake were justified. All were done by human selfishness, greed, religious bigotry, and the evil of societal dominance and control. We must find the oasis within our souls that will stop the violence that is spreading wilderness among us as a nation. What is it and where is it?

This reclaiming oasis is imbedded in this spiritual command, "You shall love the Lord your God with all your heart, with all your soul, and with all your mind. This is the first and great commandment. And the second is like it: 'You shall love your neighbor as yourself.' On these two commandments hang all the Law and the Prophets." Whether you are a Christian, a Muslim, a Hindi, a Buddhist, a Jew, a Krishna Worshipper, or a traditional religionist, this commandment is for you, this commandment is for me, and it is for all the world. It means that my love for God is tied to my love for my fellow men, your love for him is aligned with your love for me, and our love for God is totally connected to how we must love and accept each other's differences no matter what. The same Lord said, "If ye love me, keep my commandment!" We can also say, "If ye trust me, follow my lead!"

If you are a White Christian nationalist and you claim to follow Christ, then you should know that by killing people who do not look like you or believe what you believe in is against his will. "Thou shall not kill!" If you instigate hate and bigotry against your neighbor under any circumstances, remember his teaching, "Love your neighbor as you love yourself." And do good to those who persecute you; by so doing, you would have heaped coals of fire upon their heads. Anyone who claims to fight for God is a liar for God does not require us to fight for him; he is the one that fights for us. The plan of salvation and redemption is God's battle plan for the war against evil, and Satan the perpetrator of evil is doing everything to scuffle that plan. He is roaming like a roaring lion seeking whom to devour. Would you become his prey, or would you resist him and reclaim your God-given authority over evil?

John Aris Eleleme

Be Awake to the Whims of Evil in Our Society! Resist It! Condemn It! Destroy It!

If there is any time in American and world history that we the people needed to unite against an unseen force that is purposed to destroy us, that time is now! At this moment in time, we are not fighting against flesh or blood; we are engaging in the most gruesome battle against evil that is raging within us. The outcome of this battle is expressed in all that is happening in our society that has created the worst sense of fear and doubt that we have become helpless to. You may be wondering why as a nation we feel so helpless, even with things we know that we can accomplish without much argument or decisions we are able to make without being critical of each other's sense of existence and rights to existence. It is because we are facing a very devastating force that cannot be seen but can only be felt. Therefore, the call to be alert, to be awake, to be vigilant is the oasis of "wokeness" that is imbedded in his message, "Be sober, be vigilant; because your adversary the devil, as a roaring lion, walketh about, seeking whom he may devour: Whom resist steadfast in the faith, knowing that the same afflictions are accomplished in your brethren that are in the world" (Matt. 5:8–9).

The call to be awake or to be alert to the final onslaught of evil in our society is a divine call for all people across the world. It is a call for all Americans and non-Americans alike: for Democrats, Republicans, Independents, Conservatives, Liberals, Progressives, humanists, etc. Whether you believe in God or you don't, at least your sense of awareness or human instinct tells you that something huge is going on in our society and you can't just lay your hands on what it is. You are probably right! This power of darkness was foretold over two thousand years ago, and its influence is becoming more pronounced today than ever before. It is "the essence of evil" that is devouring our societal principles, generating divisiveness among us, propelling us to kill each other in the name of religion, and proposing lies, misinformation, and disinformation to cajole and deceive as many as possible for damnation. This force is demanding secrecy and anonymity as a veil to cover its activities and tendencies. Since it is a force that requires the human body to manifest, its gradual possession of unsuspecting individuals is quite astronomical.

Be aware that this veil of secrecy is the "dark web." Yes, the darkest hidden websites that are set up to entice and corrupt our young people. The sites that recruit killers who have done immense damage to our societal sense of justice, our sense of safety, our sense of unity, and our sense of tolerance. These are sites where spells of indoctrination are cast upon those who already have hate and bigotry growing in them; the sites only provide the confirmation and encouragement they needed to do evil. You may be wondering why words are so powerful as to change simpleminded individuals into deadly monsters. It is because words are spirits and possess the power to create or destroy. As it is written, "So then faith comes by hearing, and hearing by the word of God" (Rom. 10:17). It is by consistently reading, hearing, and listening to the word of God that we can be transformed through faith into people who love God with their whole minds and love their fellow men as themselves.

The same is true with those who constantly access the dark doctrines of hate and bigotry in the dark web; they become transformed into haters, bigots, racists, and self-centered brutes whose main purpose is to kill, defraud, and enslave others. They become soldiers to the "roaring lion," armed with a deadly weapon, AR-15, dipped in conspiracy theories and infused with deadly conscience and coldheartedness. At this point, their humanity is gone, and they are swift in shading the blood of the innocent as a sacrifice to the master they serve. Unfortunately, those who lack spiritual knowledge of what is going on would think that these people are mentally sick. No! They are not mentally sick, their minds are sound, and they know exactly what they are doing. They know the consequences of their actions, and to avoid those consequences, they turn their weapons on themselves after they have concluded their master's order, that is the devil. Apart from the dark web scenario, the various deceptive utterances by people meant to deceive others and very extreme ideologies that are being proposed to divide rather than unite Americans also serve as smoke veils to cover up the essence of evil.

Perhaps, we are finding it hard to understand why innocent schoolchildren are paying the price of societal lukewarmness. They are innocent and have committed no crime by attending schools to learn as future leaders of this great nation. Then why are the cold-hearted legislators in Texas, Florida, Tennessee, Kentucky, Alabama, Colorado, Georgia, Indiana, Kansas, etc. particularly passing laws allowing easy access to assault rifles and open carry of guns without permits? Why are continuous demands for background checks and banning of military-styled weapons being ignored? Your guess is as good as mine! But I can assure you that they are directly influenced by the same essence of evil: selfishness, greed, and taste for power; underneath all their inconsiderate decisions lie their worship of wealth. Their injustice against their fellow men knows no bound. If you love weapons more than the lives of your fellow men, then your claims of being devout followers of religion, whichever one you are into, is nothing more than deception; you are a liar and a rumormonger. It is written, "Not everyone who says to me, 'Lord, Lord,' will enter the kingdom of heaven, but the one who does the will of my Father who is in heaven" (Matt. 7:21). Claiming to be a devout follower of any religion without bearing the fruits of its teachings is fraudulent, and there is no truth in anyone that does that. In Christianity, entering the glorious kingdom of God is the goal of every believer; so also are the Muslims who look forward to paradise and Buddhists and Hindus whose aims are to attain the highest levels of "awakening."

Therefore, it is unjust to aim toward these perfections then ignore the evil being committed against your fellow men. Now is the time for Christians to spread the message of redemption and forgiveness as commanded by their Lord. It is time to activate the oasis of love and persuasion to counter this essence of evil. Since White Christian nationalists are members of Christian churches, it is the full responsibility of their leaders to preach vehemently to their congregations about the evil of hating other people, the divine consequences for racial and religious killings, and the evil of discriminating against their fellow men. Similarly, the rabbis and the imams have the duty of reaching out to their communities more often now than before.

Reach out to the young people and other community members with programs of friendship and simple explanation of your beliefs and breach the divide generated by any religious isolation. Remember, Christianity is not meant for Christians alone, Judaism is not meant to serve the Jews alone, Islam is not limited to Muslims alone, and Buddhism is not the sole ownership of Buddhists. All religions are meant to serve the whole world from their places of worship to their immediate communities, from lecture halls to conference rooms, from community radio and television stations to national cable networks, the message of reclamation must go out to all the people.

Although our constitution proposed the separation of church and state, it does not stop an imam from visiting a local school to speak on important topics necessary for the growth of the young people. It does not limit a reverend or bishop of a Christian denomination visiting a local youth organization to persuade them to sheath their "swords," in this case holster their guns and turn away from evil. The fight against evil must move from the pulpits and platforms to the fields; it must transcend our sacred grounds to where the battle is raging. It must move from the holy grounds to the defiled and blood-soaked crime scenes. The police cannot do this work alone without the full assistance of the religious leaders and teachers. The constitution resists making policies and political decisions based on religious sentiments or doctrines; it does not allow laws to be made to deprive citizens of their civil rights based on how some people feel religiously or culturally but insist on us making practical decisions that are focused on the general good of society. Therefore, our religious leaders must become more practical in providing services to their immediate community than just preaching doctrines and dogmas.

Religion and religious organizations can help in tending to the spiritual oasis needed to dispel the encroaching wilderness of deception and dark doctrines. It is time to get to know your members beyond their religious attendance. Know who is sick and needs help. Talk to parents who are struggling with children or teenagers who are accessing "dark websites" and teach the alternative messages of love, hope, redemption, and salvation from evil. It is time to reach out to the community, not wait for the community to come to the worship centers; meet the people where they are and not where you want them to be. It is time to start listening before providing spiritual and practical advice to young people, as well as the older people. Demography has changed, communication styles have changed, and cultural beliefs have changed, so should religious organizations change to accommodate these changes, but the message of righteousness must remain same for he is "the same yesterday, today, and forever!" If we neglect to fill the minds of our young people with the right thoughts, we should expect this essence of evil to take advantage of the vacuum. If you relent from sowing the seeds of righteousness, then expect the enemy to sow weeds and tares in the vineyard. Therefore, the call to action is open and the labor is great. It requires all hands to be on deck and the people to get in the game for our national survival.

Many have misconstrued the prophetic statement: "For there shall arise false Christs, and false prophets, and shall shew great signs and wonders; insomuch that, if it were possible, they shall deceive the very elect" (Matt. 24:24). Of course, anyone would think of people claiming to be Christ and prophets and performing miracles. You may be wrong! It is talking about the lies and deceptions being carried out by religious syndicates, the divisiveness being perpetrated online, the misinformation and disinformation that has created sociopolitical tension and chaos among the people, the rumors and rumormongering or conspiracy theories that has invaded our communication space beyond our understanding. Do not for once pretend that you have not been taken aback by how false information go viral in our social media space: the hate and disrespect that flows through the system, the death threats that permeates the fiber threads, and mind-twisting messages that are meant to deceive you, the very elect.

The anonymous writer and web blogger that manipulates you to becoming a White nationalist or a member of any hate group, in this case, is a false prophet. The truth is "love your neighbor as yourself!" The dark teachings that corrupted you to kill your fellow men with AR-15 is the false prophecy. The truth is "thou shall not kill" and "thou shall not lie!" If you claim in any manner that you are fighting for God or any religion, remember he said, "If you love me, keep my commandment." If by any means you are having issues in adjusting to the presence of other people who are not of the same ethnicity with you, remember he commanded, "If it is possible, as far as it depends on you, live at peace with everyone" (Rom. 12:18). The bottom line is that we can turn things around and start from the new beginning, we can make a U-turn even when things seem out of hand, and we can look again in the right direction for a better tomorrow.

CHAPTER 11

Applying the Principles of "Oasis" in Our Sociopolitical System

In this chapter, our discussion is on the principles of oasis and their applications in resolving our sociopolitical systemic problems. A nation without problems is a nation without growth. It is only when we put our effort into finding solutions to the issues that besiege our nation that we can become inventive, and invention leads to improvements in every facet of society then to growth. However, the worst enemy of growth is the ideological impasse which in many instances brings to a halt in growth. Unfortunately, our democratic system of governance which was designed to be a system of checks and balances tends to develop a lot more impasses than resolutions. The United States Senate, for instance, is the most debating institution in modern history, with exceptional language eloquence that turns off the simple at heart. To add salt to injury, the party platform system had split politicians, voters, interests groups, districts, states, and ethnic groups further into left-wing, right-wing, far-right, far-left, moderate, and centroid groups and created divisiveness so wide that the possibility of restoration is far beyond the horizon of the present setup. It is a terrible wilderness that has dried up all living plants on its path. Yet without doubt, we can still find, and grow the spiritual oasis that will restore and improve on all things the cankerworms have eaten.

Despite the destructive tendencies of this terrible wilderness, we can still recalibrate our efforts to grow toward a more perfect union if we follow the principles of spiritual oasis that are imbedded in every chapter of this book. So far, we have come to see the oasis as the spiritual possibilities that God instilled in every human being from the creation of Adam and Eve and through the birth of all that had graced this world. The oasis includes freedom, liberty, equality, justice, fairness, sincerity, honesty, compassion, love or charity, wisdom, truthfulness, peace, lawfulness, etc. When these are applied in our sociopolitical system, then it will be equal to none. This political and social arrest depends solely on the citizens of this great nation. It depends on the Democratic-Republicans, which are those who believe in the republic, as well as the Democratic principles that governs its domiciliates. These principles are to help every one of us to decisively defend our country against all enemies, foreign and domestic. Its value is to help us to put a stop to the manipulation of the citizenry by politicians and those who take undue advantage of the people's lack of knowledge of our sociopolitical system to rip off the republic.

As it is written, "By their fruits, you shall know them." By comparing what is happening in our society with the principles of oasis mentioned above, we can determine who the domestic enemies are, what they are up to, and how we can stop them from wreaking more havoc in our land. One of the "big three" science fiction writers, Isaac Asimov, stated, "There is a cult of ignorance in the United States, and there has always been. The strain of anti-intellectualism has been a constant thread winding its way through our political and cultural life, nurtured by the false notion that democracy means that my ignorance is just as good as your knowledge." No matter how people feel about this, Professor Asimov's statement remains true and is more pronounce in our sociocultural dealings with each other today than ever before. Democracy can only succeed when a greater percentage of the population is well-informed on how our government works and how best to make it work for the people instead of against their interests.

We can illustrate with instances where ignorance had brought more chaos than efficiency: why should the older generation vote for party platforms like the Republican Party whose intensions are to cut Social Security benefits and Medicare insurance when they are the vast beneficiaries of these government programs? Why must young Republicans or Democratic voters support candidates whose policy proposals are meant to derail infrastructure development and job creation when these are focused on providing a better future for them? Why should anyone support any government whose policies cut taxes for the wealthy and put the burden of financing the government on the rest of society? This counterproductive ideology is completely against the spiritual understanding that "to whom much is given, much is expected!" It is blatant injustice that the less-fortunate ones are duped, taxed to extreme, manipulated on all fronts, and even sentenced to jail for not paying their taxes while the wealthy ones pay less to nothing in taxes and are not languishing in jail.

A case in point was former president Donald J. Trump who paid no taxes to the federal government for fifteen years and deceptively paid only $750 in 2016 and 2017 as a requirement for getting on the ballot. For many years, Trump had refused to release his tax returns and was not investigated or prosecuted as is the case with all other American citizens. His claims that he made no money in his businesses was completely bogus. Yet it is the same person that executed the policy of cutting taxes for the wealthy, thereby increasing the national debt by $7.8 trillion. A man who could not manage his own business cannot manage the business of the nation; several deceptive bankruptcies, multiple failed projects, unending court cases of personal unpaid debts, instances of verbal corruption, and deep sense of selfishness were all indications that the wrong peg was put in the wrong hole. "By their fruits, you shall know them." America should have seen it coming; the people would have been wiser if they applied the principles of oasis as indicated instead of allowing themselves to be deceived by mere words of a liar. "Action speaks louder than words" and "Pictures tell a story better than written words."

Separating the True Guardians of the Constitution from Corrupt Deceivers

As fully explained in "The People's Court, the Supreme Court" section of chapter 3 of this book, the Supreme Court of the United States of America is supposed to be the guardian and protector of the Constitution of the United States of America. This document is the supreme law of the land that confirms the civil and human rights of all the citizens, as well as serves as the certificate of incorporation of the Democratic government of this country. As a matter of fact, the guardians or protectors are expected to protect the rights of all the citizens as indemnified in the Bill of Rights, not cowed by personal interests, regardless of religious sentiments or philosophical beliefs, or be influenced by race, ethnicity, financial or economic gratuity, and not to be corrupted by any means in decision-making regarding their legal responsibilities. According to the Online Legal Dictionary, "There are two main types of legal guardianship, both of which consist of appointing a person to act on behalf of another. These include guardianship of an estate, and guardianship of a person. Regardless of the type of guardianship, the individual is expected to act responsibly as caretaker. The arrangement of legal guardianship is meant to be temporary, as the goal is to restore the ward's rights sometime in the future. On occasion, a guardianship can be permanent, remaining in effect until the ward is deceased, though the individual acting as guardian may be replaced by the court."

In the case of the Supreme Court, the guardianship is that of an estate, the constitutional rights of all the citizens, and the certificate of incorporation of the people's Democratic government. It is a permanent appointment because the justices are appointed for life and can only be replaced when deceased or impeached. In addition to being appointed as guardians, the justices are also appointed protectors of the constitution and the rights of all the citizens. It is the highest level of responsibility invested in any one whereby the object or subject of protection is protected from all external forces, including any possibility of betrayal by the protector. In simple terms, it is defined as "someone who protects or guards, by assignment or on his own initiative. A protector may be a device or mechanism which is designed to protect. A protector may be someone who prevents interference." To better understand the true nature and importance of this noun, *Merriam-Webster Dictionary* provides other synonyms for the word protector as follows: "defender, guardian, preserver, bodyguard, guard, champion, watchdog, ombudsman, knight in shining armor, guardian angel, patron, chaperone, escort, keeper, custodian, shield, pad, buffer, sentinels, warders, harbors, watchmen, sentries, etc." All these illustrations indicate a high level of security that depicts the importance of what is being protected.

Unfortunately, the present justices occupying the Supreme Court of the United States of America have shown that they cannot be trusted with the responsibility of guarding or protecting the rights of the citizens under the constitution. The six conservative justices have been corrupted by their religious sentiments, external financial interests, and political pressures that turned them from justices who were expected to justify the rights of all citizens into judges of sociocultural grievances or religious sentiments. They have acted in the capacity of opiniated judges who decides cases not by the tenets of the constitution but by their majority status in the court. Justices Clarence Thomas, Samuel A. Alito Jr., John G. Roberts Jr., Neil M. Gorsuch, Brett M. Kavanaugh, and Amy Coney Barrett have come to believe that by being the majority in the court, they now have the right to take the rights of citizens away from them because they are the majority instead of protecting those rights based on truth, facts, and principles of fairness.

Some of these justices were nominated and confirmed for dubious and unjustified reasons. Justice Neil Gorsuch was nominated by Pres. Donald Trump after the seat meant to be filled by Pres. Barack Obama was stolen by the Republican-led Senate in 2016. For more than eight months, they delayed Obama's nomination of Judge Merrick Garland. Justice Clarence Thomas was nominated in 1991 by Pres. George H. W. Bush, not by merit but by the mere sentiment of replacing late Justice Thurgood Marshall by another Black man. Also in 2020, Justice Amy Coney Barrett was hurriedly confirmed to the court after the death of Justice Ruth Bader Ginsberg, a seat that was meant to be filled by Pres. Joseph Biden Jr., stolen again by the Republican-led Senate. Americans cannot forget the blatant lies of Sen. Lindsey Graham that "no president is allowed to fill a Supreme Court seat in an election year." The lie that deprived President Obama of his constitutional right to nominate Judge Merrick Garland. Lindsey Graham disgraced himself with "Keep the tape!" drama and rushed to confirm Amy Coney Barrett in an election year, in short, a couple of months before the 2020 presidential election which Joe Biden won. They came through corrupt means and are deciding cases by corrupt reasons as well.

In recent times, the people's confidence in the functions of the Supreme Court has been eroded drastically. For one, some justices' palely with the devil, corruption, had been exposed. Justice Clarence Thomas's business dealings with the conservative billionaire, Harlan Crow. As headlined by Alison Durkee in a *Forbes* article dated May 5, 2023, "Supreme Court Justice Clarence Thomas has come under renewed fire for having GOP megadonor Harlan Crow pay his grandnephew's tuition without disclosing it and a Washington Post report involving his wife Ginni Thomas receiving payments from conservative judicial activist Leonard Leo—the latest in a series of recent scandals involving Thomas that have fueled calls for him to recuse himself from cases or be removed from office and the court to impose a binding code of ethics." Whether these ethical issues are real or portray an appearance of maladjustment, the unseen influence of Justice Thomas's behavior are fully displayed in his recent rulings in being the only justice that voted in support of cases involving his wife, Ginny Thomas. From her efforts to overthrow the 2020 election results to her financial dealings with the conservative judicial activist Leonard Leo, Ginny Thomas has taken undue advantage of her husband's position as a Supreme Court justice, to be the only one to vote in favor of Donald Trump in an eight to one decision. A shame indeed!

It is unfortunate that the custodians of the constitution have become the very destroyers of the sacred document they were supposed to protect. A wilderness of corruption, pay-to-play tendencies, under-the-table transactions, and the highest bidder syndrome have eroded the confidence of the people in the court that was supposed to be the defender of their rights under the constitution. Disgustingly, any attempt to criticize or call to question their nocturnal behavior is met with unrighteous claim of justification by the perpetrators. They have turned the court into a battleground for cultural and religious grievances, where the defense of the principles is far from their intentions. The rights of all Americans now depend on the opinions of Samuel Alito, Clarence Thomas, and Neil Gorsuch, not on the statement of the constitution as they were supposed to be.

The fraudulent idea of Clarence Thomas that the Supreme Court decision of *Roe v. Wade* was not properly decided led to the rights of all Americans to do religion or not to do religion being sacrificed on the altar of greed. Well, the decision that was decided by highly intellectual justices became scuffled in the veil of darkness by less-intelligent custodians. They decided to abuse their power of majority in the court by twisting the arms of other justices and imposing their religious sentiments on the people. To them, how and what other people believe about abortion is of no consequence but what they as conservative Christians believe is all that matters. The continuous rigmarole on the timing of abortion, six weeks, fifteen weeks, twenty weeks, and so on, have created so much apprehension since the beginning of our nation. The truth is that the creation of man holds all the answers that we require concerning reproduction and reproduction rights.

In the beginning, God created the heavens and the earth. The story gives an account of creation from the dawn of time till now. He spoke into existence all the creation, but with man, he employed a personal touch. A personal touch because man would become a replica of God's image on earth. Genesis 1:26 gave this account as follows, "And God said, let us make man in our image, after our likeness: and let them have dominion over the fish of the sea, and over the fowl of the air, and over the cattle, and over all the earth, and over every creeping thing that crept on the earth." The creation of man was a process and not a magical situation. As a process, the time of completion of each step is as important as the process itself. As further stated in Genesis 2:7, "And the Lord God formed man of the dust of the ground and breathed into his nostrils the breath of life; and man became a living being," the process began with God forming or molding his image with the dust of the earth or miry clay. He then concluded that it was well sculptured but needed life, and his breath is all that is needed to bring it life. He stooped down and breath into his nostrils the breath of life, and man became a living being. Adam's life began when he took in God's breath of life and not before. His consciousness and human personality came alive from the breath of life and not from the mass of dust from the earth.

Although Adam and Eve were the first and only human created directly by God, his will of man multiplying and having dominion over all other living things is done through the replicating process known as birth. In reproduction, the same process holds. From the fusion of the ovum and sperm into a zygote to the formation of embryo and the growth of the embryo to the fetus is all in the process of creating the image of God. The fetus comes to life when it takes its first breath. Like the creation of the first man, a baby's consciousness and human personality comes alive after the first breath. The original godlike image of man is transferred from parents to their offspring through genetic makeup known as DNA, and the viability of fetus is the same in every human being. According to www.babycenter.com, "Unfortunately, fetal viability is not always so clear-cut. While fetal viability is generally considered to occur at 24 weeks, some doctors now consider 22 or 23 weeks a potential point of viability, thanks to amazing advances in medical technology that allow some babies to survive at younger gestational ages (gestational age simply means the time your baby was in the womb)." As far as records are concerned, the viability point is of no consequence; it is the point of first breath that matters.

It is very subjective for anyone to insist that by any humanly established laws, a woman must give birth against her own will or against her doctor's advice not to bring a baby into this world. God did not force Eve to give birth, rather, he proclaimed the consequences of her disobedience to be difficulty in childbearing. The book of Genesis's account of God's dealings with Eve's disobedience clearly stated the consequences and the limitations of her punishment. According to Genesis 3:16, to the woman he said, "I will make your pains in childbearing very severe; with painful labor you will give birth to children. Your desire will be for your husband, and he will rule over you." From painful menstrual cycles to painful childbirth, women have paid for the sins of Eve and men have paid for the sins of Adam as well. There is no evidence that God forced Eve to give birth, that decision is strictly hers and her husband. The free will to give birth or not to give birth was invested in the couple, but when such decisions are made, the process will always be painful.

To be candid, John Roberts's led of Supreme Court had done nothing more than scuffle the natural and constitutional rights of all Americans by their nocturnal decision on *Roe v. Wade*. The government has no right to determine whether a woman and her family should or should not do abortion. A bunch of old men and old women in state legislatures have no legal, constitutional, or moral rights to interfere in a family decision of any woman concerning abortion. Although from the views and opinions of these conservative justices, abortion was legalized, and it was for them to stop the legalization. In other words, they believe that it is their right to impose their Christian morality on the rest of the country. The constitution is still adamant on the issue; it is the right of all the citizens to do or not to do religion, to believe in philosophies or not to believe in any philosophy. The conservative Christians have the rights not to do abortion, no one forces anyone to carry out this process. They must preach to their congregation, their women, their men, and those that care to listen not to do abortion. It is their right to religion that justifies their right not to have abortion. But stumping upon the rights of all other citizens to make that decision to have or not to have abortion is hypocrisy.

Abortion is a medical process that is quite emotional for any woman, whether you are a Christian, a Muslim, a Buddhist, a Jew, or a believer in any other religion; the feeling is the same. The feeling of bearing a child from incest and rape is abhorring; the feeling of carrying a dead fetus until birth is cruelty; and the idea of bearing a child who is going to be dysfunctional despite a doctor's advice to abort is nothing more than being daring, but it's still the decision of the family to keep or not to keep that baby. The same people who are agitating for other people to go through this emotional stress are the same people who will transport their mistresses from their extramarital affairs to another state for abortion procedures. Without doubt, the same legislators are ready to have their women abort fetuses that they believe when born will bring shame to their families. Over and over and over again, we've had incidences where hypocrisy has shown its ugly head among state and federal legislators who have decided cases based on their numerical power and not on the truth, and this Supreme Court is no exception.

To stop this wilderness created by conservative justices in the United State Supreme Court and the aftershock of their behavior, it is time to establish a code of conduct to govern their actions. If the conservative lawmakers really believe in conservativeness, they must do away with their resistance to a formal code of conduct for the justices. Conservativeness was to preserve truth and not to trample on it. The truth is that without a code of conduct, we cannot hold these people accountable. If God who is the judge of the universe gave humanity a moral code of conduct, the Ten Commandments, and a natural code of conduct, the natural laws that governs the whole universe, why should appointed but not elected court justices of a country's highest court in the land not have a code of conduct? It amounts to the same situation of having a security detail without modus operandi or code of conduct. It may feel the same way if the banker that keeps your money and financial resources has no rules.

Why must the custodians of the constitution be without any moral, legal, standardized rule, or modus operandi to govern their behavior? They are human like everyone, their judgment may be faulted at some point, their morality may be corrupted through any means, and their sentiments may become, unfortunately, a part of their decisions. Therefore, a code of conduct will prevent them from taking gifts from those whose intentions is to corrupt their decisions. A code of conduct would have prevented them from stumping on the constitutional rights of the people they were supposed to protect due to their religious and cultural sentiments. A code of conduct would in a direct way inform the justices of the consequences of their behavior that may include impeachment and removal from the court. A code of conduct would have triggered investigations into the behaviors of Clarence Thomas, Samuel Alito, and Neil Gorsuch in selling out the peoples' rights for dollars.

When a custodian or protector of the constitutional rights of the citizens decides to relegate his responsibility to the states, then such jurisdiction has become an avenue for direct and open corruption. No state has any right to decide how the rights of Americans under the Bill of Rights are to be implemented. The Bill of Rights is a sacred portion of the sacred document, the constitution. It is only the Supreme Court of the United States of America that is entrusted with the power to protect those rights under any circumstances without prejudice or favor to anyone. Therefore, when six out of the nine justices in the court decided by the power of majority, which is not a factor in the court's decision-making, to relegate the protection of the citizens' right to practice or not to practice religion to the states, then injustice has been committed.

The injustice of allowing the will of a particular religious sect, in this case conservative Evangelical Christians, to determine the morality of the whole nation is nothing but fraud. Their argument in this matter is that they are protecting the lives of unborn babies, yet they feel no emotion when innocent children are being murdered in schools due to their unrelenting protection of the Second Amendment rights, which unfortunately has been misconstrued and misinterpreted to the damnation of our nation. They are almost dead silent when children are dying of malnutrition and avoidable childhood diseases. To them, childhood poverty is nothing but a part of life so far as it does not involve any member of their families.

To really introduce the oasis of fairness and honesty, I believe that it is time to limit the terms of anyone serving in the Supreme Court. The idea of a life appointment has unavoidably generated an undue sense of job security among the corrupt justices. They feel safe in continuing with their nocturnal activities without fear of being removed from the court. Although impeachment is one way of getting rid of these bad eggs, the sociopolitical corruption in the Congress makes it almost impossible to carry out this process successfully. A twelve-year term with a second term reelection is a better fitting duration than a lifetime appointment. This means that a seating president can select five nominees of Conservatives and Liberals or Independents for election. The people must decide who their Supreme Court justices should be through elective means and not the president's call. This shouldn't be a political campaign but a simple selection by the people through a majority vote.

To avoid political influences, the idea of two or three manifesto nights for the nominees to present their profiles to the nation and for the people to gain enough information to decide who must be sent to the court is much preferable to unnecessary debates. The background of the nominees must be fully investigated by the press and by all other institutions whose responsibilities are to search for and provide all the information to the public. In this way, we can avoid all the political corruption of the Senate, including the abusive use of the so-called "Thurmond rule" by the majority party. This was just a makeshift political move of the '60's. According to historic records, "The Thurmond rule, which is named after Sen. Strom Thurmond. In the late '60s, Thurmond blocked then-president Lyndon B. Johnson's appointment of Justice Abe Fortas as chief justice, citing the closeness of the upcoming election. The 'Thurmond rule' posits that a federal justice, such as a Supreme Court justice, should not be decided in the run-up to an election."

Mitch McConnell's led 2016 Senate applied this unconstitutional and non-legalized rule to block Pres. Barack Obama's Supreme Court nomination, Merrick Garland, from being seated in the Supreme Court but corruptly decided not to apply the same rule in stopping Pres. Donald Trump from nominating Amy Coney Barrett to the bench. For American democracy to be truly successful, truth must be the foundation of its modus operandi. It is written, "To the Jews who had believed him, Jesus said, 'If you hold to my teaching, you are really my disciples. Then you will know the truth, and the truth will set you free'" (John 8:31–32).

Politicians who lie to gain political advantages over their opponents are not only declaring themselves untrustworthy but are directly depriving those they serve of the sanctity of truth. Truth is required in making the right decisions, and manipulating the people into making nonfact-based decisions is nothing more than morality and spiritual wilderness. According to *Merriam-Webster Dictionary*, truth is the body of real things or evidence that defines events and facts. It means the form of actuality or the state of being the case and in deeper sense a transcendent fundamental or spiritual reality. From the open falsehood of the conservative ideologues in the Senate, the court became saturated with justices whose aims were tended toward imposing their will upon the people and not protecting their rights.

The peculiar nature of the present court makeup is their unrelenting determination to promote the idiosyncrasies of conservative beliefs and not actually protecting the rights of all the citizens no matter their sociopolitical ideologies, cultural affiliation, or religious backgrounds. A move that is completely alien to the very purpose of the court as a democratic institution has by implication diminished the respectable view of the court in the eyes of the people. To be sincere, the Supreme Court is based squarely on the people's trust in its function and existence. When that trust is tarnished by corrupt justices, the efficacy of the court is gone and would take more than just changing the makeup to restore what the cankerworms have eaten. It took many years of baseless grievances and unfortunate nocturnal plans to scuffle the purpose of the court. It will take even more time to reverse-engineer the manipulation that led to this unfortunate perilous situation.

Since the situation is a wilderness of falsehood filled with ticks of self-aggrandizement, imposition of a specific group's religious and cultural will on the rest of the nation, and the relentless movement of keeping America in the image of the early European settlers despite the constant demographic evolution of its population, it is time to really counter this condition with the "oasis of truth and justice." The truth is that the composition of the court must be changed to eliminate corruption. Justice demands that it must be done and must be done sooner than later. The oasis of peace will require that the court must be increased to thirteen justices to eliminate the influence of the corrupt ones or the corrupt ones must be impeached no matter their philosophical affiliation. In conjunction, this will require the people to vote for the right politicians into Congress, and this same court has through their consequential decisions scuffled that right too.

According to NPR report of July 1, 2021, by Nina Totenberg, "The Supreme Court Deals a New Blow to Voting Rights, Upholding Arizona Restrictions." The headlines display once more the impurities of the court and the daring behavior of the same culprits, simply reported as follows: "The US Supreme Court Thursday gutted most of what remains of the landmark Voting Rights Act. The court's decision, while leaving some protections involving redistricting in place, left close to a dead letter the law once hailed as the most effective civil rights legislation in the nation's history. The 6–3 vote was along ideological lines, with Justice Samuel Alito writing the decision for the court's conservative majority, and the liberals in angry dissent." Impurities indeed, viruses that have laid hold on the nation's highest court and have destroyed the people's beliefs regarding the court. When your fellow justices in the court become openly frustrated with your decisions, based strictly on your ideologies, then we can conclude that your behavior has gone too far to be tolerated. The question is, "Are these justices defenders of the constitution or abusers of its tenets?" No matter your sociopolitical or religious-cultural affiliation, you know the truth that corruption is in play here. If my voting rights, your voting rights, or our voting rights are now a matter of state decision, then the constitution is no longer valid for any purpose.

Let us be clear here, the constitution can only be invalidated if two-thirds of the United States Senate votes to make it so, if a simple majority in the United States House of Representatives decides so by vote, and if four-fifths of all the states' legislatures vote to ratify the decision. The same process holds for any and all amendments. As far as all the citizens are concerned, our rights under the Fifteenth Amendment, "The right of citizens of the United States to vote shall not be denied or abridged by the United States or by any State on account of race, color, or previous condition of servitude. The Congress shall have power to enforce this article by appropriate legislation," is still in place. There is no amount of manipulation based on vote-counting procedures, timing of elections, early voting procedures, absentee voting procedure, mailed-in voting procedures, drop box arrangements and locations, districting or redistricting rules, and registration processes can take this right away. This right is what makes America a true democracy, a country where the power belongs to the people and not rulers. Whether you are a Democrat or a Republican, a Liberal or a Conservative, rich or poor, able or disable, religious or nonreligious, White, Black, Brown, Oriental, or mixed-colored, your right to vote is my right to vote, and we are in this together.

To stop the authoritarians who have invaded the Supreme Court and our various legislatures across the country, we must become more active in identifying who these enemies of democracy are and work in unison to get rid of them. The instrument of oasis we need is "By their fruits we shall know them." Samuel Alito who is using his opinion writings to make decisions to trample upon the rights of the citizenry is displaying the fruit of injustice, falsehood, dishonesty, insincerity, self-centeredness, and lack of respect or inconsideration of other's rights. The five justices who had colluded with him in voting against the people's rights have shown that they are not the defenders of the constitutional rights but the destroyers of their tenets. They maybe wallowing in delight on their newfound power, the power of minority-majority, and that of life appointment in the court, but the fact remains that the real power belongs to the people, and it's time to clamp back that which were stolen by congressional manipulation of our political system. Restoring the congress to "the new beginning" philosophy must be the real focus in making amends to this injustice.

Repairing the Breaches of Our Congressional Dysfunction

The gathering of people in any setting requires a purpose. There is a purpose for any gathering no matter what that may be. If at the end of such gatherings the objectives are not achieved, then the purpose of gathering is defeated. The United State Congress is the gathering of all the representatives of the various districts, regions, states, constituencies, and domains that constitute the commonwealth of this republic. The gathering is for the purpose of finding solutions to the problems that we face as a nation and defining the rule of law on which our democracy is based. Remember, "a nation without a problem is a nation without growth and progress." Growth, progress, is imbedded in the learning curves traced out while searching for solutions to each situation, crises, difficulty, or even the effects of natural phenomena on our very existence.

However, the situation where representatives of the people are immersed in debating each other's views and opinions instead of stated problems and proposed solutions is nothing more than redundancy at its most devastating manifestation. Year after year, the most infuriating complains labeled against the congregation of these representatives is that nothing gets done, divisiveness that creates time wasting, inability to pass important bills that affects all Americans, and constant bombardment of blames on each other because of partisanship. The atmosphere within the edifice known as the United States Capitol Building is charged with so much resentment that you can cut through it with a swing of a sword. From the start of a day in Washington to the end of it, constant begoring and fault picking tend to float like a Lilliput across the hallways. No wander things are not getting done because no one wants to associate with each other.

According to Donald Henry Rumsfeld, who served as the Secretary of State for Defense under Gerald Ford and George W. Bush, "Don't divide the world into 'them' and 'us.' Avoid infatuation with or resentment of the press, the Congress, rivals, or opponents. Accept them as facts. They have their jobs, and you have yours." This advice should have been indemnified and placed on the walls of every hallway in the Congress as a learning device needed to teach members of the Congress the ideas known as "collaboration" and "cooperation." This perilous situation in our Congress was unfortunately installed as part of the procedural accessibility of information in the first Congress which met on March 4, 1789. Debate! It began with a debate. Since then, through the last two hundred and forty-seven years of our democracy, debate has remained the worst enemy of efficiency and reliability of the Congress.

The only institution in our political system that has refused to borrow from coffers of collaboration and cooperation is the United States Congress. As you watch the unfortunate display of vicious attacks by members of the congress on fellow members, the press, and other entities, we can begin to wonder if that is the major reason for sending them to represent us in the first place! They fan themselves after each session of debate, absorbing the feelings of having outdone the opposition, and at the end of it all, they vote on party line without conviction of any form. If this perilous situation is not resolved as soon as humanly possible, the functionality of our political system may become the straight missile by which our democracy would be shot down. The dichotomy between the Congress and other sociopolitical institutions is in the functionality procedures.

In corporations and economic-based institutions, debates or unnecessary arguments is strictly frowned out by all the subjects involved in decision-making. The main aim of such bodies is to get things done, generate new methods of commerce, discover new ways of utilizing resources more effectively, and more acceptable ways of making profits. In these settings, ideas are not debated on but discussed, compared, and contrasted for the purpose of achieving higher standards. In contrast is the confrontational debates that goes on in the United States Senate and the ridiculous divisiveness that the United States House of Representatives duel on every day. From the moment when representatives promised their districts or states that they are going to Washington to fight for them, to the moment they make their congressional statements, the euphoria of confrontation is at its maximum expropriation. Many at this point believe that their personal opinions or ideologies must take over the public space of "we the people." The idea of collaboration or cooperation is of no importance to them. The ensuing wilderness is that nothing gets done.

If the nation's lawmaking institutions are to rise to the standards that we can appreciate as "American exceptionalism," they must be taught collaboration and cooperation from the foundational levels. They can learn from the school system, just as our students are taught using cooperative learning groups. In a cooperative learning team, each member has a function and must perform the function efficiently for the team to be effective. They follow a respectful discussion protocol that allows each member to express their views and as well as appreciate the views of other members. This collaborative state provides the opportunity for everyone to be fully involved in breaking down complex ideas, analyzing situational problems, finding evidence within facts for the purpose of creating solutions, and in retrospect applying their solutions in real-life situations. In classrooms where students are taught to master this and many more collaborative procedures, differentiation of lessons is smooth and efficient. The strengths and weaknesses of every member of the team are considered in forming the teams. In this way, the students are each other's support and not variants. With collaborative methods and cooperative teams, many students who were low-level performers had accelerated to high achievers. Whether it is in elementary school, middle school, high school, or in colleges, the idea of collaborating among students have created a new generation of Americans whose philosophy of work is different from the older generations.

Today in our society, the conflict between the old ways and the new and more efficient ways of doing things is raging. The younger generations in the Congress see differently since they have experienced collaborative learning and cooperative functionality procedures. They prefer the idea of focusing on issues and not on cultural grievances, they believe in sharing ideas and disseminating workable information for the purpose of getting things done, and they believe in each other's capabilities or respect for individual opinions or views. Unfortunately, their interaction, or lack thereof, tends to create conflicts because the older generations prefer debating on issues than discussing them. The older generations prefer political maneuvering than problem analysis, inflicting cruelty on each other's opinion and views instead of applying them in problem-solving procedures and creating political labels for each other's political philosophies rather than viewing our national problems as issues that affects us all.

We can change all this by intentionally transforming the congressional wilderness into an oasis of peace, freedom, liberty, justice, equality, and truth. The truth is that members of the Congress need collaborative education, they need serious lessons on cooperative problem-solving procedures, and they need to understand that loyalty after election is to their constituencies and not to their parties. The saying that "you cannot teach an old dog new tricks" should not be allowed to lay hold in this case. The only time old dogs cannot be taught is when they choose not to learn, and it is time to make it a requirement for every member of the Congress to go through series of collaborative education programs and cooperative procedure orientations for the sake of creating a more functional, modern, and effective problem-solving procedures.

If the Senate is divided into problem-solving teams of ten members in each team, with a total of ten teams to study parts or factors of any of the country's issues in a procedural setup, it will make it easier for majority of the members to vote for related bills because they were part of the teams that created the bills based on collaborative procedures. Similarly, in the House of Representatives, members could be assigned to fact-finding teams, information-analyzing teams, solutions-generating teams, or real-life applications building blockers teams whose outcomes could be interpreted and put together into effective bills for solving our national problems. When all said and done, it will be either difficult or strange for anyone to vote against the projects they participated in creating. Therefore, we must change the modus operandi of how our Congress does business if we desire a more efficient, competent, effective, and more technologically oriented sociopolitical institution.

Indeed, we can transform our Congress to reflect other institutions that have contributed to making the United States of America the greatest economic and military power the world has ever seen. It is time to change the "nay" and the "yeh" voting procedure of the Senate into the electronic voting that gives visuals of who voted, how they voted, and the electronic or paper trails of their history of voting that allows their constituencies to hold them accountable for their votes. Both the Senate and the House of Representatives must invest in large smart boards that show photos of members and their votes. Indeed, the application of technology is required to build a better and more efficient Congress, better accessibility to the activities of the delegates is important in building the relationships with their constituents, and worthing off special interest groups.

Regardless of how members of Congress may feel about reaching out to their constituents, it is the administrative units of the United States Congress that must provide the accessibility of the constituents to their members. From setting up a better and more efficient telephone system to smooth email and social media communication devices, technological access to every Congress person must be breach-free. Also the rule that requires every member to conduct a minimum of one town hall meeting every quarter of the year must be sternly implemented. The people must be informed of what their representatives are doing in the congress to serve their interests. For example, some members of the Republican party, like Mitch McConnel and Charles Grassley, were caught on tape bragging to their constituencies that they will receive money from the Biden administration-backed American Rescue Plan—despite McConnell and Grassley not having voted for it. These politicians took the credit from other people's efforts and unjustly deceive the people into thinking otherwise. Although this deception was exposed by the press, the ignorance of the people in voting again for these corrupt politicians was not prevented. Also the redundancy of some Democratic party members in voting against the interests of their constituents would have been exposed if their activities were monitored through easy access to their offices. All these could be minimized or eradicated if voters and constituents are provided with easy access to the activities of their representatives.

In addition, the administration of the Congress must be separated from the influence of the political parties or sociopolitical ideologies. Experts in various fields should be employed to manage the facilitation of activities within the United States Capitol Building. Management of the procedural activities of the house chambers must be designed by instructional designers. The administration of information and communication technology of the complex must be handled by technologists and not individual secretaries of politicians. Ethical issues must be handled by professional legal teams and not by the political ethics committee. By taking care of these specifics, the constant begoring and partisan infightings may be avoided, and efficiency standards instilled within members, thereby increasing productivity and effectiveness.

Despite the exquisite debates and constant arguments among senators, congressmen, and congresswomen, most members' knowledge and logic are easily questionable. The unfortunate situation where laws and bills are being enacted by people who lack the true knowledge of the problems, and required solutions creates the euphoria of incompetence and mediocrity. According to the late Kofi Annan who was the seventh secretary-general of the United Nations, "Knowledge is power. Information is liberating. Education is the premise of progress, in every society, in every family." There is no better illustration of this assertion than the United States Congress.

Relatively, every new member of this body, including the older ones, is imbued with different knowledge levels of the constitution, laws of the land, socioeconomic situation, sociopolitical events, national financial conditions, even history and historical events that are some of the most important factors that directly affect their effectiveness in the congregation. Therefore, to bring all members to a common level of understanding, there must be a nonpolitical and nonpartisan parliamentary department led by real professionals to educate, inform, and train politicians and other functionaries within the Capitol Building on the process of information gathering, lawmaking procedures, and the importance of always disseminating the truth. Indeed, these professionals must be skilled in accessing national and local databases, information acquisition, data analysis and presentation, application of technology, either as information technology, communication technology or general technological applications. By having professionals inform, educate, and train lawmakers before they begin their congressional sessions, during the process of enacting bills, and in times of national emergency, we can be assured that the Congress and its members will be less tense, less confrontational, and less impasses in decision-making.

We cannot easily forget the rudeness of some members of the Congress to individuals and groups invited to testify before the congressional committees. The utter disrespect of invited professionals or individuals by congressmen, such as Jim Jordan, Steve Scalise, or Matt Gaetz, during congressional hearings must not be allowed to continue. The aggressive questioning techniques of Alejandra Ocasio-Cortez, Marjorie Taylor-Green, or Katie Porter may somehow defeat the purpose of the process if those testifying are not allowed to answer the questions and explain their views and opinions. Like the classroom cooperative procedure, it is imperative to develop a workable and more effective protocol of discussion that would allow better two-way communication procedures between the representatives and the testimonials.

A protocol where teams set out proper questioning techniques that are meant to elicit information and not to traumatize persons testifying is far more effective than the all-out warfare, tension-soaked, confrontation-induced, language-abused, and disrespectful dramatic displays that has eroded every sense of humanity among members of the Congress. This is where educational system developers, communication experts, informational technologists, and professional psychologists' expertise must come into play. There must be an established departmental unit entrusted with the responsibility of teaching, educating, training, or psychologically preparing members of the congregation on the rudimentary communication procedures needed to conduct an efficient, effective, and competent interview session. We as American people, the owners of the American government, the supposed beneficiaries of the purpose of the government, are in all respect deserve to have a functional government that is bipartisan in decision-making.

Therefore, to have bills and legislated laws that are bipartisan, the Congress must follow collaborative processes and cooperative procedures that will integrate members into units that will produce such modus operandi. Our legislative institutions can have smooth transitions from one Congress to another if members are prepared to follow protocols at the beginning of every congressional year, during which effectiveness in the body's functions can be achieved and the ability to serve the people can be assured. We demand a Congress that is respectful and respectable, as well as technologically efficient. America deserves a lawmaking institution that is trustable and can be trusted in carrying out the functions of governing with less conflicts, chaos, impasses, and confrontations. We need bipartisanship and not party lining. Finally, we need humanity to reign in place of cruelty, acceptability to replace despicability, equity and justice instead of cultural grievances, and team productivity against debate-laden redundancy.

Finding Oasis in the Wilderness:
The Conclusion of the Whole Matter

A simple but lesson-inducing story of a wealthy ranch owner as is told by the master teacher, Jesus Christ, to his disciples and a great crowd that gathered to hear him speak could be the best way to bring this matter to a conclusion. "For the kingdom of heaven is like a landowner who went out early in the morning to hire workers for his vineyard. He agreed to pay them a denarius for the day and sent them into his vineyard. About nine in the morning he went out and saw others standing in the marketplace doing nothing. He told them, 'You also go and work in my vineyard, and I will pay you whatever is right.' So, they went. He went out again about noon and about three in the afternoon and did the same thing. At about five in the afternoon, he went out and found still others standing around. He asked them, 'Why have you been standing here all day long doing nothing?' 'Because no one has hired us,' they answered. He said to them, 'You also go and work in my vineyard.'

"When evening came, the owner of the vineyard said to his foreman, 'Call the workers and pay them their wages, beginning with the last ones hired and going on to the first.' The workers who were hired about five in the afternoon came and each received a denarius. So when those came who were hired first, they expected to receive more. But each one of them also received a denarius. However, When they received it, they began to grumble against the landowner. 'These who were hired last worked only one hour,' they said, 'and you have made them equal to us who have borne the burden of the work and the heat of the day.'"

Although the lord of the vineyard was taken aback by the grumbling workers, he calmly but methodically explained his agreement or contractual obligations to them, which were agreed to before they began to work in the farm. "But he answered one of them, 'I am not being unfair to you, friend. Didn't you agree to work for a denarius? Take your pay and go. I want to give the one who was hired last the same as I gave you. Don't I have the right to do what I want with my own money? Or are you envious because I am generous?' So the last will be first, and the first will be last."

The promise of eternal life is the same for whosoever will. As it is written, whether you joined the lifeboat yesterday, the promise is the same. Whether your family boarded two hundred years ago, your reward is one stretch of timelessness. Even an individual who made it an hour or two before the lifeboat sails is entitled to eternity and all the privileges associated with it. Whether your skin color is white, black, brown, or oriental is of no importance, the promise is the same, everlasting life. Whether you are a wealthy person or a poor person, your accumulated wealth or poverty is of no consequence; eternity is the promise. As far as the master of the vineyard is concerned, whether you were salvaged or redeemed at 6:00 AM, employed into his household at 9:00 AM, given an opportunity to labor for him at 12:00 PM, blessed for an opportunity of a lifetime at 3:00 PM, or provided with a passport to heaven at 5:00 PM nick of time, your reward is the same, eternally privileged everlasting blissful life. In his reward, there's no comparison for all the redeemed are in the first class, nothing more, nothing less.

Since the United States of America is a symbol of God's promise of final freedom, liberty, equality, equal justice, and fairness to all people, it is comparable to a vineyard or an oasis in a wilderness. Whoever gets here enjoys the same promise of freedom. Freedom from oppression, whether it is political or ethnic, is the same "free from domination." However you got here, the same "liberation from tyranny" is promised. No matter the injustice committed against you, the promise of justice and fairness is what this great nation presents to all that have graced its borders. If your ancestors were part of the *Mayflower* Pilgrims that arrived Plymouth Rock in November of 1620 in search of a better environment to live and to thrive, the promise of equal opportunities for them and all the generations that came along is the same promise for everyone who arrived through the variety of other ways.

For the first Africans who arrived the continental America in chains, against their own will, the promise of freedom and liberty was for them despite the deprivation they suffered under the cruelty inflicted on them by the criminals who raided their continent and raped and killed their women and children for no just cause. The same promises remain for their descendants, the African Americans, despite the incivility, cruelty, racism, discrimination, and evil committed against them by the descendants of the original perpetrators. They may have arrived this country in AD 1619, but in AD 2008, they arrived the new beginning, the year one of their sons becoming the president of the country that inflicted on them the most heinous crime against humanity. It is time for them to lay hold on God's promise of an oasis filled with his blessings to educate themselves, expand their domain of influence, and to prove that all men were created equal. For many years, great and talented Africans and African Americans have contributed to the building of the United States of America with no reservation. Therefore, this great oasis that God has planted in the middle of the wilderness included them, and no one should tell them otherwise.

Let us not forget the indigenous Americans who are the natives of this beautiful land. They protected this land through the tenets of their religious belief on the "great spirit" who made the whole world and charged them to preserve the land, not to kill animals for sport but for food, show compassion to strangers, and provide help and assistance to those who need them. Although their welcoming of strangers led to them being massacred by the cruel Europeans who tagged along with the *Mayflower*, God's promises of a new beginning are also for them and their descendants. Heaven recognizes them as the only natives of this land because for any ethnicity to be a native of any land, they must have dwelled there for more than one thousand years. Historically, no other subrace, ethnicity, or cultural entity has lived up to a thousand years on this land, except the Native Americans. Therefore, we are either born citizens or naturalized citizens of the United States of America.

In addition to the multicultural diversity that makes America a unique place in the world, the early Asians who landed this land came in search of a better opportunity. According to Pew Research Center, "Chinese were among the first Asian immigrants to the United States. The California gold rush that began in 1848 attracted Chinese merchants and sailors initially, and larger scale immigration began in 1852 when 52,000 Chinese arrived." They came to oasis when the land needed them the most. Their contributions to the building of America are the same as that of the Europeans, Africans, Native Americans, Latin Americans, etc. American railway systems owe them just as the high-rising buildings, plantations, and industries owe the Black people, the Jews, Italians, the French people, etc. In essence, they merit the same denarius payment that all the laborers in God's vineyard deserve. This oasis demands that the Asians must love every other citizen as they love themselves; do good to all men without the indentation of discrimination and racism. It requires all other citizens to love and appreciate the Asian as we love ourselves.

American union will not be complete without the Latin Americans. It is time for all those who live in America's western hemisphere to understand that coming to America should not be only for economic reasons but because they believe in freedom, liberty, equality, and equal justice of all people under the law. They must see America as a country that belongs to the world, developed by people that came from all over the world, established under the ideology of Democratic-Republic to fit all the cultures and traditions that makes up this great nation. It is time for the oasis to view the Latin Americans not as low-level workers but as people who are equally as talented as any other. They must be given equal opportunity to pursue their happiness like other people and be judged equally and fairly under the law.

Perhaps we can truly understand that most of the resources that built America came from outside the shores of this great country. Human resources or types of brain drain from Europe, Africa, Asia, North America, and South America have contributed to making America the best scientific and technologically oriented society in the world. Without the scientific escapades of Albert Einstein and the ingenious project management of the Army Corps of Engineers and scientist J. Robert Oppenheimer, the United States of America wouldn't be the leading country in the invention and continuous development of nuclear weapons. We have the Manhattan Project signed into law by Pres. Franklyn Roosevelt in 1941 to thank. Also we have Dr. James Naismith to thank for the great invention of basketball and the development of the game. Today, Americans and non-Americans alike enjoy the competitive NBA games without reservation. Where would we be without video games? German-born Ralph Baer invented the concept for playing games on TV screens in 1966, and he and two colleagues created the "Brown Box," a very early version of the video game. We can appreciate the famous work of Scottish-born Alexander Graham Bell who invented the telephone after immigrating to the United States in the 1870s. Today, the cell phone is almost second nature to all citizens who cannot do without its applications.

We may not have the space to list all, but from early video screens to modern-day online research, immigrants have helped develop technology throughout American history. Google is no different. Michigan-born Larry Page and Sergey Brin, who was born in Russia, created the world's most popular search engine in 1998. Where would the world be without the famous inventions of Africans and African Americans? We have Alexander Miles to thank for automatic elevator doors patented in 1887. The blood plasma storage equipment invented by Dr. Charles Richard Drew, an African American famously known as the "Father of the Blood Bank" whose work revolutionized blood donation and transfusion in the 1940s indelible in American history. And without Dr. Mark Dean, chief engineer and one of the designers on the original IBM personal computer team, modern computing wouldn't be the same.

Let's not forget Marie Van Brittan Brown who invented the home security system and filed a 1969 patent with husband Albert Brown. These people were looked on as non-Americans despite being born in the United States of America. They contributed immensely to the greatness of the United States of America. From far and wide, they came in droves and in spots with more to give than they received and deserve the same reward of freedom, liberty, equality, equal justice under the law and most importantly the respect of a grateful nation.

Like the reward of a denarius, our general American rights promised in the constitution is equal and does not depend on who came first or came last. The blessing is the same; the opportunity must be the same, equal. The first ten amendments of the constitution, the Bill of Rights is for all the citizens no matter your color, race, status in society, or cultural or political affiliations. These rights indicate that the entity known as the United States of America is a Democratic-Republic that belongs to all Americans and American citizens. The benefit of the republic is the commonwealth of the people and must be equally distributed. The government which is the administering institution of the commonwealth is the government of the people, by the people, and for the people (Democracy). It is time for individuals, politicians, ethnicities, cultural domains, and political affiliates to understand that for anyone to be free, all must be free. For liberty to be the sounding bell of jubilee, all men must be liberated from government oppression, individual or group antagonism, including racism and tribalism. It is time to look at each other from God's eyes of equality and not divisiveness. It is time to know that we all deserve a denarius no matter who we are, what we are, the color of our skins, our status in society, our cultural and religious background, and our political ideologies. When we all come to this truism, then our dream of growing into a more perfect union will come to life. We will pledge our allegiance to God whom we trust and to the republic to which America is built as one nation that is indivisible, with liberty, and equal justice under the laws and constitution of the United States of America.

John Aris Eleleme

Let the Oasis Blossom, Let Freedom Reign, and Let Peace Be Still

A certain farmer decided to plant flowers along a meadow or a pathway of his farm. He planted yellow marigold all throughout both sides of the winding road. In three months, the meadow became a picture of painted yellow that caught the attention of many who passed through this special road. Some stood for a while to enjoy the blanket of yellow, and others just glanced through with less attention. For some time, the meadow became the talk of the community. However, after several months of excitement, the people's attention began to weaned as they got so used to the yellow flowers that they don't even pay attention to them anymore.

One evening, a stranger approached the farmer and asked, "Do you notice that the attention of the people have shifted from your meadow?"

The farmer replied, "I notice that they don't even look at them anymore!"

The stranger pressed ahead, "Maybe, one type or one color of flower could not hold their attention if it should. What must you do to change it?"

The farmer thought for a while then looked up at the stranger and said, "I need multiple colors, and I need a variety of flowers with eye-catching designs to make the difference."

The stranger responded, "I think that is a great idea!"

The farmer looked around for a while, and when he turned around, the stranger was gone. This experience stunts the farmer so much as to propel him to begin the work of changing the landscape the following day. He ordered new flower seeds: red roses, white roses, lotus, jasmine, sunflowers, daisy, tulips, magnolia, lavender, flax, balsam, butterfly pea, and Crossandra. He did not stop there; he requested for golden shower, pot marigold, forest ghost, star jasmine, night-blooming jasmine, Jasminum sambac, and crape jasmine. He spent months designing the meadow with geometrical shapes of variation of flowers, variation of colors, and variation of inspirational letterings.

Finding Oasis Within the Wilderness of our Sociopolitical Ideologies

In addition, the farmer lined the sides with benches for people to sit and admire his work. He planted trees with foliage to shade the people from direct sunlight, set up water fountains for effects, and beautiful lighting designs to inspire whoever visits. The flowers blossom into a mosaic of beautiful rainbow colors that catches and maintains the attention of the people. It became a meadow of inspiration for all people since they observed their preferred flowers grow among the rest of the mosaic of colors. This spot draws thousands of people each year for its ability to dig deep into the people's inner selves, provide them with the inspiration they require, and propel them to reach greater heights. The flowers grew on the same soil, absorbing the same nutrients, sharing the same space without complaining; they were equally planted without preference but requirement. They grew and produced the inspiration the people needed to make changes in their lives. I believe that none of the flowers claimed superiority over the others or antagonized others to submission but accepted each other's presence and grew in unison.

The demography of the United States of America is no more dominated by the yellow marigold or one race. It is a multiracial society that is more of a mosaic of colors that must fit into one beautiful rainbow. It is a country that is strong and unique with its multiracial, multicultural, and multiple sociopolitical ideologies. Its strength is in the variation of colors and talents than the single claim from any one of its subgroups. Let our existence as a people be like this beautiful flower meadow, with clusters of flower beds lined with variations and variations of beautiful flowers. As individuals, let us become inflorescent of flowers arranged beautifully on any of the systems of branches that litter the trees. When we absorb the oasis of wisdom that all men were created equal, then we can begin to fit into the whole design of what America is all about.

Like the farmer, we really needed to consider a change in our attitudes, beliefs, cultures, traditions, and sociopolitical ideologies that seem to become outdated and impracticable in the modern world. We need to change how we think about other people, become more appreciative of other cultures and traditions, as well as make changes to our ways of life that are no longer practicable. In my deep appreciation of Jim Rohn's statement about change, I can as well conclude with his idea that, "You must take personal responsibility. If you cannot change the circumstances, the seasons, or the wind, you can change yourself. That is something you have charge of." Sometimes, the wilderness becomes overwhelming, so we give up. However, for us to change the circumstances, we must begin the process of making personal decisions that will change them. According to Leo Tolstoy, "Everyone thinks of changing the world, but no one thinks of changing himself."

The farmer thought through the situation of changing the world of flowers around him by changing his perspective of how they coexist. He changed his view of planting only the flowers that he loved to planting variations of them. His idea of one bright color changed into a mosaic of colors that attracted and maintained the attention of all that behold them.

Fellow citizens of this great country, it is time to really appreciate the blessings that God has bestowed upon us by learning from the flowers of the field; they sow not, they reap not, they decide nothing, and yet their uncomplaining attitude of growing alongside each other creates the most beautiful mosaic of colors that keeps the eyes spellbound for as long as they scan through their beds, lines, and inflorescent of branches. Let us change from nepotism of only employing people we know to that of giving everyone that merits the positions their due respect. Nepotism creates a wilderness of tribalism, selfishness, and discrimination. Let us change from raising walls against each other to building bridges for all to walk across the sociocultural barriers that has created so much of the wilderness of hate, divisiveness, and cruelty among us as a nation. Let the oasis blossom, let the flowers florist in you and me, let the colors merge into the mosaic that allows us to be "different but equal," and let us understand that our strength lies in our multicultural, multiracial, multiethnic, and multireligious backgrounds.

To lose the wilderness, we must learn to plant the oasis. C. S. Lewis provides a perspective to this by stating, "It may be hard for an egg to turn into a bird: it would be a jolly sight harder for it to learn to fly while remaining an egg. We are like eggs at present. And you cannot go on indefinitely being just an ordinary, decent egg. We must be hatched or go bad." We cannot make any change to anything if we remain on the same spot, conserve the same ideas from the wilderness that we are complaining about, or refuse to look beyond our noses. Like a journey of a thousand miles, it begins with a step, next step followed by the next step, then the next step, and so on.

To understand and appreciate other citizens, you must step out of your cultural and religious cocoon and take a pip into their world. Taking the steps does not require magic or spiritual miracle. It requires practical movement toward change. According to Jon Bon Jovi, "Miracles happen every day, change your perception of what a miracle is, and you'll see them all around you." It does not need a miracle to greet someone who is not of your race or ethnicity; start a conversation that will create that friendship and understanding of each other's cultural and political beliefs. It only takes the courageous move of extending a hand of friendship and keeping an open mind.

We can only eliminate the wilderness by growing the oasis one step at a time. Isaac Asimov in his assertion stated, "It is change, continuing change, inevitable change, that is the dominant factor in society today. No sensible decision can be made any longer without considering not only the world as it is, but the world as it will be." We can only let the bell of freedom ring when we eliminate the chains of enslavement, be it political or social, be it religious or economic; those chains must be loosened. According to Frank Herbert, "Without change, something sleeps inside us, and seldom awakens. The sleeper must awaken." This is the time to wake from the slumber of hate, bigotry, racism, ethnicity, and tribalism. This is the moment of truth where we must understand that freedom requires liberation from all the factors that hold us bound.

As this concluding part stresses, freedom for anyone must mean freedom for all the people. Freedom for all the people must mean freedom for every individual no matter what their status is, no matter what the color of their skin is, no matter what their economic status is, and no matter their level of knowledge or educational attainment. It means that all Americans must walk any American street without fear of being hewn down by an irate person who believes that he owns the country and no one else should exist. It means that qualifications, benefits, privileges, and opportunities must not be decided by race or status in society. It means that the responsibility of maintaining the government of the people must be borne equally by all the people. The rich must pay their equal share of taxes as are those in the middle class, and the less fortunate in society must always be given consideration. As it is written, "To whom much is given, much is expected!" It is injustice to place the burden of nation building squarely on the shoulders of a section of society while the upper class get away with political ideologies that prevent them from paying their fair share of taxes.

America will always find the advice and philosophical views of Ronald Reagan useful in any situation, any crises, or among any generation. Reagan stated, "Freedom is never more than one generation away from extinction. We didn't pass it to our children in the bloodstream. It must be fought for, protected, and handed on for them to do the same." For them to do the same or better. Therefore, we must teach our children to bear the torch of freedom from homes, schools, workplaces, courthouses, and government hallways. Let them know that by defending a fellow student against bullies, no matter their race, is fighting for freedom. Teaching them that to avoid discriminating against other people in workplaces and positions of authority is fighting for freedom, and it is their responsibility and duty to stand in that gap whenever they are needed. Even the generations that have perpetrated injustice in the past must know that it is not too late to change. Do not go to your grave with injustice in your heart. According to Ronald Reagan, again, "We can't help everyone, but everyone can help someone." Pass it on through your children, grandchildren, and relatives whose minds are open for wisdom.

It is true freedom that leads to real peace. For freedom to be truly free, it must generate peace, even peace that passes understanding. Many did not realize that freedom and peace go hand in hand. According to the Oxford English Dictionary, "Peace is freedom from turbulence or disturbance; It is a state of tranquility. It is a state or period in which there is no war or war has ended." Also Wikipedia defines it as "a concept of societal friendship and harmony in the absence of hostility and violence. In a social sense, peace is commonly used to mean a lack of conflict and freedom from fear of violence between individuals or groups."

We must not misunderstand the real physical warfare from the spiritual warfare that rages within each of us daily. To overcome the wilderness that grows without end in our hearts, we must allow the oasis of peace to expand. Dalai Lama described this phenomenon in a simple term as follows: "We can never obtain peace in the outer world until we make peace with ourselves." It is when you make peace with the idea that all men were created equal that you begin to love your fellow men as yourself. By being at peace with having the resources of the nation equally distributed among all the ethnic groups in the country will we refrain from corruption and self-centeredness. By understanding the rights of every American and American citizens as stated in the Bill of Rights is for all and not for few, then we would refrain from stepping on the rights of others by not creating unjust laws that take their rights away. It is when we realize the constitution began with "we the people" that we will be at peace with the idea that America is a Democratic-Republic that belongs to the people of United States of America, all the people, 100 percent of them.

When we all finally come to terms with democracy as government of the people, by the people, and for the people, then we will be at peace on the fact that political parties are just platforms that launches people into public offices and not control their loyalties. For there is only one loyalty, loyalty to the people that we serve. There is only one worship, worship to God whom we trust. We cannot love our fellow men as ourselves if we love not the God who created us all; we cannot love God if we do not love our fellow men.

On the Mount of Blessings, he stated, "Blessed are the peacemakers, for they will be called children of God." According to Annette Griffin, "The Hebrew word for peace, Shalom, means much more than just absence from strife. It means completeness or wholeness." It is by total agreement with him that we can be at peace with each other. Helen Keller once stated, "I do not want the peace which passes understanding, I want the understanding which bringeth peace." Although I partly agree with Helen, we must note that to have the understanding that bringeth peace, we must experience the peace that passes understanding. Therefore, it is the truth in knowing that all men were created equal that will bring the inner peace of accepting each other no matter the assumed race. There is only one race, humanity. There is only one God, the one that created all things!

It is this level of spiritual understanding that will break the chains of divisiveness that has split us into bounds and pieces that does not allow us to grow toward a more perfect union. To grow into a more perfect union, we must be fitted into places like the flowers of multiple colors. The best of us must be chosen to represent each community within this country no matter their ethnicity or status in society. Letting an incompetent politician represent your community because of party affiliation creates a wilderness of chaos; voting for a person because of ethnicity and not capability is nothing more than effervescence of backwardness. Let the oasis of peace that passes understanding lead us to step across the aisles to select the best and not the ones we like or prefer. Let the oasis of peace that passes understanding be the guard that prevents us from accepting inferior talents into our Ivy League schools while the talented ones are left out because they are not from rich families. It is the peace of making the right decision without fear or favor to anyone that will create the change that we require as a nation.

Be not deceived to think that one religion is the only one that should stand the test of time. For all religions lead to him that created all things, and it is this understanding that will lead to peace among us as a nation. According to Dr. Juan Cole, "Peace is one of the major things in Islam and everything is done in the name of God/Allah to reach peace. In Islam, praying and fasting for example is for inner peace, helping others is also for peace. Everything is done for peace and as mentioned, it's one of God's/Allah's names." In Judaism, Shalom is one of God's names, the God of Peace. He is the peace that passes all understanding, the understanding that will lead me to love you as myself and lead you to love me as yourself. Also the Buddhists believe and practice peace like any other major religions.

According to Theresa Der-Lan Yeh in her contributing writing to *The International Journal of Peace Studies*, Volume II, 2016, "The Buddha looks at the external causes of conflict as consequences derived from a general orientation common to all living beings: avoiding harm and obtaining happiness. Anything contrary to this would result in disturbing one's peace and lead to conflict. If people want to live an ultimately happy life with no harms toward themselves at all, the Buddha teaches, they should start with avoiding causing harm to others, physically and verbally at the personal level, since people are afraid of physical violence, and resent harsh words; and the physical and verbal harm we inflict upon others usually leads to hate and conflicts that, in turn, would bring harm to us and cost our happiness. As stated in one Buddhist Scriptures."

We must allow peace to reign within us before we can pass the peace to other people. Like the meadow of flowers, we must hate no one, proclaim no superiority on anyone, declare no superiority on none, be it individuals or groups, and feel no inferiority because of any injustice committed against you but fight to claim back your God-given equality.

Finally, we must absorb the same nutrients from the same soil, be watered by the same fountains, give credence to each other's existence, protected by the same trees with foliage wide enough to provide the umbrella of comfort we all need. By so doing we can continue to grow toward a more perfect union as indicated in the Constitution of the United States of America.

THE END

ABOUT THE AUTHOR

John Aris Eleleme has served as an educator for close to twenty-five years. Mr. Eleleme holds a degree in Bachelor of Science in Mathematics and a degree in Master of Science in Instructional Design and Technology. For many years and across three school districts, John has worked with middle school students, high school students, as well as adult students, providing the foundational instructions they needed to excel in mathematics and science. Also Mr. Eleleme has served as the head of the Department of Mathematics and Technology at Access Schools in Calabar. His desire to teach, inform, instruct, and provide a sense of direction to both the younger generation and the older generation led to the writing of this very important book. We all know that American history or world history cannot replace civic education. It is only with civic education that we can understand why America is the champion of Democracy, have a feel of the structure of our government, and what our responsibilities, rights, and privileges are within the structure. With the foundational knowledge of civil society, the citizens will be able to wield the power allotted to them under the constitution to exert their authority on the government as the sole owners of American government.

www.ingramcontent.com/pod-product-compliance
Lightning Source LLC
Chambersburg PA
CBHW071217151224
19048CB00008B/114